WOLFPACK

WOLFPACK

THE U-BOAT WAR AND THE ALLIED COUNTER-ATTACK 1939 – 1945

DAVID JORDAN

SPELLMOUNT
Staplehurst

British Library Cataloguing-in-Publication Data:
A catalogue record for this book is available from the British Library

Copyright © Amber Books Ltd 2002

ISBN 1-86227-158-5

First published in the UK in 2002 by
Spellmount Limited
The Old Rectory
Staplehurst
Kent TN12 0AZ

Tel: 01580 893730
Fax: 01580 893731
Email: enquiries@spellmount.com
Website: www.spellmount.com

1 3 5 7 9 8 6 4 2

Editorial and design by:
Amber Books Ltd
Bradley's Close
74-77 White Lion Street
London N1 9PF

Project Editor: Naomi Waters/Chris Stone
Design: Zoë Mellors
Picture Research: Lisa Wren

Printed in Italy

Picture Credits

Aerospace Publishing: 80.
AKG: 6-7, 104 (b), 111, 113 (t), 172.
POPPERFOTO: 8, 10 (t), 14, 17, 51, 52-53, 62, 63, 64, 69, 70, 73, 74, 78-79, 81, 82, 90-91, 92, 95, 97,
104 (t), 108, 110, 122-123, 130, 138 (both), 143, 146 (b), 149, 155, 156-157, 160 (t), 162 (t), 167.
Bruce Robertson: 13 (b).
Suddeutscher Verlag: 12, 13 (t),15, 16, 24 (both), 30-31, 33, 34-35, 36 (t), 36-37, 42, 43, 49, 56-57, 59, 72,
83, 86, 101 (both), 112, 113 (b), 117, 136, 146 (t), 148, 151,169, 171 (t), 173.
TRH Pictures: 8-9, 10-11, 18, 19, 21, 22 (both), 23 (both), 25, 26-27 (both), 28, 38, 40-41, 44, 45, 47, 50,
55, 58, 60, 61, 65, 71, 76, 85, 87, 89, 98-99, 100, 103, 107, 109, 115, 116, 118, 119, 120-121, 125(both),
126, 129, 133, 134, 135 (both), 137, 139, 140, 141 (both), 142, 144, 145, 147, 150, 153, 159, 160 (b), 162
(b), 164, 165, 168 (both), 170, 171 (b).

All artworks supplied by: Aerospace Publishing & Tony Gibbons.

CONTENTS

CHAPTER ONE

SO NEAR, SO FAR: THE STORY OF U-BOATS IN WORLD WAR I

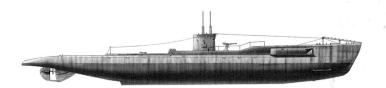

World War I saw the development of the submarine as an effective weapon system. Such was its rise that the U-boat came close to winning the war for Germany.

The rise of the submarine as a major weapon system stemmed not from a major sea battle, but from the steady aim of a previously unremarkable man, Gavrilo Princip. On 28 June 1914, he assassinated the heir to the Austro-Hungarian throne and began the process that plunged Europe – and ultimately the world – into just over four years of war. Princip's actions were not the cause of the war, merely the catalyst which ended the increasing tensions between the major European powers and drove them to mobilize their forces. The result was World War I.

World War I has received a bad press among historians. It is generally regarded as having achieved very little apart from large-scale casualties and creating an unstable and distressed post-war Europe. As a result – directly or indirectly, depending upon viewpoint – Adolf Hitler was able to take power in Germany and lead the world into another conflict. Despite the horrors of World War II, the later conflict has been treated more favourably by history. It is generally considered that, for the

LEFT: German U-boats at anchor in 1914. Those seen here made up much of the German submarine force. The lack of numbers was to prove a serious problem for much of the war.

Allies at least, the war had a point – ridding the world of Nazism. These descriptions, however, merely scratch the surface of the complexities of the two wars. Despite the major differences in the way in which the two wars were fought, there were many similarities. Nowhere is this more striking than in the way in which the Germans sought to use the submarine as a potentially decisive weapon. In both conflicts, the German submarine arm caused serious concern to the Allies, particularly given the serious threat to Britain posed by the possible cutting of the maritime supply routes upon which Britain depended.

The German submarine campaigns of World War I played a large part in shaping the naval strategy of World War II. Without understanding how the U-boat arm operated between 1914 and 1918, one cannot fully comprehend the way in which the Germans and the Allies were to approach naval warfare between 1939 and 1945. In both cases, the end result was the same – the ruin of Germany. This was something that had been feared by German leaders from the early years of the twentieth century, and helped to create the circumstances in which World War I began.

Of all the major powers in 1914, Germany faced perhaps the greatest dilemma. The system of alliances that had developed over the preceding 20 years had left the German

empire facing the prospect of a two-front war against France and Russia. This was not something that the Germans wished to contemplate, so they came up with a plan. As John Bourne has noted, this was the most famous military plan since the Trojan horse, although its instigator, Alfred von Schlieffen, never lived to see it implemented. Bearing in mind how events progressed, it is perhaps as well that he did not.

The plan was bold. To avoid a two-front war, the Germans would launch a sweeping attack on France, knocking the French out of the war within a matter of weeks. This would permit attention to be turned to the Russians. The third member of the Triple Entente, Britain, would have no ability to continue the conflict without a continental ally – if Britain chose to become involved at all. Given Britain's rather chequered diplomatic past (Britain had fought alongside or against almost every nation in Europe apart from Germany by 1914), there was some concern among French politicians that 'perfidious Albion' might choose not to become embroiled in a major war, alliance commitments or not. While it was hardly in Britain's interests to see a German victory in Europe, given the implications for Britain's imperial possessions from a massively aggrandized Germany with an ambitious Kaiser, becoming entangled in a major war

RIGHT: Kaiser Wilhelm II provided great support for the creation of the German Navy. The Kaiser was a naval enthusiast, and the naval race between Britain and Germany after 1897 owed much to his desire to see a German Navy that was able to sustain the overseas empire that he hoped to develop.

LEFT: Surface units of the Royal Navy exercising in the Solent in early 1914. The size and power of the Royal Navy was unrivalled. The U-boat appeared to offer a relatively cheap and effective means of countering British numerical strength without going to the expense of attempting to match the Navy ship for ship.

BELOW: The *U21* was one of a class of four similar submarines (led by *U19*). *U21* was one of the first submarines to employ diesel engines, instead of the petrol engines used before. *U19* survived the war, but foundered in the North Sea in February 1919 as she was sailing to Britain to surrender under the terms of the Versailles settlements.

was hardly desirable either. Although the Germans may have hoped that the British would not become involved, the Schlieffen plan ensured that they did. The *casus belli* was the need for German forces to plough through Belgium to ensure that the French forces were outmanoeuvred.

Britain had guaranteed Belgian neutrality in 1839, and it used the violation of Belgium's territorial integrity to justify the decision for war. Even this took some agonized debate in political circles before the decision to commit was reached. The question of 'gallant little Belgium' swung the argument. On 4 August 1914, Britain declared war on Germany. This single action, stemming from more than a decade of rising tension between the two powers and their allies, completely altered

U21

Country:	Germany	**Armament:**	One 86mm (3.4in) gun, four 508mm (20in) torpedo tubes
Launch date:	February 1913		
Crew:	35	**Powerplant:**	Diesel/electric, driving two shafts
Displacement:	660 tonnes (650 tons) surfaced, 850 tonnes (835 tons) submerged	**Surface range:**	9265km (5000nm) at 10 knots
		Performance:	15.4 knots surfaced, 9.5 knots submerged
Dimensions:	64.2m (210ft) x 6.1m (20ft) x 3.5m (11.5ft)		

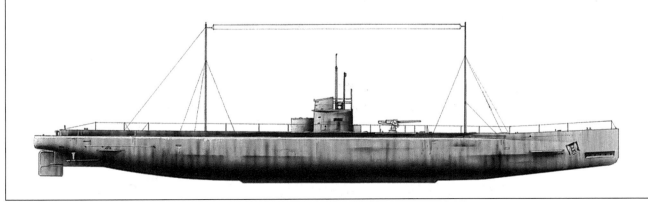

the British manner in warfare. It forced the world's leading maritime power to despatch an Expeditionary Force to France and to employ its land forces in a manner that it had studiously managed to avoid since 1815 and the Battle of Waterloo.

Britain's geography and imperial commitments meant that it had become the leading maritime power in the world by 1914. The Royal Navy intended to be able to defeat the combined forces of the next two largest navies combined, although it did not achieve this 'two-power standard' before the outbreak of war. Maritime power was essential to Britain's trade links with its empire, and, since the 1870s, this trade had included foodstuffs that British agriculture did not have the capacity to replace should the supply be affected. Napoleon had attempted to starve Britain into submission, but failed (the Royal Navy returning the compliment with more success). With the French threat removed after 1815, it appeared that there was little prospect of Britain's seaborne trade being threatened. This all changed after German unification.

For most of the nineteenth century, naval power was not of great importance to the German states. Prussia's military reputation was based upon its army, and none of the states had any overseas interests that demanded possession of a battle fleet. After unification in 1870–71, Imperial Germany began to develop a small fleet, but this was commanded by army generals and remained

ABOVE: Admiral Alfred von Tirpitz (1849–1930), the father of the Imperial German Navy. With the support of the Kaiser, Tirpitz was responsible for developing the German Navy from a small coastal force into an ocean-going fleet.

RIGHT: Elements of Germany's High Seas Fleet exercise in the Baltic prior to the outbreak of war. Although the High Seas Fleet was of impressive size, it was limited in potential by the might of the Royal Navy.

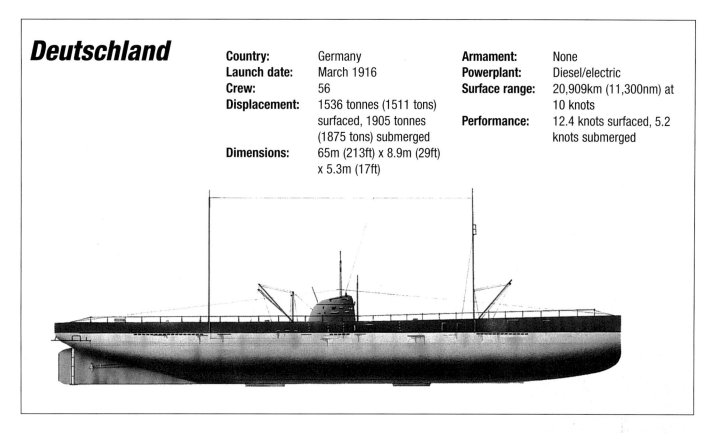

Deutschland

Country:	Germany	Armament:	None
Launch date:	March 1916	Powerplant:	Diesel/electric
Crew:	56	Surface range:	20,909km (11,300nm) at 10 knots
Displacement:	1536 tonnes (1511 tons) surfaced, 1905 tonnes (1875 tons) submerged	Performance:	12.4 knots surfaced, 5.2 knots submerged
Dimensions:	65m (213ft) x 8.9m (29ft) x 5.3m (17ft)		

small. Chancellor Otto von Bismarck took the view that Germany's geographical position demanded strong land forces and cautious relations with neighbouring states. In these circumstances, it was unsurprising that the navy received little attention, while the German army increased in size. Bismarck took a careful and pragmatic view of events. While this suited Kaiser Wilhelm I, his son took a very different view.

Kaiser Wilhelm II was eager to see Germany take its place as a major power and became progressively more frustrated with his Chancellor. Matters came to a head in 1890, when Bismarck was dismissed, and Wilhelm embarked upon a dramatic change in German policy. Henceforth, Germany was to acquire colonial possessions, which the Kaiser took as being a sign of a nation's greatness. There was something of a problem, in that the other European nations – especially the British – had colonized most of the prime locations well before German unification. Africa, however, remained almost untouched by imperial designs, and it was to this continent that Germany turned. The resulting scramble for territory between the major powers was at best undignified, with Britain regarding the entire process as being a potential threat to the Empire and imperial trade. If European powers were able to build or obtain suitable naval facilities along the African coast, the implications for British imperial policy would be severe.

British discomfort was not helped by the Kaiser's fascination with maritime affairs. Wilhelm correctly noted that one of the prerequisites for great power status was a strong navy, and, from 1897, the Imperial Navy received the attention previously denied to it. The most prestigious vessel any navy could possess was the big-gun battleship. The Kaiser found a ready supporter in the form of the Minister for Marine, *Grossadmiral* Alfred von Tirpitz. Tirpitz argued for a major

ABOVE: *Deutschland* was built when the Germans recognized that large cargo-carrying submarines could offer an effective means of evading the surface blockade imposed by the Royal Navy. *Deutschland* was converted from the *U155*, and made two runs to America before the United States entered the war. This rendered the cargo-submarines useless, and they were converted back for military use. *Deutschland* was scrapped in England in 1922.

increase in the size of the German Navy based upon what he called the 'risk theory'. This theory held that it was necessary to build a large enough fleet to ensure that Britain would not be prepared to risk the Royal Navy in a war with Germany. Even if the British were prepared to take on the Germans, they would face the uncomfortable prospect of suffering such heavy losses that they would be vulnerable to the French and Russian fleets. Tirpitz contended that this would ensure that the British would not seek to interfere with Germany's empire building.

Tirpitz's aims were probably more aggressive than this. Williamson Murray has noted that Tirpitz's private papers seem to suggest another agenda. Tirpitz felt that the

BELOW: The German High Seas Fleet on manoeuvres. The length of the line here demonstrates the size and power of the fleet built up by the Kaiser, of which this was only a fraction. It is salutary to think that even this force was outnumbered by the Royal Navy.

Germans could outbuild the British in an arms race; given Britain's worldwide commitments, the German High Seas Fleet would be able to concentrate superior forces in the North Sea and destroy Britain's maritime supremacy. This all rested upon the assumptions that Britain, France and Russia would be unable to reach an accommodation and that a German naval build-up would go unchallenged. The British, however, regarded the German building programme as a serious challenge and embarked upon a major construction programme of their own.

The naval race became more intense when the Royal Navy dramatically altered the concept of the battleship by launching HMS *Dreadnought* in 1906. The German Imperial Navy followed suit, building battleships of its own, and the race continued unabated. This resulted in the remarkable situation whereby the British government proposed to build four battleships, while the Admiralty argued that six was the minimum necessary. The two parties ended by compromising with eight (four to be built and four to be built if they were deemed to be needed – they were). Along with battleships, units of all other types, ranging from battlecruisers to in-shore torpedo boats, were built as each nation tried to ensure superiority at sea.

Britain recognized that allowing the Germans to gain the advantage could have disastrous consequences upon the supply of food and raw materials; the Germans fully appreciated that an effective blockade by the Royal Navy was likely to destroy any prospect of an easy victory. A glance at the size of the mercantile fleets of the two nations gives some idea of just how important control of the sea was – Britain led the way, having 47.9 per cent of the world's total tonnage, while Germany was in second place with 11.9 per cent. Shipping was essential to both countries, and the spectre of an enemy hindering maritime trade was an uncomfortable thought for political leaders in Berlin and London.

No great perceptiveness was required to recognize that the numerical superiority enjoyed by the British Grand Fleet presented Germany with a serious problem, and this was increased further by British diplomacy. The Royal Navy's position in the North Sea was enhanced with the conclusion of an alliance with Japan in 1902 which permitted the Far Eastern squadron to return to home waters; in 1904, an *entente* with France was reached, followed three years later by a similar accommodation with Russia.

These developments did not deter Tirpitz from seeking ways to defeat the Royal

LEFT: The High Seas Fleet in port. Unfortunately for German ambitions, the sight of ships tied up alongside was all-too familiar during the war, as the fleet was forced to remain in harbour for fear of losing in an engagement with the British. Although the High Seas Fleet sank more ships than it lost at the Battle of Jutland, the battle was a strategic defeat, with the German fleet still unable to gain command of the sea.

Navy's Grand Fleet. He believed that the Royal Navy would seek to impose a close blockade of Germany, which would demand that the High Seas Fleet engage the Grand Fleet in battle. Before this was done, however, numerical parity would need to be obtained. The Germans anticipated that the Royal Navy would unwittingly assist by remaining true to its aggressive heritage. In this scenario, the Grand Fleet would rapidly seek to engage the High Seas Fleet, which would be waiting around Heligoland Bight. Before the British managed to get within range of the major surface units, they would encounter a mixture of destroyers, torpedo boats and submarines, drawn up in three defensive lines. The outer line consisted of the destroyers, which would provide early warning of the British approach, and then draw the enemy forces towards the second line, composed of the submarines riding at mooring buoys. As the British approached, the submarines would cast off, submerge, and launch their torpedoes. Coupled with torpedoes fired from the destroyers and the torpedo boats that made up the third defensive line, it was intended that the Grand Fleet would suffer sufficient losses to ensure that the High Seas Fleet was not at a grave numerical disadvantage. This would thereby increase the chances of success when it sailed to meet an already depleted enemy.

Within this scheme, the submarine played a key part. Submarines offered a relatively cheap means of coastal defence, but, although they had been employed in the American Civil War, it was only the technological advances of the later nineteenth century that turned them into viable weapons. One of the major difficulties confronting designers was the means of propulsion. Using internal combustion engines provided necessary power, but these consumed the oxygen in the vessel, with obvious effects upon the submarine's ability to stay submerged. This difficulty was overcome from the 1870s, with the development of the first effective storage batteries, which permitted the use of electric motors. These solved the problems of consumption of oxygen in the submerged submarine, but the power output of the motors was low, as was the endurance that they offered. The solution came in combining internal combustion engines and battery-powered motors, although the use of petrol engines was problematic because of the volatile nature of the fuel; this difficulty was overcome with the introduction of the diesel engine.

Once the submarine had become more practical, it offered navies the opportunity to acquire a relatively cheap means of

BELOW: The *U1* at sea. The first German U-boat was not completed until 1906, thanks to some doubts about the value of the submarine. The use of kerosene motors meant that *U1* could not be an effective operational vessel, and she was used for experimental purposes and training throughout the war. *U1* was sold in 1919 and refitted as a museum exhibit.

UC74

Country:	Germany	**Armament:**	One 86mm (3.4in) gun, three 508 mm (20in) torpedo tubes, 18 mines
Launch date:	October 1916		
Crew:	26		
Displacement:	416 tonnes (409 tons) surfaced, 500 tonnes (492 tons) submerged	**Powerplant:**	Diesel/electric motors, driving two shafts
Dimensions:	50.6m (166ft) x 5.1m (17ft) x 3.6m (12ft)	**Surface range:**	18,520km (10,000nm) at 10 knots
		Performance:	11.8 knots surfaced, 7.3 knots submerged

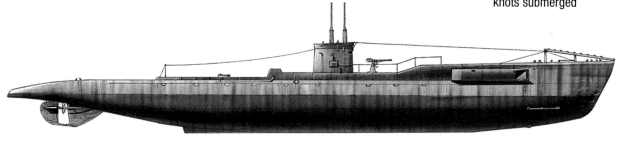

ABOVE: *UC74* was one of six U-boats built for mine-laying operations. *UC74* was interned in Spain at the end of the war, then surrendered to the French, who scrapped her in 1921.

BELOW: The *U15* passes through the Kaiser Wilhelm Canal. Worthy of note is the tall exhaust on the deck, which had to be demounted and stored before the boat could submerge.

countering the supremacy of powerful surface fleets. Tirpitz did not, at first, display much interest in the submarine, preferring to concentrate upon the building of surface units. It was not until 1904 that the German Imperial Navy ordered its first *Unterseeboote*, or U-boat. The diplomatic successes enjoyed by the British ensured that the initial reluctance to build submarines was quickly overcome, and they became a key part of the German strategy for defeating the Grand Fleet. Unfortunately for the Germans, the Royal Navy did not respond as anticipated. By 1914, the British had recognized that the submarine and torpedo boat made close blockade extremely dangerous. As a result, it was decided to apply steady pressure through distant blockade. This would have the desirable outcomes of interdicting German maritime trade and bottling up the High

Seas Fleet, which, it was believed, would have to come out to battle, where it could be defeated. As a result, the German naval command began to consider a more aggressive use of its submarines.

In August 1914, the Germans possessed a total of 28 U-boats, while a further 16 were in various stages of construction. The first four U-boats built were too small to be effective and were therefore reserved for training purposes, leaving 24 operational submarines, or *Frontboote*, divided between two flotillas. Following the plan to see more aggressive use of the *Frontboote*, they were sent on patrol, tasked with the location of the Royal Navy's patrol lines. Once this was achieved, the U-boats were to engage any capital ships that they encountered, continuing the idea of using the submarine to reduce the numerical supremacy of the Grand Fleet.

The first of these operations began with the submarines from the 1st Flotilla leaving Heligoland early on the morning of 6 August 1914. No ships were sighted on the first or second day as the submarines, keeping 11 kilometres (seven miles) separation between them, steered northwest. At midday on 8 August, *U15* sighted three battleships. The submarine submerged to attack and launched a single torpedo at HMS *Monarch.* The torpedo missed the target, and the three battleships manoeuvred out of sight. By that evening, all the U-boats had reached the northerly limit of their patrol, and they turned to trace their course back towards Germany. The journey was not to be completed in one go, as the U-boats had been ordered to stop on the line of latitude that intersected the South Orkney islands. There they would remain surfaced for 39 hours in the hope that units of the Grand Fleet would inadvertently blunder across them, permitting engagement. It should be noted that the image of the submarine cruising silently beneath the surface was far from accurate: commanders would try to remain on the surface if they possibly could. They submerged only when it would provide an advantage, such as surprise, or, of more immediate concern to the crew, to ensure that the submarine was not itself attacked and sunk.

This aspect of submarine warfare in the first half of the twentieth century is often forgotten. While the submarines obviously could and did operate effectively underwater, they suffered serious disadvantages when below the surface. Underwater speed and endurance were decidedly limited, making it difficult to keep up with targets. Finding the targets was also extremely difficult underwater, as only one man, using the limited field of vision offered by the periscope, could try to locate them. By contrast, there would be more than one pair of eyes available if the submarine was on the surface, and the low profile of the boat in the water meant that detection by the enemy was unlikely. Once a potential target was sighted, it was far better to pursue it and attack on the surface, as the greater available speed made engagement and escape much easier. Consequently, commanders would seek to attack on the surface wherever possible. This gave the option of using the deck-mounted gun against targets which were not worth a torpedo. The major attribute of the submarine, then, was its ability to hide beneath the waves when it was to its advantage, rather than simply just possessing the means to travel and attack underwater. The key was exploiting this ability correctly, as getting it wrong presented a grave threat to the boat and crew.

Staying surfaced proved to be the undoing of *U15,* for, at 0340 hours, it was sighted by the cruiser HMS *Birmingham. Birmingham* ran straight for the U-boat, which appeared to be unaware of the danger it faced. *Birmingham* struck *U15* a glancing blow across the stern and turned tightly to enable guns to be brought to bear. As *Birmingham* turned, *U15* attempted to get under way, moving painfully slowly as the attacking cruiser manoeuvred into position. *U15* was unable to dive before *Birmingham* closed in and rammed her amidships, cutting the submarine in two. The two halves of the stricken U-boat remained surfaced for a short while, before disappearing beneath the waves. All the crew were lost. Little more than an hour later, *U18* was presented with the chance of evening the score when

she sighted another British cruiser, but this vessel disappeared into a passing rain squall and was lost to view before anything could be done. This proved to be the last sighting of any British ships before the patrol returned to port on the afternoon of 12 August, minus another of its number. *U13* simply disappeared at some point that morning, never to be heard of again.

These results did little to suggest that the U-boat would become one of the most significant weapons of World War I. The failure to discover where the British patrol lines were suggested to the German High Command that the Royal Navy was patrolling well beyond the effective range of its submarines. This gloomy conclusion led to the U-boats resuming defensive operations once more. This was to be a brief

ABOVE: *U48* off the Sardinian coast. The crew are manning the deck gun, which was the preferred weapon against low value targets, to save on the limited supply of torpedoes available.

U9

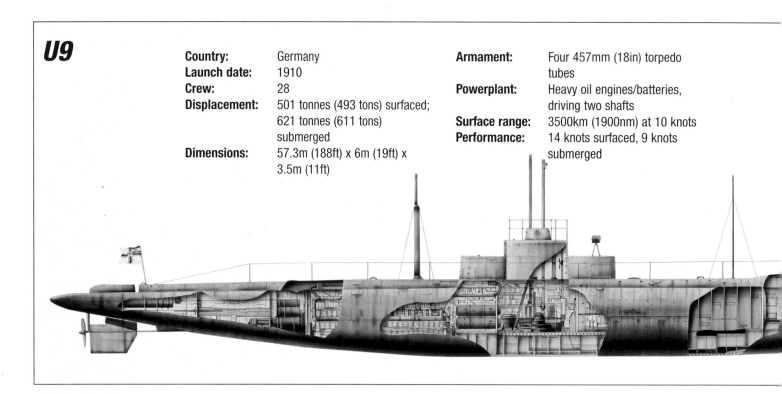

Country:	Germany	Armament:	Four 457mm (18in) torpedo
Launch date:	1910		tubes
Crew:	28	Powerplant:	Heavy oil engines/batteries,
Displacement:	501 tonnes (493 tons) surfaced;		driving two shafts
	621 tonnes (611 tons)	Surface range:	3500km (1900nm) at 10 knots
	submerged	Performance:	14 knots surfaced, 9 knots
Dimensions:	57.3m (188ft) x 6m (19ft) x		submerged
	3.5m (11ft)		

ABOVE: *U9* was almost obsolete before war broke out, being powered by heavy oil engines which limited the boat's effectiveness. Because of this *U9* was retired for use in training duties. The boat was scrapped in 1919.

RIGHT: Otto Weddigen and the crew of *U9*. The *U9* scored the first major success for U-boats in World War I, sinking three British cruisers on 22 September 1914.

reverse, as, on 30 August, reports that heavy ships were anchored off Rosyth led to the despatch of two boats on 2 September with orders to enter the Forth estuary and attack any warships that were found.

Three days later, *U21*, commanded by Otto Hersing, came across the small cruiser HMS *Pathfinder* going about its business off St Abb's Head. The sea was particularly rough, but Hersing produced an excellent firing solution for the single torpedo he fired. The

torpedo struck *Pathfinder*'s magazine and sent it to the bottom. A fortnight later, *U9* struck an even more significant blow. Just after first light on 22 September, Johannes Spiess, *U9*'s Officer of the Watch, alerted the boat's commander, Otto Weddigen, to the sight of a masthead and a smoke plume to the south. Weddigen decided to submerge to periscope depth and slowly approached the plume of smoke. As the distance closed slightly, Weddigen saw more masts and

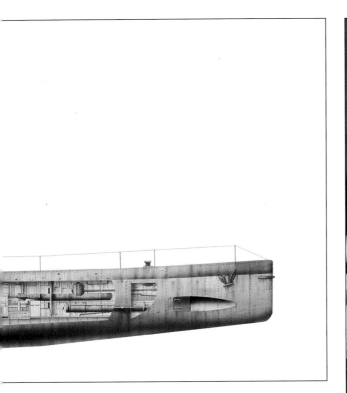

concluded that he was approaching three cruisers. The cruisers maintained their course, moving ponderously along their patrol lines. After about 50 minutes, *U9* was within range of the middle of the three vessels. Weddigen took a final look through the periscope and ordered the firing of a single torpedo. The weapon ran true and struck the target, the armoured cruiser HMS *Aboukir*, which almost immediately took on a list to port. The *Aboukir*'s companions, *Hogue* and *Cressy*, in a move as reckless as it was commendable, moved in to take on survivors.

While his crew reloaded the torpedo tube, Weddigen maintained a steady right-handed turn to bring the submarine's bow onto the second vessel, the *Hogue*. At 350m (1150ft), Weddigen fired both bow tubes and called for both motors to be reversed to avoid collision with the target. Without the torpedo ballast tanks fitted to later U-boats, *U9*'s by now lighter bow broke the surface, giving the *Hogue's* crew the chance to open fire. Weddigen rapidly made the necessary corrective action to bring the boat under control and back under the surface before the British gun crews found their range. Within five minutes, both *Aboukir* and *Hogue* had gone to the bottom.

Incredibly, *Cressy* appeared completely unaware that her two companions had been attacked by a submarine and sailed determinedly towards survivors. Weddigen ordered the reloading of tube two with the last spare torpedo and manoeuvred his boat so that the aft torpedo tubes – so far unused – were facing *Cressy*. At a range of about 1000m (3280ft), Weddigen fired both aft torpedoes. Although these were spotted, *Cressy* was only able to evade one of them, taking a hit forward on the starboard side. Weddigen was unsure whether this had done the job and turned *U9* to bring the bow onto the target. The final torpedo was fired at the now stationary *Cressy* and struck home. *Cressy* rolled to starboard and went under. Torpedoes exhausted, Weddigen headed north to clear the scene and surfaced some 15 minutes after the last of the unfortunate British cruisers had gone to the bottom, taking 1460 men with them. The attack was condemned by the British as an example of 'German Frightfulness', but this moral judgement disguised more profound concerns.

Even before *U9*'s dramatic success, the report of a sighting of a periscope in Scapa Flow had prompted the Commander in Chief of the Grand Fleet, Admiral Sir John Jellicoe, to order the fleet to sea and to Loch

ABOVE: Admiral Sir John Jellicoe commanded the Grand Fleet before becoming professional head of the Royal Navy. His innate caution led to criticism that he mishandled the Battle of Jutland. When the U-boat threat was at its height in 1917, his reluctance to introduce convoys led to considerable losses. Although Jellicoe did introduce the convoy system eventually, he lost the confidence of politicians, and was removed.

Ewe on the northwest coast of Scotland, where it would be out of range of the U-boats. The report was incorrect, but demonstrated the concern with which Jellicoe regarded the submarine threat. The day after *U9*'s three victims had sunk, there was another (and again inaccurate) report of a periscope being sighted. Jellicoe ordered the fleet to sea, heading for Loch Swilly in Ireland. They

returned to Scapa in early November, only to receive another rude shock before the month was out. On 23 November, *U18* managed to penetrate what defences there were at Scapa Flow, only to find that the anchorages where she might have expected to find rich pickings were deserted. On the way out, her periscope was sighted, and she was rammed twice – first by an armed trawler and then, more

U151

Country:	Germany	**Armament:**	Two 150mm (5.9in) guns, two 86mm (3.4in) guns, two 508mm (20in) torpedo tubes
Launch date:	April 1917		
Crew:	56		
Displacement:	1536 tonnes (1511 tons) surfaced, 1905 tonnes (1875 tons) submerged	**Powerplant:**	Diesel/electric motors, driving two shafts
		Surface range:	20,909km (11,300nm) at 10 knots
Dimensions:	65m (213ft) x 8.9m (29ft) x 5.3m (17ft)	**Performance:**	12.4 knots surfaced, 5.2 knots submerged

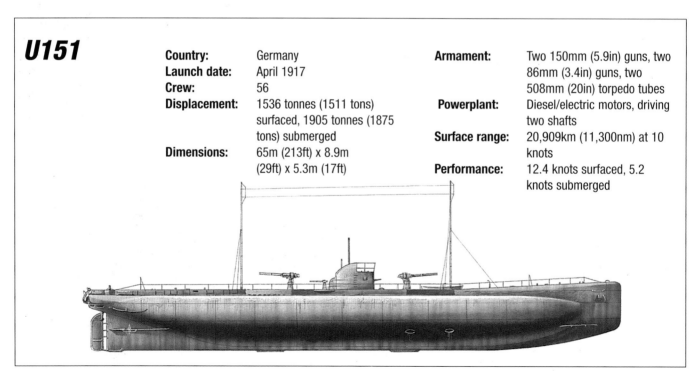

decisively, by a destroyer. *U18* was damaged and lost all motive power as she was carried by the current onto the Skerries, where the crew scuttled their boat.

From the German perspective, U-boat operations in 1914 may not have been successful in terms of tonnage sunk. All the ships that were lost were old units and not part of the Grand Fleet, while the U-boats had suffered losses. They had, however, made a much more significant contribution in the moral effect imposed on the Royal Navy. The ability of enemy submarines to penetrate Scapa Flow was a tremendous shock to the Admiralty and simply confirmed Jellicoe's suspicions that the submarine was a serious threat to his command. A small force of boats had driven the world's most powerful fleet out of its anchorage twice, temporarily altering the strategic balance. However, the failure to sink any major surface units was a significant matter – the High Seas Fleet was still outnumbered, and Britain maintained effective protection of commerce and trade routes. Although it did not seem especially significant at the time, the U-boat's major contribution to World War I had been signalled on 20 October in an event that had passed almost unnoticed.

The steamer *Glitra*, heading for Stavanger with a cargo of coal, was intercepted and brought to by *U17*. The submarine commander, Feldkirchner, despatched a boarding party, which opened the ship's seacocks, allowing it to sink. Before this happened, Feldkirchner allowed all the crew to take to the lifeboats and then, to ensure that they had the best chance of survival, towed the lifeboats closer to the shore. This rather polite event was in stark contrast to the image of the rapacious U-boat callously sending unarmed civilian vessels to the bottom with little thought for the wellbeing of the crew. Indeed, in the first six months of the war, only 10 merchantmen were lost to U-boat attack, which was largely carried out in an extremely polite fashion without loss of life.

The U-boats followed 'prize regulations', which meant that they were required positively to identify the ship that they were targeting. This demanded that they surface and board the vessel in which they were interested. Only once the U-boat commander was satisfied that the ship was a legitimate victim was he able to sink it; in so doing, he was required to make sure that the ship's company was given the opportunity to leave the ship before it was sent to the bottom. These demands meant that the value of surprise was completely lost, and it is not surprising that the German naval command felt that this approach negated the tactical advantages offered by the submarine. On the whole, this part of the campaign seemed unremarkable, and the view of Rear-Admiral Alexander Duff that Germany would be unable to do much harm to merchant shipping with submarines seemed perfectly reasonable at the time.

BELOW: The crew of a sunken steamer are interrogated by the crew of the *U35*. Although there were claims that the U-boat was a terror weapon, with surprise attacks being made against defenceless merchant ships, the reality was different. During restricted U-boat warfare, the submariners had a duty to ensure that the crew had the best chance of survival, and often provided food and water for the lifeboats. In some cases, lifeboats were towed nearer to shore to reduce the amount of time that the survivors spent adrift.

U140

Country:	Germany	Armament:	Two 150mm (5.9in) guns, six 508mm (20in) torpedo tubes
Launch date:	November 1917		
Crew:	62	Powerplant:	Diesel/electric motors, driving two shafts
Displacement:	1961 tonnes (1930 tons) surfaced, 2523 tonnes (2483 tons) submerged		
		Surface range:	32,873km (17,750nm) at 8 knots
Dimensions:	94.8m (311ft) x 9m (29ft) x 5.2m (17ft)	Performance:	15.8 knots surfaced, 7.6 knots submerged

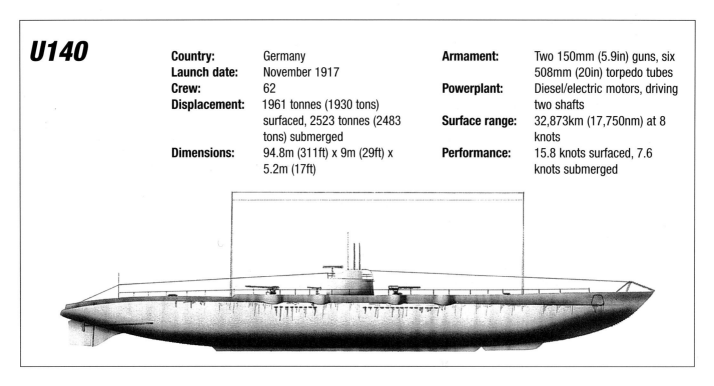

ABOVE: The U140 was built as a submarine cruiser, and was one of the few U-boats to receive a name: Kapitanleutnant Weddigen, in honour of the skipper of U9. After the end of the war, she was surrendered to the United States, where she was sunk as a gunnery target.

Duff's prediction was overturned when the German Admiralty began to press for aggressive submarine warfare against all merchant vessels, be they from neutral countries or not, unhindered by prize regulations. This would enable U-boats to attack when submerged, preventing the target vessel from escaping, greatly increasing their effectiveness. There was some opposition to this plan, notably from the Imperial Chancellor, Bethmann Hollweg, and Admiral von Pohl, the Chief of the German Naval Staff, who both feared that this would antagonize neutral countries, particularly the United States.

THE MOVE TO UNRESTRICTED WARFARE

Pohl's view changed on 2 November 1914, when Britain declared that the whole of the North Sea was to be regarded as a war zone. All supplies bound for Germany would be stopped, even if they were aboard ships from neutral countries. This would have the effect of cutting Germany off, with the important side effect of preventing the importation of food. Pohl took the view that the British attempt to starve Germany out of the war merited a more robust response. This was to be in the form of unrestricted submarine warfare.

The nature of the campaign was significant, as it meant that ships would be sunk without warning. It also meant that the crews of merchant ships could no longer rely upon U-boat commanders making any attempt to save them from their fate. On 4 February 1915, although concerns over the reaction of the United States remained,

Germany declared that all ships in the vicinity of the British Isles were likely to be attacked without warning. Britain and Germany were now following the same maritime policy – they would attempt to starve the enemy out of the war by destroying their maritime trade. For both nations, the effects were serious, but for Germany they proved disastrous. There had already been concerns about how the United States would react, and events over the next two years demonstrated that Bethmann Hollweg had been right to be concerned. The United States would not take kindly to attacks on its vessels, and, within three months, this had been demonstrated by what is still the most readily recalled submarine attack in military history – the sinking of the Lusitania.

The Americans were far from happy with the notion of unrestricted submarine warfare, and a series of diplomatic exchanges between Washington and Berlin nearly undermined the submarine campaign before it began. The implied threat of a US military response prompted the Germans to promise that vessels which could be clearly identified as neutrals would not be attacked. This led to an immediate protest from the German naval command. They pointed out that around a quarter of imports to the United Kingdom were carried by neutral ships; to guarantee that neutrals would not be attacked undermined the whole basis for the campaign. Furthermore, many British ships were already flying the colours of neutral states to prevent attack, and it did not take much imagination to realize that the whole British merchant fleet might do the same to protect itself. Finally, while the promise to Washington was fine in theory, quite how a submarine commander was meant to distinguish between neutral and Allied ships while looking through a periscope was unclear. Consequently, the German naval staff argued that the unrestricted campaign would have to be called off.

The result of the Imperial Navy's protest was to secure a compromise. It was declared that genuinely neutral ships would not be attacked, nor would hospital ships or vessels of the Belgian Relief Commission (which was heavily funded from the United States). However, while these limits were in place, U-boat captains were quietly told that they would not be blamed if they made mistakes and attacked ships that were supposedly safe. It should be pointed out that this was not so much duplicity on the part of the Germans as a practical recognition that the difficulties of identifying ships meant that genuine mistakes would inevitably be made.

THE LUSITANIA

The unrestricted U-boat offensive of 1915 was hampered by the lack of submarines available to the Germans. The greatest number of boats at sea on any one day was 12, while the overall average was just over seven per day. This was unlikely to be enough to bring the British Empire to its knees, but the small fleet still managed to sink more than 762,000 tonnes (750,000 tons) of shipping. Among these sinkings were two highly significant incidents that helped to end the campaign prematurely.

On 1 May 1915, the American tanker *Gulflight* was torpedoed. Although it made harbour, the master died of a heart attack and two other crew members jumped overboard and were drowned. The attack provoked considerable anger in Washington, but this was nothing compared to the outrage caused six days later when a British steamer was sunk. On 7 May, *U20*, commanded by *Kapitanleutnant* Walter Schwieger was operating in the Western Approaches. Early in the afternoon, a four-funnelled steamer was sighted some 22.5km (14 miles) away. After some consideration, the identity of the ship was narrowed down to two possibilities: either the *Lusitania* or the *Mauritania*. According to the most up-to-date reference source available – the 1914 *Jane's Fighting Ships* – these vessels were both armed merchant cruisers. The Germans were convinced that the ships were being used as troop transports, and, with these two considerations in mind, Schwieger felt that he was faced with a legitimate target. *U20* ran at high speed towards the ship until it was some 700m (2296ft) away. At 1510 hours, a single torpedo was fired, striking the steamer, which stopped and heeled to starboard. Within 20 minutes, the ship sank. Still unaware of the precise identity of the target, *U20* left the scene.

The stricken ship was the *Lusitania*, and she took 1201 passengers with her. Of these, 128 were US citizens, a number of whom were notable society figures. If this were not enough, the ship was unarmed and certainly not being used for trooping. Although the swift nature of the ship's demise prompted some speculation that armaments or war materials were being

LEFT: A U-boat halts an American steamer, prior to sending a boarding party to inspect the cargo. If the cargo was deemed to be war material for an enemy power, the steamer's crew would be permitted to take to the ship's boats before she was sunk. The laws of war demanded that the submarine inspect the cargo before taking action; once unrestricted submarine warfare was introduced, this was impossible.

ABOVE: The *Lusitania*, perhaps the most famous victim of submarine warfare. The *Lusitania* was sunk in May 1915, having been identified by *U20* as an armed merchant cruiser. The sinking claimed the lives of many Americans, and caused outrage in Washington. The possibility of America entering the war effectively brought the first unrestricted submarine campaign to a close, as the restrictions on submarine operations imposed by the German government made it impossible for the campaign to be effective.

RIGHT: The engine room crew of a U-boat at work. The picture demonstrates the cramped conditions within a submarine, where every spare centimetre of space was utilised. The picture does not convey the unpleasant atmosphere that the crew had to endure.

carried, the most recent consensus is that *Lusitania* was operating in a purely civilian capacity. The repercussions were enormous.

The American reaction was vehement, with President Woodrow Wilson effectively demanding an instant end to the unrestricted campaign. Once again, a difference of opinion between the German foreign ministry and the naval staff arose. The naval staff, convinced of the merits of unrestricted warfare, was determined that all American pressure should be resisted, while the foreign ministry was more willing to compromise so as to keep the Americans from intervening in the war. Matters were not helped by highly effective British propaganda, which suggested that the German nation as a whole was glorying in the drowning of women and children. American

feeling was intensified by the sinking of the liner *Arabic* on 19 August, with two US citizens being among the 44 casualties.

After considerable diplomatic effort, on 28 August, Chancellor Bethmann Hollweg managed to persuade Wilson that U-boat commanders would no longer endanger the safety of neutral ships and passenger liners. The new head of the naval staff, Admiral Bachman, argued that the restrictions imposed by the latest guarantee to the Americans made the campaign unworkable, and that the campaign would have to be abandoned forthwith. Bachman may have been working on the assumption that the Chancellor would not dare to risk the public reaction to the ending of the campaign, but failed to realize that the Chancellor had

other options. Bethmann Hollweg dismissed Bachman and replaced him with Admiral von Holtzendorff. Holtzendorff was not only a personal friend of the Chancellor, but also, even more importantly, thought that the claims for the unrestricted U-boat campaign were excessive.

Although more than 360 ships were sunk between July and September 1915, the campaign had not had a great impact upon the British. Neutral ships had not been dissuaded from continuing to trade with Britain, and the economic pressure was nowhere near enough to make Britain consider lifting its blockade of Germany. Had the campaign continued unabated, the situation may have changed for the worse as sinkings increased. As it was, the sinking of another liner on 6 September tipped the balance. The liner *Hesperian* was sunk with 32 casualties, in direct contradiction of the promises made to Wilson, and Holtzendorff promptly ordered the withdrawal of all U-boats from the English Channel and the Western Approaches. In addition, he gave instructions that operations in the North Sea could only be conducted according to Prize Regulations. This meant that attacking without warning was impossible, and it prompted von Pohl, now Commander in Chief of the High Seas Fleet, to withdraw all submarines from the North Sea rather than comply with the new restrictions. This marked the end of the first attempt at unrestricted submarine warfare.

Although the campaign was brought to a close by Pohl's withdrawal of the U-boats from the North Sea, the lack of U-boats in service meant that the campaign was already beginning to lose impetus. When assessing the campaign, it became clear that more U-boats were needed for any subsequent attempt to blockade the British Isles. It was also obvious that attacking while submerged was a far more effective option than engaging ships on the surface. Surfacing gave the intended victim a greater chance of escape: 54 per cent of vessels that were attacked by surfaced U-boats managed to escape, while this figure fell to 42 per cent for those attacked without warning. Surfacing also gave enemy ships the opportunity to attack the submarine; seven out of the 15 boats lost between February and September 1915 were sunk as a result of surfacing to carry out their attack.

THE BRITISH RESPONSE

For the British, it appeared that the first U-boat campaign was only a minor cause for concern. The Germans had seriously antagonized American opinion, and they

had not come close to threatening the continuance of British trade. This perhaps ensured a rather complacent approach to anti-submarine warfare. There were no really effective countermeasures for dealing with submerged submarines, as there was very little that could be done to locate them. By May 1916, some 450 vessels made up from a variety of sloops, armed yachts and trawlers, and a few destroyers conducted 'offensive patrols' against submarines in the Western Approaches. While the number of ships employed sounds impressive, this needs to be put into perspective: the vast area that the ships had to cover made the likelihood of encountering a U-boat extremely small. Even if the ships happened to be in the vicinity of an enemy submarine, as they had no effective means of finding a submerged U-boat, the chances of actually engaging an enemy vessel were even more remote.

While the Western Approaches were guarded in this largely unsatisfactory manner, the English Channel's anti-submarine measures relied heavily on minefields. Although the minefield seemed to be a useful deterrent to submarines, the reality

ABOVE TOP: As part of the British anti-submarine effort, a number of small merchant craft were equipped with concealed weapons, to allow them to attack U-boats. These 'Q- ships' were not worth a torpedo, and it was hoped that U-boats would surface to sink them with their deck guns, whereupon the Q-ship would reply using its own armament.

ABOVE: A concealed gun on a Q-ship. Although the Q-ships enjoyed some initial successes, as soon as the Germans were aware of the ruse they became much more careful.

ABOVE: A German propaganda poster demonstrating the imbalance between the number of merchant ships built and those sunk by the U-boats. The calculation was simple: sink more merchant ships than the British could build, and Britain would be starved of vital imports. If a sufficient amount of imports were stopped as a result, Britain would be forced to seek peace.

RIGHT: A British mine is displayed, having been washed ashore. At first, British mines were hopelessly unreliable, often failing to explode. Eventually, a copy of a German mine was made, which proved far more effective, although even these were unsuccessful in making large areas of sea impassable to U-boats.

was rather different. The mines were moored and could be seen at low water, which made navigating around them a relatively simple proposition. Even if a submarine were to hit one, the British mines were scandalously unreliable, often failing to explode when struck – hardly the best advertisement for a 'contact' mine. On top of this, the mines had a habit of sinking to the bottom of the sea, where they were useless, or simply drifting away. Despite these obvious failings, the British seem to have been unconcerned about the poor quality of both the mines and the minefields, an oversight that was to prove regrettable.

Behind the mines, there was a line of ships equipped with so-called 'indicator nets'. These used long lines of netting equipped with a carbide flare that would light when a U-boat fouled a section of the net. In theory, once the flare had indicated the presence of a U-boat, the patrol craft would close in and sink the submarine with gunfire or by ramming. This presupposed that the submarine captain would choose to surface to free himself from the netting; if he chose to remain submerged, the matter was greatly complicated. There were no depth charges available, so the patrolling ships would have to attempt to sink the submarine using explosive charges attached to a long looped wire. This imprecise method managed to account for one submarine (*U8*), but no more.

By the end of the first unrestricted campaign, the most effective countermeasure was the 'Q-ship', a small ship fitted with concealed guns. The reasoning behind them was that, because of their size, they would not be considered worth a torpedo by U-boat captains. A submarine would surface to sink the ship with its deck gun, whereupon the Q-ship would engage the submarine at point-blank range, with lethal results. Although Q-ships were to prove relatively effective, they sustained losses when fighting it out with the U-boats.

This deficiency in effective counter-measures, caused by some technological difficulties and a degree of complacency, was to have serious effects in the last three years of the war.

THE SECOND OFFENSIVE

If the British hoped that the end of the unrestricted offensive of 1915 marked the end of their troubles, they were to be disappointed. By the end of the year, the Royal Navy's blockade of Germany was causing the German leadership anxiety, particularly over the effect on the food supply. At a meeting on 30 December, the Chief of the General Staff, Erich von Falkenhayn, offered two solutions to the problem. The first was to be a major offensive against the French army at Verdun, which was planned to 'bleed the French Army white', while his second proposal was for a resumption of the U-boat campaign in home waters.

By this time, Admiral von Holtzendorff had modified his views on unrestricted submarine warfare. He now believed that a properly conducted campaign stood a good chance of making Britain sue for peace. This reversal of opinion came about thanks to calculations Holtzendorff made based upon the results of the campaign of 1915. He concluded that a campaign that sank somewhere in the

LEFT: King George V (centre) and Edward, Prince of Wales (far right) on board the USS *New York* in 1918. The broad smiles for the camera would not have been there a year earlier, when the U-boats appeared likely to cut the lifeline between the United States and the United Kingdom.

region of 162,500 tonnes (160,000 tons) of shipping a month would leave the British facing losses that could not be made good by new shipbuilding, no matter how hard they might try. Although the support of Holtzendorff was significant, it did not lead to immediate adoption of the plan.

Bethmann Hollweg argued that the opinion of the United States had to be considered and doubted that the elegant simplicity of the calculations would hold true in actual practice. The disagreement required the Kaiser to make the final decision. Wilhelm agreed that the campaign would provoke the United States, but felt that Holtzendorff's calculations were not

unreasonable. He ordered that a new campaign should start on 29 February 1916, but with certain limitations. While enemy ships within the war zone were to be destroyed without warning, those outside the zone could only be attacked in similar fashion if they were armed. To placate American opinion, enemy steamers were not to be attacked by submerged submarines at all. Once again, the Navy was unhappy with the restrictions, and Tirpitz resigned as Secretary of the Navy. Despite this, the restrictions were not modified, and the new campaign started as planned in the new year.

Despite the clearly identified need for more U-boats, the first day of the second

BELOW: A sister-ship to the *U140*, the *U139* was named the *Kapitanleutnant Schweiger*. Unlike the *U140*, *U139* had a profitable post-war career, being pressed into service with the French navy as the *Halbronn*.

U139

Country:	Germany	**Armament:**	Two 150mm (5.9in) guns, six
Launch date:	December 1917		508mm (20in) torpedo tubes
Crew:	62	**Powerplant:**	Diesel/electric motors, driving two
Displacement:	1961 tonnes (1930 tons)		shafts
	surfaced, 2523 tonnes	**Surface range:**	23,390km (12,600nm) at 8 knots
	(2483 tons) submerged	**Performance:**	15.8 knots surfaced, 7.6 knots
Dimensions:	94.8m (311ft) x		submerged
	9m (29ft) x 5.2m (17ft)		

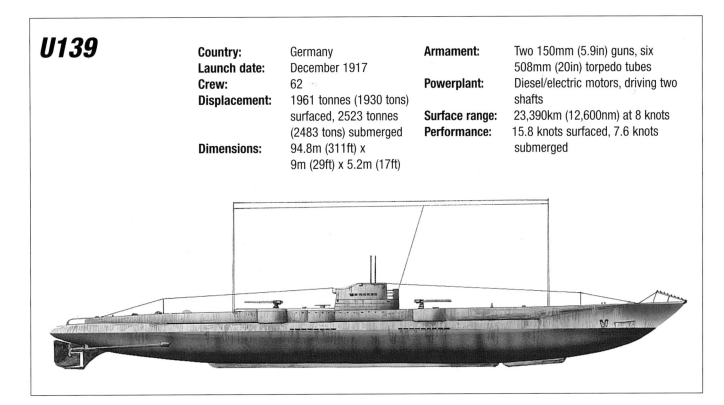

ABOVE: A boat of the *UC1* class demonstrates the small size of most U-boats – note the crowded conning tower as the crew take some fresh air.

offensive began with only one submarine at sea. Nonetheless, the offensive seemed to be progressing well. Although Holtzendorff's calculated figure of 162,500 tonnes (160,000 tons) per month was not being met, there was good reason to suppose that it would be once more U-boats were in service. Unfortunately for German plans, this was never put to the test, as another crisis in relations with the United States intervened. On 24 March, *UB29* sighted a steamer about to enter Dieppe. Through the periscope, it appeared to be a troopship, and the captain had no hesitation in torpedoing what he thought was a legitimate target. The ship, though, was not a troopship, but the liner *Sussex*. The attack caused 50 casualties, including some Americans. Washington's reaction was one of fury – although the word 'war' was not mentioned in President Wilson's signal, the implication that this was a likely result if such attacks continued was clear. The German government immediately

ordered that no attacks were to take place without the inspection of the ship, ending attack without warning and removing all the tactical advantages it offered.

As a result of ill health, Pohl had retired as commander in Chief of the High Seas Fleet. It fell to Admiral Reinhard Scheer, his successor, to show the Imperial Navy's disapproval by calling off the whole submarine campaign. Once again, there may have been the hope that the public reaction would cause the Chancellor difficulty, but this was not the case. The second offensive ended before it had any chance to have an effect on the war; it was not long, though, before the question of unrestricted warfare arose again.

RESUMPTION OF ACTION

As 1916 progressed, Germany's military situation worsened. The campaign at Verdun, while as sanguinary as von Falkenhayn proposed, was unsuccessful, and, on 1 July, the British launched an offensive on the

Somme which applied yet more pressure to the German Army. In addition, the Russians had made advances in the east against Austria-Hungary, presenting a further threat to the Germans. The failure at Verdun saw the replacement of Falkenhayn by General Paul von Hindenburg and General Erich von Ludendorff. The two new commanders argued that an unrestricted campaign to apply severe pressure to Britain was necessary.

Bethmann Hollweg was concerned that such a campaign might drive neutral states such as the Netherlands and Denmark into the war against Germany, but, for the first time, he accepted that an unrestricted campaign was the only solution to the problem of the British blockade. Hindenburg was similarly concerned about the possibility of the neutrals joining the war on the Allied side and arrogantly informed the rest of the German political and military leadership that he and Ludendorff would decide the exact time when the unrestricted offensive could begin. In the interim, a restricted campaign should continue. This was a major turning point, as it marked recognition by all the parties in the strategic decision-making process that the best hope of winning the war was by launching a ruthless campaign of submarine warfare against British maritime trade: the question was not *whether*, but *when*. The answer was 1917.

THE UNRESTRICTED CAMPAIGN

Even the restricted campaign showed some promise for the Germans. Ocean-going U-boats began to cause considerable concern, as they started to engage shipping

LEFT: *U25* takes on torpedoes prior to heading for operations in the Mediterranean. Submarine operations around Italy were far less successful than hoped for, and the same pattern was repeated in World War II.

in the Bay of Biscay, while *U53* went as far as the eastern seaboard of the United States. *U53* sank five steamers off Nantucket light vessel, provoking further public outrage in the United States. This was probably less of a concern in Berlin than previous reactions, as the decision to launch an unrestricted campaign had already been taken. As the number of U-boats in service increased during the year, the success of the limited campaign was such that it gave Holtzendorff hope that around 610,000 tonnes (600,000 tons) of shipping could be sunk each month. He also predicted that twice this amount of neutral tonnage would be dissuaded from trading with the United Kingdom.

Holtzendorff claimed that, if his assessment were accurate, the level of shipping to Britain would be reduced to crisis levels within five months. In support, Hindenburg and Ludendorff argued that the threat from the United States could be ignored. Despite the threatening noises emanating from Washington, the military readiness of the United States was not high enough to permit the despatch of a critical number of troops to Europe in the short term. Additionally, US troops could only reach Europe by sea, and they would be subjected to the depredations of the U-boats. By October 1916, there were 96 U-boats in service, compared to just 30 in June. The

offensive had claimed 768 ships by this date, of which 500 were neutrals.

These losses were serious enough, but the effort to intimidate neutrals had finally borne fruit. More than two million tonnes (two million tons) of tonnage was lost to British trade as a result, while warnings of U-boats had caused serious delays as ships remained in harbour. The Admiralty became increasingly concerned that the campaign would begin to have serious effects on the importation of food and was moved to form an Anti-Submarine Division (ASD), under Rear Admiral Duff. Sir John Jellicoe, now the First Sea Lord, saw three ways of stopping the U-boat campaign. The first was by preventing submarines from putting to sea; the second by sinking them; or, finally, by protecting the merchant ships directly, rather than permitting the continuance of ships operating independently of escort. There was some historical precedent that suggested that this was the best way of preventing commerce from being strangled by an enemy navy, but the Admiralty seemed reluctant to adopt the practice of convoying ships. It would not be long before the unrestricted campaign compelled it to reconsider.

By October, the Royal Navy's blockade of Germany was having serious effects. It was clear that the winter of 1916–17 was likely to see serious food shortages – it in fact

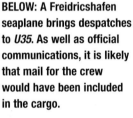

BELOW: A Freidricshafen seaplane brings despatches to *U35*. As well as official communications, it is likely that mail for the crew would have been included in the cargo.

U160

Country:	Germany	**Armament:**	Two 104mm (4.1in) guns, six 508mm (20in) torpedo tubes
Launch date:	February 1918		
Crew:	39	**Powerplant:**	Diesel/electric motors, driving two shafts
Displacement:	834 tonnes (820 tons) surfaced, 1016 tonnes (1000 tons) submerged	**Surface range:**	15,372km (8300nm) at 8 knots
		Performance:	16.2 knots surfaced 8.2 knots submerged
Dimensions:	71.8m (235ft) x 6.2m		

became known as the 'turnip winter', as the turnip became the staple foodstuff – and something had to be done to break the stranglehold. Without some form of action, it was possible that Germany could be starved into peace. Coupled with the fact that the situation regarding the neutral nations seemed better, the Kaiser was persuaded to agree that the unrestricted campaign could begin on 1 February 1917.

ALL-OUT SUBMARINE WARFARE

When the campaign began, the U-boat force was far stronger than before. There were 105 U-boats available, with the prospect of more to come. The effect of the submarines was dramatic. Between the start of the campaign and April, an average of 658,821 tonnes (648,414 tons) of shipping was sunk per month, exceeding Holtzendorff's calculations. Neutrals 'practically abandoned' trading with Britain, while those who were in British ports refused to leave. To make matters worse for the British, only 10 U-boats were lost, and three of these were accidents not involving any action by the Royal Navy. Although the campaign finally provoked the United States to enter the war as a co-belligerent of the Allies, this development would be of little benefit if the submarine campaign continued to enjoy such success. The technology available for anti-submarine operations had improved, but it had not evolved far enough to make a substantial difference. The solution would be found in strategy, rather than equipment, and consideration of how to approach the U-boats became ever more urgent.

The first solution proposed by Jellicoe, that of preventing the submarines putting to sea, was practically impossible to achieve. Apart from capturing or destroying all the bases, this method was dependent upon minefields. Incredibly, despite the failings of British mines, nothing had been done to address the problem. It was not until the spring of 1917 that the Royal Navy finally had a reliable mine, which was achieved by the simple expedient of copying a German design – which was proven to work. Even though the design was perfected, it took until December 1917 for there to be enough: a full 10 months after unrestricted warfare had begun.

This left the other two solutions: hunting down and sinking the U-boats or convoying the merchant ships. The technology for locating submarines was still primitive at the start of the unrestricted offensive, with the hydrophone being the only available tool. The model in use in 1917 was better than the first type, but it could still only detect the beating of submarine propellers. It could not provide any indications of bearing or depth, which meant that prosecuting a contact was far from easy. The use of signals interception by the Admiralty's Room 40 provided some indication of where U-boats were, but this obviously did not have the same immediacy as a detection device on a ship. In light of this, it seems odd that the third solution, convoy, was not viewed with any favour.

The Admiralty had several major objections to convoying ships. The first was over the nature of convoys. The biggest

ABOVE: *U160* was the first of a class of fast U-boats to be built in the last year of the war. The high speed enjoyed by these submarines was perfect for attacks on the surface, giving the ability to evade enemy defences. *U160* was surrendered to France after the armistice, and was scrapped in 1922.

ABOVE: The final humiliation: the High Seas Fleet, escorted by units from the Royal Navy, heads towards Scapa Flow to surrender. The German crews managed to salvage something from the surrender, scuttling their ships before the British could take them over.

perceived failing was a shortage of suitable escort vessels. The Admiralty pointed at the huge number of shipping movements each month, which suggested that a huge increase in the escorts would be required. In addition, there were doubts about the sea-keeping ability of the merchantmen, with a suspicion that this would lead to the convoys breaking up. Another concern was rooted in the belief that the Royal Navy was an offensive arm and that convoying was a purely defensive measure not in keeping with the traditions of the service. This assessment ignored the fact that convoy had been a prime part of the Royal Navy's activities in the days of Nelson, and there had been few complaints about a lack of action then. Finally, the Admiralty contended that putting ships into convoys would present the U-boats with easy targets.

At face value, these objections appeared reasonable, but there were doubters. The Secretary to the War Cabinet, Sir Maurice Hankey. presented the British Prime Minister with a paper arguing in favour of convoying merchantmen in February, but Lloyd George had not seen fit to act upon it. As a result, the sinking of unescorted merchant vessels continued to increase, while only doom and despondency could be found at the Admiralty. When Admiral Sims, who would command the US Navy forces in European waters, visited Britain after the US declaration of war, he was shocked to discover that Jellicoe apparently could see no solution to the crisis. In fact, Jellicoe had some ideas, but his natural pessimism meant that he held out little hope of success. There were three possible answers. The first of these, building ships at a faster rate than they were sunk, had been dismissed as improbable by Holtzendorff

French industry depended upon British coal. France had few coal reserves of its own, and much of what it had was under German control. The British did not have these difficulties and had happily obliged in supplying the French since the outbreak of war. The sinkings saw the supply reduced drastically, and France's war industry slowed. It was decided to convoy the coal ships, and, from 10 January 1917, convoys of up to 45 colliers were escorted across the channel by armed trawlers. By the end of April, only five out of 2600 coal ships had been sunk.

The unexpected success of convoys in an area thick with U-boats persuaded Rear Admiral Duff that it was at least worth trying convoys elsewhere. Furthermore, research by Commander R.G.H. Henderson demonstrated that the number of ship movements that would need to be convoyed were far fewer than had been supposed. The original figures had covered all shipping movements, which ran into thousands, while the number of ships that would be covered by the convoys was in the hundreds. The success of the coal convoys and the revised figures persuaded Duff to propose that an ocean convoy from Gibraltar should be attempted; a doubtful Jellicoe approved the plan on 27 April. After the war, Lord Beaverbrook's rather eclectic approach to historical accuracy gave rise to the story that the British Prime Minister himself had visited the Admiralty and ordered the adoption of convoy. David Lloyd George did nothing to correct the story, but his visit to the Admiralty took place three days after Jellicoe agreed to the Gibraltar convoy.

The Gibraltar convoy arrived absolutely unscathed on 20 May; four days later, a convoy was escorted across the Atlantic from Hampton Roads, Virginia, and it too arrived without loss. By the end of July, there had been 21 Atlantic convoys, but only two ships had been lost. Despite this success, the introduction of convoying was initially slow, and independent sailings continued, with commensurately high losses. By November, however, 90 per cent of British shipping was in convoy, and losses had decreased dramatically. This did not mean that victory had been achieved.

The Germans responded to the increasing use of convoy by attacking merchant ships when they had reached coastal waters and the convoy was dispersed. This change of tactics enabled the Germans to inflict a loss rate that caused some concern, but the worst was over. No tactical counter to the convoy itself was discovered, blunting much of the effect of the offensive. With the

when he made his calculations for the campaign. Jellicoe was similarly dubious, but this did not prevent a reorganization of shipbuilding to try to achieve the goal. Quite how the loss of experienced seamen was to be made up was not explained. Jellicoe's second proposal was to mine the Heligoland Bight, but although the quality and quantity of mines were at last improving, the mines were always spotted by the Germans, who simply navigated around them. The third solution was to introduce experimental convoys. Once again, Jellicoe was not hopeful of success.

CONVOY

Ironically, the convoy system was already in place. U-boats operating in the English Channel had inflicted serious losses on coal ships heading for France during the last months of 1916. This was a grave matter, as

UB4

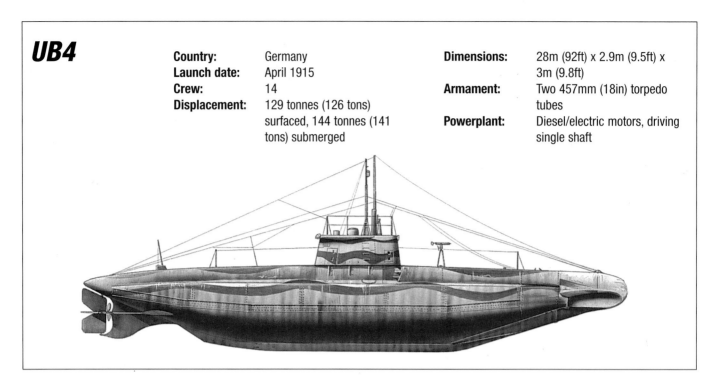

Country:	Germany	**Dimensions:**	28m (92ft) x 2.9m (9.5ft) x 3m (9.8ft)
Launch date:	April 1915		
Crew:	14	**Armament:**	Two 457mm (18in) torpedo tubes
Displacement:	129 tonnes (126 tons) surfaced, 144 tonnes (141 tons) submerged	**Powerplant:**	Diesel/electric motors, driving single shaft

ABOVE: The *UB4* was one of the small coastal boats that were built in 1914. Only three of the eight boats in *UB4*'s class survived the war. *UB4* was sunk by the British armed trawler *Inverlyon* in August 1915, after a short career of only four months.

benefit of not much hindsight, it was clear that a concentration of U-boats to meet the concentration of ships would have been the best answer. Before this conclusion was reached, though, the German Naval Staff remained convinced that the solution was simply to increase the number of U-boats. This was not enough. Although the threat from submarines remained almost until the end of the war, the Allies managed to contain the unrestricted campaign at a sustainable level. It is important to note, however, that they did not manage to defeat it.

The means of containing the threat lay entirely in the convoy, the Admiralty's mistrusted tactic. With hindsight, it is puzzling to understand the reluctance to adopt the convoy system. Although involving surface raiders rather than submarines, historical examples demonstrated that an attack on enemy shipping demanded two things. The first was that the surface raiders find enemy merchant shipping; the second was that they sank it in large enough amounts to deny supplies to the enemy. The solution was elegantly simple: concentrate the trading ships behind the protection of the Royal Navy. This would mean that the surface raider would be very lucky to survive the encounter, given the superiority of the defence. If the enemy chose not to engage, this was all well and good, as he would have failed in his key aim of sinking merchant shipping. The British navy of Nelson's day saw nothing wrong with this principle; the navy of Jellicoe's day did, but on flimsy grounds.

By 1914, the Royal Navy preferred to talk about protection of trade routes and felt

that the only worthwhile sort of action was offensive action. This meant going out, finding the enemy and engaging him (victoriously, of course). The convoy, with ships tied to merchant vessels, was defensive and unlikely to meet with success. This thinking was to miss the point. Given the extent of Britain's maritime trade by 1914, the U-boats – replacing surface raiders in the equation – would often manage to find a ship that was carrying something to Britain. The ship, sailing independently, would have no defence against attack; if the submarine attacked without warning, only a failure of the torpedo (or its firing plot) would save it. Unless the U-boat was unlucky, it could repeat the performance several times.

Although there was a relatively large number of anti-submarine vessels available, using them in an 'offensive' manner meant that they patrolled purposefully up and down what had been identified as the key trading routes. The problem here was that, for all the determination shown, it was easy to avoid the patrols in the vast expanse of ocean. The U-boat commanders simply attacked ships sailing independently and carried on without much concern.

Concentrating the merchant ships did offer a tempting target to the enemy submariner, but it presented a major challenge. Instead of having to thrash about the sea desperately trying to locate a submarine with the primitive technology available, convoy escorts simply had to wait for the submarine to come to them. In fact, the convoy made the ultimate expression of offensive action – sinking the enemy – a far easier prospect. In addition, concentrating the merchantmen meant that the U-boats had a far more difficult time in finding their targets. Whereas the German submarines could at least be certain that there would be a merchantman sailing independently somewhere in their operating area (although they might not find it), the convoy system denuded the seas of this easy prey. This was always obvious to the Germans, who saw that the question was not one of 'offence' or 'defence' or 'routes' or 'lines of communication', but the simple one of sinking ships at such a rate that the enemy could not make good the losses. Despite having the evidence presented to them in the course of 1917 and 1918, it seems that the British Admiralty did not quite take this on board, with a lack of appreciation of the importance of anti-submarine vessels in World War II. It is fair to say that, in World War I, the Royal Navy did not so much win the battle against the submarine as eventually make sure that it did not lose it. Given the wider context of the war, this was good enough to be vital.

THE END OF WAR

Although the level of losses caused by U-boats remained disconcerting until almost the end of World War I, they were acceptable. For the British, the war would not be lost for want of supplies, while events conspired against the Germans. In March 1918, Ludendorff launched a massive offensive on the Western Front. Although it was an outstanding success to begin with, the Allies resisted with considerable determination. A mixture of dogged rearguard actions and problems within the German ranks halted the advance. When German soldiers captured British supply dumps, they were amazed to discover how well stocked they were. This had two effects: it demoralized the German soldiers, who were convinced that the British were suffering grave shortages, and it caused them to be less willing to accept what they were told by their leaders. Also, the German soldiers stopped to remove the food and personal equipment they needed from the Allied stores, causing crucial delays in some sectors of the front. By the end of June, the offensive was virtually at an end, and the Germans were all but spent. The casualties of the Spring Offensives were unsustainable.

In July, the French launched a counterattack, and, on 8 August, British Empire forces achieved a stunning victory at the Battle of Amiens. Ludendorff described this as the 'Black Day of the German Army' and was right to do so. In circumstances where troops were falling back, the impact of submarine warfare was reduced. By the end of October, it was effectively over. By 11 November, the High Seas Fleet had mutinied; communist uprisings had broken out in various cities; the Kaiser had abdicated; and the new republican government had signed the armistice. In 1919, the punitive Versailles Treaty was imposed upon the German nation, and it was generally agreed that a similar conflict should never happen again. Nineteen years later, to the horror of most of the world, another one did.

LEFT: The beginning of the end: German workers and sailors protest at Kiel, calling for an end to the war. The decision to send the High Seas Fleet on a virtual suicide sortie as a last, defiant gesture, prompted a mutiny. Coupled with other rebellions, the Kiel mutiny led to the Kaiser's abdication and the creation of the German Republic in November 1918.

CHAPTER TWO

THE SECOND ROUND: SEPTEMBER 1939 – MAY 1940

World War I was not the last major conflict to afflict Europe. When World War II broke out, the U-boat was to play a major part in the conflict once again.

Although the fighting stopped on 11 November 1918, World War I did not officially end until the signing of the peace treaties in 1919. The most famous of these was that dealing with the former German Empire, signed at Versailles on 28 June 1919. The Versailles settlement ranks among the most resented treaties in modern history, and it was an undoubted contributory cause in the rise to power of Adolf Hitler and World War II. The reasons for the resentment are not hard to find. The Germans had no choice in signing the treaty and no option to negotiate. As a result, they found themselves being given sole responsibility for starting the war, forced to pay huge reparations to the victorious powers (which were never fully delivered) and stripped of all but a notional military capability. The U-boat arm was particularly affected by the latter clause, as Germany was forbidden to possess any submarines. Those it had were to be surrendered to the Allies. After some contention between victors and vanquished, Germany surrendered 176 U-boats.

LEFT: U-boats preparing for operations at Kiel harbour. When war broke out again in September 1939, there was a shortage of submarines, just as there had been in World War I.

RIGHT: Admiral Erich Raeder, head of the German Navy. Raeder laid the foundations for Hitler's navy and although he focused primarily on the surface fleet, he did much to assist in the creation of the new U-boat arm. Constant disagreements with Hitler led to his dismissal in 1943.

The French Navy retained 10, which stayed in service until the 1930s, while the rest were sold for scrap.

In Britain, the Admiralty favoured the complete abolition of the submarine. Cynics might suggest that this option was favoured as it would prevent the Royal Navy from ever having to worry about taking stultifying 'defensive' measures such as convoy. Although they would not have any hard evidence, they could also suggest that there was another motive – abolishing the Royal Navy's own submarine branch. The higher echelons of the Royal Navy held a generally unfavourable opinion of submariners. Despite – or perhaps because of – the fact that several British submariners had been awarded the Victoria Cross – in stark contrast to the surface fleet – it seemed that the Royal Navy regarded the men of its underwater arm as oddball characters. As well as acknowledging the major strategic benefit of the abolition of submarines, it is sometimes tempting to wonder whether or not the chance to dispose of a branch of the Navy that was not fully understood crossed the minds of senior Admiralty figures.

GERMANY AND THE RESURRECTION OF THE U-BOAT

The Germans were not as poorly disposed towards the submarine, with naval opinion largely recognizing the contribution made by U-boats. Given the terms of the Versailles settlements, though, regard for the submarine was irrelevant, as what was left of the German Navy could hardly set up a submarine service without a swift reaction from the victorious powers. Or so it seemed.

As has been well recorded elsewhere, the Germans displayed considerable ingenuity in continuing to develop a whole array of weapons that were banned or limited by the treaty, using alliances with foreign companies and dummy companies in Germany that were not quite what they seemed. A submarine construction office was set up in The Hague in April 1922, with the full connivance of the commander in chief of the Navy. By 1932, when Admiral Erich Raeder had become the professional head of the German Navy, the government had approved the development of a new U-boat arm, although this would only take place when the political situation was favourable. This was less improbable that it might have seemed.

The aftermath of World War I was not kind to the victorious European nations. Britain and France were indebted to the United States, which withdrew to isolationism. By the 1930s, if not before, the depressed economic situation led to an increasing feeling in many quarters that the war had not been worthwhile. The sheer scale of casualties had horrified popular opinion, and it was largely agreed that every effort to

prevent a repetition of the horrors of 1914–18 should be taken.

It was the growth of this sentiment that had persuaded the German government that it might be possible to add U-boats to its armoury without much international opposition. It also coincided with the rise to prominence, and then power, of Adolf Hitler and the Nazi Party. As is well known, Hitler was able to appeal to many Germans by offering an apparent solution to the grave state in which Germany found itself, in part by seeking to restore German pride. Hitler's attacks on the conditions of the Versailles settlement struck a chord with the German people; when Hitler achieved absolute power, the aggressive undermining of the Versailles settlement began.

This did not meet with the sort of hostile reaction from Britain and France that might have been expected. Initially, Hitler was regarded as a notable statesman (although some of his views appeared extreme), and there was some sympathy in London at least for the argument that Germany had been unjustly treated by the peace treaties. On 16 March 1935, Hitler announced that he was rearming, breaking the limitations set at

Versailles. Although there was some adverse comment in Britain and France, nothing was done to prevent this. Indeed, on 18 June 1935, Britain reached an accommodation with Hitler over naval forces. The Anglo-German Naval Agreement permitted Germany to build a navy that was 35 per cent of the total size of the Royal Navy, while the submarine fleet could be 45 per cent the size of that of Britain's.

It is not unfair to say that the Anglo-German Naval Agreement presented a number of problems. The first was diplomatic, as the French were outraged at Britain's rapid acquiescence to the agreement. The second problem was one facing the Germans, who had never imagined that they would be allowed to build a meaningful fleet of submarines. This meant that plans for the German Navy would have to be reconsidered, with the creation of a distinct submarine arm. The man chosen was Karl Dönitz.

Dönitz's credentials for the job were appropriate. He had been given command of the mine-laying U-boat *UC25* in March 1918, moving onto *UB68* in September. While attacking a convoy in the Adriatic, *UB68* had become uncontrollable. Dönitz

LEFT: *U5*, a type II boat, seen at Kiel harbour. Commissioned in 1935, *U5* served mainly in a training role, although it conducted four operational patrols between the outbreak of war and May 1940. The boat was lost with all hands in March 1943 when it failed to return from a training exercise.

UC25

Country:	Germany
Launch date:	1916
Crew:	28

LEFT: *UC25*'s importance to submarine warfare lay in the fact that it was commanded by Karl Dönitz, the man who led the U-boat arm until 1943, when he became the head of the German Navy.

BELOW: HMS *Walker*, a veteran of two world wars. *Walker* was built in 1918, and gave valuable service throughout World War II. The ship was most famed for sinking *U99*, commanded by the 'ace' Otto Kretschmer in 1941.

had no option but to order abandonment, and he and the majority of the crew were rescued by the sloop HMS *Snapdragon*. After his release from a prisoner-of-war camp, he returned to Germany and renewed his career with the much-reduced German Navy. Although Dönitz's record was good, he was not the only officer with the necessary qualifications to take overall command of the new branch. His case may have been helped by the fact that he had served under a number of officers who had been involved with the covert continuation of the U-boat programme after Versailles. At least one of these officers had provided him with a glowing report, which may have further promoted his chances. Although Dönitz's might not have been a name instantly

associated with submarines, little more than a decade later his name would be the first to be linked with them. While Europe began to come to terms with the implications of a rearming Germany, Dönitz began to build his forces so that they could play a full part in any future war.

BRITAIN AND SUBMARINE WARFARE 1919–39

Although the British Admiralty hoped for the abolition of the submarine, it discovered that there was to be no agreement. The French were of the opinion that there was no reason to object to submarines as long as they were employed in accordance with the laws and customs of war. They suspected that the British wished to maintain a naval

Displacement:	406 tonnes (400 tons) surfaced, 488 tonnes (480 tons) submerged
Dimensions:	49.4m (162ft) x 5.2m (17ft) x 3.7m (12ft)
Armament:	Three 500mm (19.7in) torpedo tubes, 18 mines, one 86mm (3.4in) gun
Powerplant:	Diesel/electric, driving two shafts
Surface range:	9430km (5100nm) at 7 knots
Performance:	11 knots surfaced, 9 knots submerged

efforts at the end of World War I, sought to develop some effective means of locating submerged submarines. As the situation became more serious, the Allied Submarine Detection Investigation Committee had taken over the task. Its solution was 'asdic' – an acronym derived not from the equipment, but the name of the body that had created it. Asdic sent out a pulse of sound and, by measuring the time between generation of the pulse and its return after reflection off an underwater object, provided the precise range and bearing of a target. The system had not been fully developed by the end of the war, but, unlike many other projects, it was not cancelled with the end of hostilities. From 1923, a working asdic device began to be fitted to Royal Navy destroyers, and, after 1932, all destroyers were fitted with the system when funding allowed this to be done.

Unfortunately for the Admiralty, this was not the solution to the submarine threat that it assumed. The level of confidence in asdic was impressive. Although the device could not provide any indication of the depth of the target – a fairly important variable – the Admiralty contended that asdic overcame the problem of the submarine once and for all. In 1935, the Parliamentary Secretary for the Admiralty, Lord Stanley, told the House of Commons that, if another war were to break out, the Admiralty would not introduce mercantile convoys. This stemmed almost entirely from the belief that the submarine threat had been defeated, although Stanley repeated the arguments against using convoy that had been used prior to its introduction in

supremacy that other nations could not hope to threaten without submarines, and they may have been correct. The Admiralty continued to press its case, but there was little chance of success. This did not mean that anti-submarine warfare was given a high priority in the Admiralty's considerations. Although the submarine had come close to crippling Britain's war effort in 1917, by the end of the 1920s, the concentration, once again, was upon the battleship and so-called 'big-gun' fleet action. As a result of this, the Admiralty managed to miss completely the most important warship type in not just one major war, but two.

The reasoning behind abandoning consideration of anti-submarine warfare seemed plausible at first sight. The Anti-Submarine Division (ASD) had, as part of its

BELOW: The *Flower* class of ships became the mainstay of the escorts, with over 100 being built between 1939 and 1942. They were designed for use as coastal escorts with the ability to conduct minesweeping operations, but found themselves used as open-ocean escorts. The short hull meant that the weather conditions found in the Atlantic made for a difficult time for the crews.

FLOWER

Country:	Britain	**Armament:**	One 102mm (4in) gun, one two-pounder anti-aircraft mounting
Launch date:	First unit 1940		
Crew:	85		
Displacement:	179 tonnes (176 tons)	**Powerplant:**	Single-shaft, four-cylinder triple-expansion steam unit
Dimensions:	62.5m (205ft) x 10.1m (33ft) x 3.5m (11ft)	**Endurance:**	6389km (3449nm)
		Performance:	16 knots

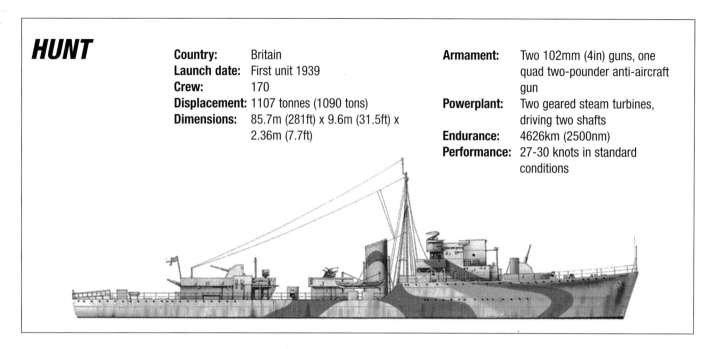

HUNT

Country:	Britain
Launch date:	First unit 1939
Crew:	170
Displacement:	1107 tonnes (1090 tons)
Dimensions:	85.7m (281ft) x 9.6m (31.5ft) x 2.36m (7.7ft)
Armament:	Two 102mm (4in) guns, one quad two-pounder anti-aircraft gun
Powerplant:	Two geared steam turbines, driving two shafts
Endurance:	4626km (2500nm)
Performance:	27-30 knots in standard conditions

ABOVE: The *Hunt* class was designed after the belated recognition that the Royal Navy needed more escort vessels. The first unit, of 86 in total, entered service in 1939. Initially, the *Hunt*s were designed for speed, and suffered from poor endurance. Later units were provided with more bunker space, and the class was much improved as a result.

1917. This confidence was all very well, but was in fact overconfidence. Between 1919 and 1939, no major naval exercise was conducted to practise the defence of a merchant convoy against submarine attack, and this omission hid a number of issues.

The major point that appeared to be ignored was that asdic worked only against submerged submarines. When the Royal Navy had conducted exercises using its own submarines, they had tended to stay below the surface, where asdic could detect them. There seem to have been little consideration as to whether a future enemy would launch attacks while running on the surface at night. The reasons for not practising night surface attack in peacetime can be understood, as the risk of collision between submarine and the destroyer was high, given that the destroyers would have been operating without external lights showing. Little effort was made to fire practice torpedo shots, with the effectiveness of attacks being worked out mathematically, based upon the calculations made by the submarine commander as he plotted his firing solution. Lulled into a false sense of security by a mixture of asdic and unrealistic exercises, the Royal Navy remained convinced that the threat from submarines had been effectively overcome.

The situation was not all bleak. By 1937, the Deputy Chief of the Naval Staff, Admiral Sir William James, had dealt with the issue of convoy once and for all. James had served as head of the Admiralty's signals intelligence organization, Room 40, between 1917 and 1918. As Room 40 had done much work against U-boats through signals interception, James was not unfamiliar with the issues of anti-submarine warfare. He was also

unconvinced that the threat posed by U-boats had gone. He was given the opportunity to put forwards his views with the creation of the Shipping Defence Advisory Committee, which was established in 1937. At the second meeting of the committee, James declared that, on outbreak of war, the convoy system would be instituted, as it provided the most effective form of protection against attack, be that from surface units, aircraft or submarines.

While James's intervention was important, it did not mean that the problems were

over. An escort policy would be in place when war occurred, but the provision of escorts to carry it out was another matter. The financial stringency attached to all defence projects during the 1920s and 1930s meant that the Royal Navy had been forced to make hard choices as to where it spent its money. As the submarine threat was regarded as being of little importance, it is hardly surprising that escort vessels did not figure highly in procurement priorities. It was only in February 1939 that the Admiralty managed to secure enough funding for escorts, ordering 40 destroyers of the *Hunt* Class and 56 corvettes (the *Flower* class). As events were to demonstrate, this was definitely a case of 'better late than never'.

A PAINFUL PROCESS: DEVELOPING MARITIME AIR POWER

The final problem that the British faced related to the use of aircraft against submarines. During World War I, they had proved to be extremely useful. Although their offensive capabilities were lacking, the mere presence of air patrols had forced U-boat commanders to be particularly wary, and in many cases the vessels remained submerged, with a consequent reduction in endurance and effectiveness. There was little dispute that aircraft were an effective tool in the battle against submarines, but this consensus was overwhelmed by the

controversy over naval aviation that occurred in the inter-war period.

On 1 April 1918, the Royal Flying Corps and the Royal Naval Air Service were united in the world's first independent air arm, the Royal Air Force (RAF). The War Office and the Admiralty, both of whom strenuously objected to the formation of the new arm, had previously controlled the air services. All the aircraft in British military service, whatever their role, were put under the RAF's control. When the war was over, the RAF maintained control of all military aircraft, while the two established service ministries did their utmost to argue that the RAF should be disbanded and its air assets returned to the army and navy.

Despite his initial doubts about the service, the Chief of the Air Staff, Sir Hugh Trenchard, sought to ensure that his service survived. He recognized that, if the RAF specialized in air support of the army, the War Office would point out that there was little point in having a separate service for this task. If the new air arm involved itself with naval matters, the Admiralty would do the same. As a result, Trenchard settled upon strategic bombing as the primary role for the RAF, as it was a task that neither of the other services could perform. A few token squadrons were assigned to army cooperation tasks and for working with the Royal Navy. While the British Army largely grumbled

BELOW: A Lockheed Hudson, serving with 269 Squadron of RAF Coastal Command. The Hudson provided the first effective land-based patrol plane in RAF service. Although it did not have the range required for operations over the mid-Atlantic, the Hudson gave distinguished service until the end of the war.

ABOVE: The crews of newly-commissioned U-boats stand ready for inspection. The smart turnout is totally at variance with the more casual attire of most U-boat crews on operations. This lack of 'spit and polish' was not through lack of professional pride, but for the need for practical clothing in the unpleasant conditions within the U-boats.

quietly about this, the Admiralty was far more vocal. A long battle for control of maritime air assets was fought, culminating in victory for the Admiralty in 1937, when it was given control of the newly formed Fleet Air Arm.

While this made the Admiralty more content, there was one notable problem, namely that the Fleet Air Arm only controlled aircraft operated from ships. Land-based maritime air power was still in the hands of the RAF, in the form of Coastal Command. Like the other services, the RAF had not been able to find enough money to fund all the aircraft types it needed. Maritime reconnaissance and anti-shipping squadrons were far down the list of priorities, and Coastal Command was not particularly well equipped. In 1938, it was recognized that the situation merited some action, and the RAF started to look for a readily available land-based maritime patrol aircraft. It soon transpired that the British aircraft industry would be unable to provide anything suitable, and orders were placed with the Lockheed Corporation of the United States for a derivative of the Lockheed L-14 Electra transport aircraft. There was considerable opposition within Britain to the purchasing of an American aircraft (although this was not the first foreign type ordered for service), but there was no indigenous

alternative. Lockheed quickly produced the new aircraft, which was known as the 'Hudson' in RAF service. The Hudson arrived in service just in time for one squadron to have been formed by the outbreak of World War II.

War Again

At the outbreak of war, the Kriegsmarine had just 39 frontline U-boats, reprising the situation where Germany simply did not have enough submarines to be effective. Despite this, an immediate offensive against British shipping was planned. The first stage of this began with the announcement that any ship in the war zone around the United Kingdom and France would be at risk of attack, whether it was flying a neutral's flag or not. This was all very well, but Dönitz was concerned that the lack of boats would make the task very difficult. He managed to convince Raeder that the lessons of World War I demonstrated that a large number of submarines was required, calling for at least 300 boats that would be capable of operating in the Atlantic. In turn, Raeder persuaded Hitler of the merits of the case.

Although approval was granted, there was one significant caveat: Hitler would not grant the U-boat building programme absolute priority, as he was determined that the needs of the army should be met first. While Hitler's position was understandable, it meant that there were not enough materials available to build U-boats at the rate Dönitz envisaged. Indeed, by April 1940, only 13 new boats had been commissioned, which meant that there had been an overall reduction in the force levels thanks to operational losses. Coupled with the lack of boats, Hitler insisted that Prize Regulations be observed. This did not stem from a surprising and little-known element of altruism in Hitler's character, but rather from his desire to avoid causing antagonism to Britain, France and the United States. While this may seem odd, it needs to be remembered that Hitler initially hoped that Britain and France would seek terms with Germany once the conquest of Poland was complete. Unfortunately for Hitler, his view that the two European powers had nothing left to fight for once Poland fell was not shared in London or Paris. Overall, this meant that the initial potential of the U-boat arm was limited in much the same way that the restrictions on unrestricted warfare had hampered the potential of submarines in World War I.

Despite these problems, Dönitz was determined to press on, and an attempt to sink as many merchant ships as possible before the British instigated convoys was launched. Eighteen submarines left Germany even before the outbreak of hostilities, which meant that the U-boats were able to land an early blow. Although it stunned the British, it did so for all the wrong reasons and contributed to an earlier introduction of the convoy system than Dönitz had predicted. U-boats had been at sea since 24 August, under the strictest instructions that, if war broke out, they were to observe Prize Regulations.

On 3 September, the Type VIIA submarine *U30* was operating some 400km (250 miles) northwest of Ireland, when her commander, Julius Lemp, sighted a large vessel in the distance. In the poor light, it was difficult to make any positive identification, but Lemp was convinced that the ship was a legitimate target. He was aided in reaching this decision by the zigzag course adopted by the ship and the fact that it was outside the normal shipping routes. In fact, the target Lemp thought he had was anything but legitimate under the Prize Regulations: it was the passenger liner *Athenia*. The *Athenia* had set sail from Glasgow on 1 September, heading for Montreal. The news of the German invasion of Poland led to a delay in leaving British waters while a decision on how to react was reached by the French and British governments. The *Athenia* was given Admiralty instructions to avoid normal

BELOW: A *Type VIIA* U-boat is overflown by a Heinkel 155 seaplane. The level of co-operation between air units and the U-boats was not as good as it might have been during the war, largely as a result of the intransigence of Hermann Göring.

RIGHT: Survivors of the torpedoed liner *Athenia* leave their rescue ship for the shore. The sinking of the liner on the first day of the war suggested that the unrestricted warfare of 1917 and 1918 was being implemented once more, and provided the Allies with excellent anti-German propaganda. In fact, the *Athenia* appears to have been the victim of mis-identification and over-enthusiasm rather than a policy of targeting liners.

shipping lanes, hence Lemp's sighting of the ship so far away from normal routes.

When the *Athenia* reached Canada, it was to be converted into an armed merchantman, whereupon there would have been no doubt as to the legitimacy of attacking it. On 3 September 1939, though, the ship was carrying 1130 passengers, all of whom were civilians. Around 21:40 hours, *U30* launched two torpedoes, one of which stuck in its tube. The other struck *Athenia* in the aft end of the engine room, instantly crippling the ship. It went down rapidly. Only when the U-boat's radio operator began picking up distress calls did Lemp fully realize that he had torpedoed a civilian ship. There were 118 fatalities, and, to compound the propaganda disaster, they included 85 women and children. Twenty-two of the victims were US citizens.

The British response was to revive the notion that the Germans were not prepared to observe the bounds of civilized behaviour in war (little realizing how accurate this charge would prove to be against the Nazis). It was perhaps hoped that the United States would be prompted to abandon its isolationism in favour of the Allies once again. Hitler was furious and ordered Joseph Goebbels, the Propaganda Minister, to make the best of the circumstances. Goebbels's claimed that the *Athenia* had either been sunk by a British mine or possibly even by a submarine, with the intent of smearing Germany. Very few people were convinced.

As Lemp was killed later in the war, the precise reason for torpedoing the *Athenia* will probably never be known. Given the

problems of observation through a periscope at night, it is quite possible that Lemp misidentified the ship, and he later stated that he thought that the vessel was an armed merchantman. As Peter Padfield has noted, however, this was an explanation offered when mistakes were made; indeed, it was the reason given for the sinking of the *Lusitania*. Padfield has also noted that Lemp was a little impetuous. When presented with a relatively easy target, the temptation was to conclude that it was a legitimate target, and he engaged it without fully weighing up the possibilities. When Lemp returned, he was

ROYAL OAK

ordered to doctor his log so that all mention of the incident was officially expunged.

Of greater importance than the public reaction was the British decision to instigate convoys immediately. This decision was unsurprising. The sinking of *Athenia* appeared to suggest that unrestricted submarine warfare was again on the agenda. Although the lessons from 1917 and 1918 had not been fully learned (or forgotten), the basic premise that ocean and coastal convoys offered some solution remained, and these were begun far sooner than the Admiralty had intended or the Germans had hoped. Nevertheless, arranging convoys took time, and, before the system became fully operational, a large number of merchant vessels had to sail as independents. As a result, 43 ships were lost in September sailing without escort. From the early convoys, only one merchantman was lost.

The Germans were aware that convoys would be instigated relatively quickly, with radio intercepts suggesting that the convoy system would be in operation from October. To counter this, Dönitz decided to test his theory that the concentration of merchant ships and escorts demanded a concentration of attacking submarines. The idea of the wolfpack was to receive its first operational test. This proved to be disappointing. It was hoped that nine U-boats could be concentrated to attack a convoy travelling to the United Kingdom from Gibraltar, assembling in the South West Approaches. The lack of available boats scuppered the operation before it began, as

LEFT: Gunther Prien, the commander of *U47*. Prien came to fame for his attack against the *Royal Oak* in Scapa Flow, which made him a national hero. Lost on 7 March 1941, his death was kept secret for several weeks, so as not to damage German morale in a month when two other 'aces' had been lost.

two of the submarines had to stay in dock for longer than intended, while three others – *U40*, *U42* and *U45* – were sunk before they could join the pack. The four remaining boats were reduced to three when *U47* was detached for a special mission, leaving just *U46*, *U48* and *U37*. On 17 October, *U46* sighted a convoy (HG 3) and called up the other two boats. They attacked just after 16:30 hours, each sinking one ship before aircraft forced them to depart the area. The first pack operation had achieved a little, but the success was limited by the lack of boats available. It had also been

BELOW: The *Royal Oak* joined the Royal Navy in 1916, and participated in the Battle of Jutland. She remained in service after World War I, and was on patrol duty in northern waters. Although *Royal Oak* was an old ship, her loss to *U47* in the U-boat's daring raid on Scapa Flow was still a serious blow to the Royal Navy.

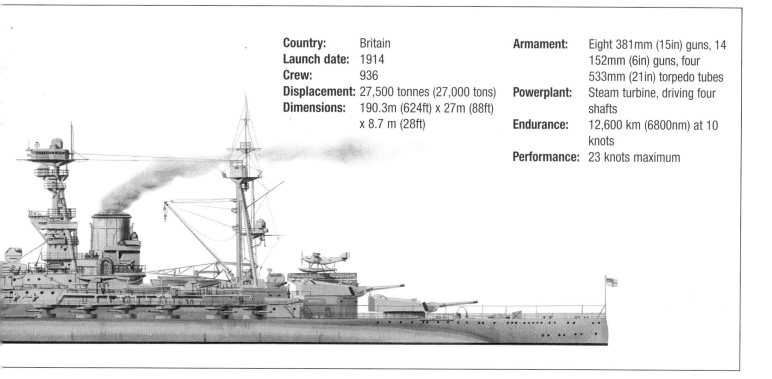

Country:	Britain	Armament:	Eight 381mm (15in) guns, 14
Launch date:	1914		152mm (6in) guns, four
Crew:	936		533mm (21in) torpedo tubes
Displacement:	27,500 tonnes (27,000 tons)	Powerplant:	Steam turbine, driving four
Dimensions:	190.3m (624ft) x 27m (88ft)		shafts
	x 8.7 m (28ft)	Endurance:	12,600 km (6800nm) at 10
			knots
		Performance:	23 knots maximum

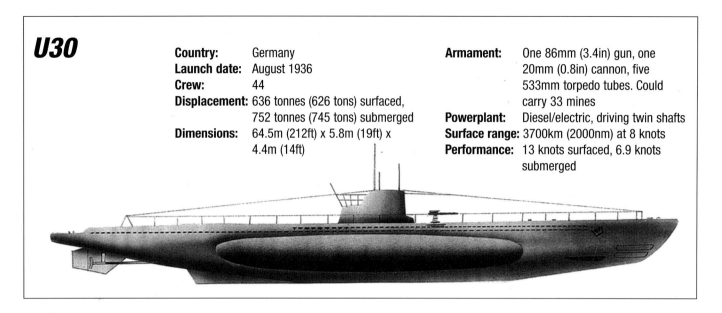

U30

Country:	Germany
Launch date:	August 1936
Crew:	44
Displacement:	636 tonnes (626 tons) surfaced, 752 tonnes (745 tons) submerged
Dimensions:	64.5m (212ft) x 5.8m (19ft) x 4.4m (14ft)
Armament:	One 86mm (3.4in) gun, one 20mm (0.8in) cannon, five 533mm torpedo tubes. Could carry 33 mines
Powerplant:	Diesel/electric, driving twin shafts
Surface range:	3700km (2000nm) at 8 knots
Performance:	13 knots surfaced, 6.9 knots submerged

ABOVE: *U30* was famous for sinking the first ship of World War II, the liner *Athenia*. The sinking was used for propaganda purposes by the British, who claimed it illustrated the brutality of the Nazi regime. The crew of the *U30* were ordered to destroy the part of the logbook that detailed the attack, since the high command tried to claim that the British sank their own ship so they could blame Germany.

overshadowed by the activities of *U47* on its special mission.

U47 AND THE *ROYAL OAK*

As in World War I, the Royal Navy's anchorage at Scapa Flow appeared to be a prime target. Dönitz pondered whether or not an attack against the ships there would be effective, and he was pleasantly surprised to discover from reconnaissance photographs that it would be possible for a submarine to enter the harbour – just. As a result, he enquired whether or not the enthusiastic Gunther Prien, commander of *U47*, thought he would be able to oblige. Prien said that he could. As a result, *U47* was detached from the planned pack operation and left Wilhelmshaven, carefully timed to arrive at the flow on the night of 13–14 September, when the tidal conditions would be at their most favourable for an attempt to penetrate Scapa Flow.

U47 spent most of 13 September resting on the bottom of the sea, surfacing in the evening so as to approach on the surface. On opening the hatch, Prien was startled by the level of illumination provided by the *aurora borealis*, and he briefly pondered whether or not the light level would be low enough to enable him to succeed in evading detection. Prien did not lack confidence and, despite this interesting thought, pressed on. Just outside the Scapa Flow, at around 23:00 hours, he was forced to dive to avoid a steamer. *U47* waited for the steamer to clear the area and surfaced again 25 minutes later, trimmed low in the water so as to offer the smallest possible silhouette. Prien carefully negotiated his way to the entrance of the Flow and then slowly made his way past the blockships sunk at the entrance. After a brief scare when the U-boat caught a cable – a problem which was quickly overcome –

Prien found himself in Scapa Flow. It was 00:27 hours on 14 September.

The Admiralty had not maintained Scapa Flow's defences as well as it might have over the course of the previous 20 years. It was this factor that enabled Prien to enter, as the blockships that had been sunk to prevent ingress by a U-boat had shifted with the tides, offering the narrow entrance that Prien had exploited. Unfortunately for *U47*, the Admiralty was aware that Scapa Flow was not as secure as was possible, for, when Prien scanned the harbour, he discovered that it was emptier than had been anticipated. The majority of the fleet had been sent to Loch Ewe, just as in World War I. Prien saw three tempting targets: two battleships, in the form of the *Repulse* and an unidentified R-class, and the seaplane carrier *Pegasus*. In fact, Prien's eyes deceived him, possibly as a result of the freakish light conditions. The *Repulse* was not in the anchorage. The *Royal Oak*, though, most certainly was. Prien fired three torpedoes from 2743m (9000ft). One failed to leave its tubes, but the others ran smoothly. After three-and-a-half minutes, the crew of *U47* heard a single explosion.

On board the *Royal Oak*, there was confusion. The idea that there might be a submarine shooting at them did not occur to the ship's officers, who concluded that there must have been an internal explosion, possibly in a paint locker. While they were trying to work out where the explosion had occurred, Prien was swinging *U47* round to fire his stern tube at the target while the upper bow tubes were reloaded. The torpedo from the stern tube missed. At about 01:10 hours, the bow tubes had been reloaded, and Prien turned about again. Around 10 minutes later, the three remaining torpedoes were fired – the two reloads plus the one in a lower tube that had not been fired on the first attack run. The three torpedoes left the submarine, and at least two of them hit.

One struck alongside 'B' turret, about a third of the way aft. A few moments later, an explosion in one of the secondary magazines inflicted fatal damage on the *Royal Oak*. The old battleship began listing to starboard, and, in less than 20 minutes, she had slipped beneath the water, taking more than 800 men with her. Prien saw headlights on the shore, and, convinced that they were stabbing through the darkness right at him, he decided that it was time to leave. In fact, the orientation of the road meant that it was unlikely that there were any headlights, and it seems that the unusual light conditions, coupled with the stress of the situation, confused Prien. *U47* made for open water, and, after another scare when it momentarily appeared that there was not enough room to break through, the obstacles were cleared and *U47* was safely out of Scapa Flow. She set course for home, returning to a hero's welcome.

THE GENESIS OF PACK OPERATIONS

Although spectacular, such operations were hardly in keeping with Dönitz's plans for a tonnage war. Dönitz understood that, if U-boats were to make a decisive contribution to World War II, they would have to conduct a 'tonnage war' just as they had during the periods of unrestricted submarine warfare in World War I. The calculations behind such a strategy were simple: by sinking more shipping tonnage than the enemy could produce, the U-boats would reduce the amount of imports to the United Kingdom to such a level that the British war effort would suffer. If the tonnage sunk was great enough, the British would have no option other than to seek terms, as their industry would grind to a halt and their population would face starvation, no matter how severe rationing controls might be. A key obstacle remained, namely the convoy.

Dönitz was well aware that this one measure had ensured that the submarine campaign of 1917 and 1918 had not succeeded, and this prompted his desire for pack tactics. In 1939, Dönitz's problem was the inability to concentrate forces against the convoy, by virtue of the lack of submarines available. The second effort at pack tactics failed before it began for this very reason. Nothing if not practical, Dönitz decided to abandon pack operations until he had enough units to conduct them effectively. U-boats went out individually, attacking independents, in much the same way as they had before unrestricted warfare began in 1917. It was quite clear that the

BELOW: A line of U-boats at anchor in home waters. The U-boat arm suffered from a lack of available boats at sea, since not enough had been built before the war to sustain intensive operations. After every patrol, the U-boats needed replenishment and servicing for their next foray against shipping, which kept a large proportion alongside.

TYPE II

Country:	Germany	**Armament:**	One 20mm (0.8in) cannon, three 533mm (21in) torpedo tubes
Launch date:	1934 (first in class)		
Crew:	25		
Displacement:	258 tonnes (253.8 tons) surfaced, 306 tonnes (301.1 tons) submerged	**Powerplant:**	Diesel/electric, driving two shafts
		Surface range:	3700km (2000nm) at 8 knots
Dimensions:	40.9m (134ft) x 4.1m (13ft) x 3.8m (12ft)	**Performance:**	13 knots surfaced, 6.9 knots submerged

ABOVE: The *Type II* was a single-hull coastal boat. It proved to be a strong, manoeuvrable submarine, and various improvements were made as production progressed, most notably with regards to increasing the type's range. Production ended in 1941.

BELOW: One of the most important submarines ever designed, no fewer than 709 *Type VII* submarines were built between 1934 and 1945, but only 10 were VIIAs, before production switched to the VIIB.

increasing number of convoyed vessels would make the U-boats' task far more difficult, possibly going so far as to render them ineffective, and Dönitz was anxious to overcome this problem. He was aware that the problem of concentrating his forces could only be solved by the construction of more U-boats. Given Hitler's refusal to prioritize, this would take time, but Dönitz appreciated that there was one simple step that could be adopted to enhance effectiveness of the submarine arm – namely to abandon the demand that the boats observe Prize Regulations.

For this to happen, Dönitz needed Hitler's permission. He argued that the Prize Regulations had only been enforced because it was hoped that Britain and France would make peace once the conquest of Poland was completed. It had been felt that

launching immediate unrestricted submarine warfare would militate against this, by angering opinion in London and Paris. As the two allies had not sought peace, Dönitz argued, the need for restraint had gone. Hitler was not altogether convinced and gave his approval in stages. On 23 September, he agreed that all merchant ships using their wireless should be sunk – the significance being that the Admiralty had instructed merchantmen to send immediate reports if they sighted a U-boat. On the following day, approval to attack units of the French fleet was granted. Dönitz was aided greatly by Hitler's decision to visit Wilhelmshaven on 28 September, and he took no time in telling the Führer that the U-boat could be the weapon that dealt a 'mortal blow' to the British, if only he had enough. Hitler made no comment, but was impressed with the

TYPE VIIA

Country:	Germany	**Armament:**	One 86mm (3.4in) gun, one 20mm (0.8in) cannon, five 533mm (21in) torpedo tubes
Launch date:	1936 (first in class)		
Crew:	44		
Displacement:	516 tonnes (507 tons) surfaced, 651 tonnes (640 tons) submerged	**Powerplant:**	Diesel/electric, driving two shafts
		Surface range:	3700km (2000nm) at 8 knots
Dimensions:	64.5m (211ft) x 5.8m (19ft) x 4.4m (14ft)	**Performance:**	13 knots surfaced, 6.9 knots submerged

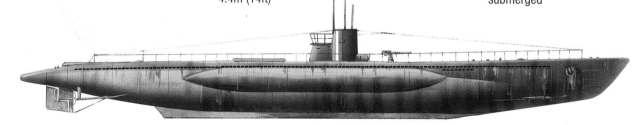

professionalism and enthusiasm that he found. Nonetheless, this did not extend to granting Dönitz's wishes. Hitler still refused to make U-boat construction a priority, leaving overall command of allocation of resources to his deputy, Hermann Göring. Göring's mastery of the intricacies of the strategic situation rarely proved adequate during the course of the war, and he saw little reason to push U-boat construction up the list of priorities.

If Hitler's visit did not achieve the results that Dönitz had hoped for, it may have been helpful in other ways. On 30 September, U-boat commanders were informed that they no longer needed to observe Prize Regulations when operating in the North Sea. By the middle of November, the requirement to observe Prize Regulations had been removed, and unrestricted submarine warfare was, to all intents and purposes, in force, although no announcement to this effect was made. Although this meant that the effectiveness of the campaign was increased, Dönitz was extremely cognisant that he required more U-boats to succeed. As it turned out, it was not just an increase in the number of U-boats that was required, but also the provision of working torpedoes. Before the second week of the war was over, two incidents gave a full demonstration of both of these demands.

On 14 September, *U39* was operating off the Orkney Islands, when, to the surprise of the crew, the aircraft carrier *Ark Royal* appeared. There could be no doubt that this was a prize target, and the crew took particular care to ensure that the firing solution for their torpedoes was correct. Two torpedoes were fired from around 800m (2600ft) from the *Ark Royal*. Unfortunately for the *U39*, the torpedoes did not work as they should have done, as both exploded short of the target. To make matters worse, one of the escorting ships, the destroyer *Foxhound*, reacted so quickly that the *U39* could be seen clearly from the bridge as depth charges were released against it. *U39* was blown to the surface, and, by good fortune, the crew were rescued before the submarine foundered. This was the first German submarine loss of the war, but the result could have been very different had the torpedoes worked. The next day, *U31* sighted an outbound convoy in the Bristol Channel and radioed for assistance. To his chagrin, Dönitz was able to send only three more boats. The small group was unable to exploit the situation and no attack developed.

These disappointments were slightly alleviated on 17 September, when *U29* encountered the aircraft carrier HMS *Courageous*. *Courageous* was not an obvious vessel to be on anti-submarine patrol, but this peculiarity did not detain *U29*. Three torpedoes were fired from a range of just under 3000m (9800ft) and struck home. *Courageous* sank in 15 minutes, taking 518 crew members with her. This was a salutary lesson for the British Admiralty and set nerves on edge, as *U27* discovered to its cost on 20 September. *U27* had attacked and sunk a number of fishing trawlers. This did not go unnoticed, and, given recent events, it was not unexpected, as John Terraine puts it, that the Commander in Chief of the Home Fleet 'reacted very strongly, as might be supposed'. Ten destroyers accompanied by an assortment of aircraft were sent to hunt down the submarine. The destroyers *Fortune* and *Forester* sank *U27*, which made a game

attempt to fire back. To the frustration of the crew, all three torpedoes failed, and they went into captivity without further ado.

THE TORPEDO PROBLEM

The failure of torpedoes to work became an increasing concern for the U-Boat Command. On 10 November, *U56* returned to Wilhelmshaven complete with a very irate commander. Kapitänleutnant Zahn bitterly reported that his torpedoes had proved useless. On 30 October, he had found the flagship of the Home Fleet, HMS *Nelson*, sitting invitingly ahead of him, broadside on. He had fired three torpedoes at a target that he could hardly miss. Two of the torpedoes duly did not, but, rather than the satisfying sounds of explosions, the crew of *U56* had heard two loud 'clangs' as the torpedoes hit *Nelson* before sinking to the bottom. The third torpedo had, somehow, managed to travel under the battleship and had exploded at the end of its run, to be followed by an eager destroyer. Although this did give *U56* the chance to slip away, it was hardly the point.

Although Zahn had not reported back by

ABOVE: HMS *Courageous* sinks after being torpedoed by *U29* on 17 September 1939. *Courageous* had been employed on anti-submarine duties, showing the confusion that existed within the Admiralty over how best to deal with the U-boat threat.

RIGHT: The archaic-looking Swordfish was one of the most effective carrierborne aircraft of World War II. Known affectionately as the 'Stringbag', Swordfishes were used to cripple the Italian fleet at Taranto in 1940. Increasingly effective air defences meant that using the Swordfish as a torpedo-bomber became ever more dangerous, but it remained an effective anti-submarine weapon until the end of the war.

FAIREY SWORDFISH

Country:	Britain
First flight:	1934
Crew:	3
Powerplant:	One Bristol Pegasus radial engine
Armament:	One fixed forward-firing 7.7mm (0.303in) machine gun, one

7.7mm (0.303in) machine gun on flexible mount in rear cockpit, one 457mm (18in) torpedo

Performance: Maximum speed 222km/h (138mph), service ceiling 3260m (10,700ft), range with torpedo, approx 885km (550 miles)

31 October, Dönitz had noted his opinion that up to 30 per cent of the torpedoes were 'duds'. After Zahn's return, it became quite clear that an investigation into the problem was required. Before any solutions were arrived at, though, the problem was to become far more serious, effectively leaving the U-boats without a weapon.

THE BRITISH RESPONSE

Even in the face of the problems of lack of numbers and unreliable torpedoes, the

RIGHT: The crew of *Type VIIC* U-boat load torpedoes while in port at Narvik. Prior to the German occupation of Norway, operations in Norwegian coastal waters had been hampered by serious reliability problems with torpedoes, which often failed to explode.

Germans gained some help from the uncertain anti-submarine policy adopted by the British. Despite the decision that convoys were worthwhile, a strong body of opinion in the Admiralty was still obsessed with the notion that the convoy was a purely defensive measure. In a repetition of World War I, anti-submarine vessels were formed into hunting groups, which ploughed up and down trying to find U-boats. The U-boats proved just as elusive as in the previous conflict. Although there were some encounters, there were not enough to justify the diversion of resources from convoy protection that the hunting groups represented. Had enough escort vessels been built during the last years of peace, this would not have been such a problem.

A sign of the confused thinking about offensive submarine hunting came with the assignment of fleet aircraft carriers. Although the Fairey Swordfish was among the embarked aircraft, employing these fighters on anti-submarine sweeps was not the best use for them. This policy was ended only when *U29* sank HMS *Courageous*, jolting the Admiralty into the realization that the anti-submarine patrol was no place for a large and valuable asset. Apart from this, though, no change was made to the policy of using the majority of anti-submarine assets for patrolling, rather than attaching them to convoys. Although convoys often enjoyed the protection of just two escorts, the success rate against submarine attack was impressive. Nine U-boats fell victim to the early convoy escorts, while the hunting groups managed to destroy just three, of which two were in

LEFT: An Avro Anson of the RAF. The Anson enjoyed a long and illustrious career with the RAF, with the last of the type leaving service in 1959. Coastal Command was forced to use the Anson as a patrol aircraft in the early months of the war, since there was nothing else available for the task. The Anson performed creditably, but was soon replaced by more suitable machines such as the Hudson.

coastal waters before the groups had reached their main patrol area – hardly a decent exchange ratio when the U-boats had claimed a major surface unit in return.

THE ROLE OF COASTAL COMMAND

The problem of locating U-boats was hardly helped by the lack of suitable aircraft in Coastal Command. When war broke out, the Coastal Command possessed 16 squadrons with a total of 265 aircraft. Many of these were ill suited to the task. One squadron of the Lockheed Hudson was available, with more on the way, but the bulk of the reconnaissance aircraft came from the nine squadrons of Avro Ansons. While the Anson was an admirable aircraft that stayed in

service until the 1950s, it was far from ideal for anti-submarine work, not least because of its relatively short range. Five squadrons were equipped with flying boats. Two of these units had the obsolescent Saro London and Supermarine Stranraer, while the remainder were equipped with the Short Sunderland.

The Sunderland was more than suited for the task in hand, with its ability to stay airborne for more than 12 hours. It could carry 907kg (2000lb) of anti-submarine weapons and was more than able to defend itself. As the war progressed, the Sunderland gained more and more machine guns, living up to the nickname of 'Flying Porcupine' bestowed upon it by the Luftwaffe.

TYPE VIIC CONNING TOWER

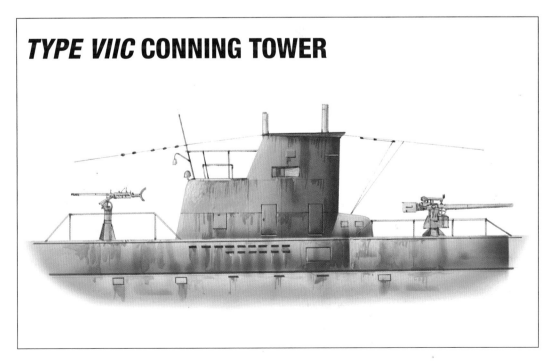

LEFT: The conning tower of the *Type VII* was located directly above the main control room, in an echo of the earliest submarines, where the commander had ports in the tower to permit vision when running just below the surface. These ports were not fitted in the *Type VII*, though, which had to rely upon the attack periscope.

ABOVE: A Short Sunderland receives attention from its groundcrew. The Sunderland was the mainstay of early Coastal Command operations, and gained a formidable reputation. The machine gun armament was increased over time, and Luftwaffe pilots nicknamed the Sunderland 'the Flying Porcupine'. The Sunderland in this picture is a later version, carrying fixed machine guns in the bow to enable it to engage the flak-gun crews carried by U-boats from around 1943 onwards.

There was one other squadron in Coastal Command, but this was equipped with the Vickers Vildebeest. By 1939, the Vildebeest looked very much as though it had escaped from a museum. It was lightly armed, poorly armoured and slow. Its chances of survival against modern fighter aircraft were negligible. Despite this, the one squadron equipped with the type was the only one that was capable of conducting torpedo attacks against surface vessels. The Vildebeest epitomized the procurement problems facing Coastal Command before the war, and it was to be a struggle to bring the force up to strength. The Sunderland and Hudson marked a start, but far more of them would be needed, as would aircraft with greater range. As a result of this unhappy situation, Bomber Command was persuaded to loan Coastal Command No. 58 Squadron, equipped with Armstrong Whitworth Whitleys. Bomber Command was a little reluctant about the transfer, and No. 58 Squadron returned to its parent command in February 1940. It was not until the autumn of 1940 that Coastal Command was able to have Whitleys of its own.

The command also needed more weapons suited to attacking submarines before there could be much hope of success. Although there were two types of anti-submarine bomb in service, these were ineffectual. Coastal Command aircraft did not have bomb sights suited to aiming the bombs from medium altitude against targets as small as a U-boat. Furthermore, the bombs had an unfortunate habit of exploding just after release from the aircraft, and it is probable that they inflicted more damage on the RAF than on the U-boat arm. The Air Officer Commanding-in-Chief of Coastal Command, Air Marshal Sir Frederick Bowhill, pointed out the failings of the anti-submarine bombs. The reaction was a little startling – somewhere in the Air Ministry, officials refused to believe that the anti-submarine bombs were not working and hampered Bowhill's attempts to have them replaced with aerial depth charges. Some depth charges were available to Coastal Command, but these were of 1918 vintage. As well as the disadvantage of their age, the depth charges had all the aerodynamic qualities of a dustbin and aiming them was difficult, to say the least. As a temporary expedient, a set of fins was designed to fit the depth charges to improve their aerodynamics, but these were nothing more than a stopgap measure and

suspended to allow the U-boat arm to support the invasion of Norway and Denmark. While the campaign was a success for the Germans, the U-boats proved disappointing. The torpedo failures that had been a concern in earlier operations became more notable.

U47 sighted two cruisers and two transports on 15 March, and fired four torpedoes at what Gunther Prien's log called a 'wall of ships'. To his astonishment, there were no hits. Just after midnight the following day, he used the cover of darkness to approach on the surface and fired four more torpedoes. Again, there were no hits. Prien was extremely concerned, as his crew had made extra-careful checks of the firing plot and torpedo settings after the first failure. It seemed to suggest that there were major problems with the torpedoes, and matters only got worse. Four days later, *U47* sighted the battleship HMS *Warspite* and two attending destroyers. *Warspite* would have been an important victim, but the two torpedoes fired, again, failed to sink the ship. One did explode at the end of its run, but served only to alert the two destroyers, which responded by launching a series of depth-charge attacks, causing the *U47* some discomfort.

U47 was not alone. On 10 April at 12:30 hours, *U48* fired three torpedoes at a British cruiser, but all of them missed. Undaunted, *U48* tried again at 21:15 hours, firing three more torpedoes at another cruiser; this time all of them exploded prematurely. About an hour later, *U51* crept up on a destroyer and fired two torpedoes that failed to detonate. Four days later, *U48* had another attempt, this time against the battleship HMS *Warspite*, but both torpedoes failed. *U65* also reported that

were not particularly successful. It was not until the spring of 1940 that purpose-designed depth charges began to arrive in Coastal Command squadrons.

THE NORWEGIAN CAMPAIGN

On 4 March 1940, the campaign against merchant shipping was temporarily

BELOW: The Anson enjoyed a production run of seventeen years, and was adapted for the coastal patrol task. Nearly 7000 machines were built.

AVRO ANSON

Country:	Britain	**Performance:**	Maximum speed 302 km/h (188mph), service ceiling 3260m (19,000ft), range approx 1271km (970miles)
First flight:	1935		
Crew:	3–5		
Powerplant:	Two Armstrong Siddeley Cheetah radial engines	**Armament:**	One fixed forward-firing 7.7mm (0.303in) machine gun, one 7.7mm (0.303in) machine gun in dorsal turret, up to 500lb of light bombs or depth charges

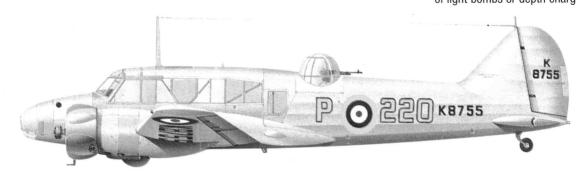

HMS *Warspite*

the two torpedoes it had fired at a transport had failed to go off. The litany of failures meant that the U-boats could not hope to be successful. On 17 April, Dönitz withdrew his U-boats from Norwegian waters, and a full-scale investigation into the problem began.

THE TORPEDO PROBLEM

It transpired that *Warspite* had been attacked on four occasions without the slightest success. Fourteen attacks against cruisers had failed, while the failure rate against destroyers and transports was 10 for each type. Only one transport had been sunk. Further investigation revealed that two-thirds of the torpedoes fitted with magnetic fuses had failed. This was not the only problem; Prien's failed attacks had been with impact fuses.

The most serious problem was with the fusing system. During World War I, torpedoes had relied upon impact fusing, that is to say, the torpedo would not explode unless it hit the target. This could be frustrating, since even a very near miss would have no effect. As a result, torpedo designers developed magnetic pistols, which would detonate the torpedo when it passed within close range of a large metallic object. This obviated the need for a direct hit, given that the explosion of a torpedo beneath a vessel would almost always inflict damage and in many cases would be just as effective as a hit. The problem faced by U-boats was that the detonators simply refused to work. They either failed altogether or

exploded prematurely. It transpired that, as well as having unreliable fuses, the torpedoes often ran well below their correct depth. This meant that, despite the careful firing solutions worked out by the boat crews, the torpedoes were running too far below the surface to strike the targeted vessel, rendering the impact fuses useless. It was quickly worked out that this could also be a problem even with functioning magnetic detonators – if the target sat high in the water, the torpedo might run so far below it as to prevent even the more sophisticated fuse from working. The investigation resulted in the court-martialling of the two officers responsible for accepting the new torpedoes into service, but this failed to get to the root of the problem. It did at least mean that improvements were made to the torpedoes, but they took time to reach the torpedo rooms of the U-boats.

The easiest problem to overcome was that of the impact fuses. It was soon discovered that the action was defective when the torpedo hit the target at certain angles, and this could be cured quite swiftly. Unfortunately, if the torpedoes were running below their set depth, a working impact fuse was irrelevant. This problem took longer to solve. After some thorough investigation, it was recognized that the running fault was caused by the changes of pressure in the valves that controlled the torpedoes' fins. The valves were not airtight, so were subjected to pressure changes every time a

Country:	Britain
Launch date:	November 1913
Crew:	1124
Displacement:	30,600 tonnes (30,116 tons) standard load
Dimensions:	196.9m (645ft) x 27.6m (90ft) x 9.1m (30ft)
Armament:	Eight 380mm (15in) guns, 12 152mm (6in) guns, eight 100mm (4in) guns
Powerplant:	Steam turbines, driving four shafts
Range:	7080km (3800nm)
Performance:	24 knots

submarine submerged or surfaced. The problem appeared to be at its worst when the U-boats spent a long time underwater, as they had done during the Norwegian campaign. The solution was to modify the valves, but this took some time to achieve.

The magnetic fuses were more troublesome. The fault afflicting them came not from shoddy workmanship, but from a more formidable problem – the Earth's magnetic field. This varies from place to place and is particularly strong in northern latitudes, such as Norway. The fuses had been confused by the Earth's magnetic field and had detonated as a result. The solution lay in adjusting the sensitivity of the fuses for different latitudes between the North Cape and the Bay of Biscay. The sensitivity could not be altered much more, so the simple expedient of not using magnetic fusing north and south of these lines of latitude had to be adopted.

THE END OF THE FIRST PHASE

By May 1940, it was clear that the first phase of the campaign had not been as successful as hoped for the Germans. The pre-eminent difficulty was the lack of operational submarines. Without an increased number of these, attacking convoys would prove difficult, as it would be impossible to concentrate enough to overwhelm the convoy defences. The situation would have been made worse had the British Admiralty not clung to the ideas of 'offensive' and 'defensive' anti-submarine warfare and

ensured a reasonable number of escorts for the convoys. Despite the poor strategy for dealing with the threat, the Royal Navy had not been idle – it had overcome the losses inflicted by the U-boats by building replacements and pressing captured German vessels into service. The lack of reliable torpedoes had ensured that a number of valuable targets had escaped unscathed, and this had caused a dip in morale among the crews.

The efforts of the British had accounted for at least 17 U-boats; Coastal Command had sunk one, while the bulk of the total was made up by 16 successes by Royal Navy surface units. These losses were serious, given that the rate of production meant that Dönitz was unable to gather enough submarines to use in packs against convoys. His determination to meet convoys with concentrated forces could not be realized until he had enough submarines. Overall, the British could be said to have won the first round in the tonnage war.

The submarine campaign, despite a number of notable successes, had been little more than a nuisance, and it was unlikely to bring the British empire to its knees if it continued in the same vein. Dönitz was not downcast, though. He recognized that the first eight months of war marked a beginning, rather than the full story. As new submarines arrived in service, the campaign would intensify, and the U-boats would have more effective torpedoes. In little more than a month, the strategic situation had changed dramatically in favour of the Germans, and with it the fortunes of the U-boat arm improved immensely as well. The key to this new phase owed nothing to submarines, but to an old-fashioned land conquest: the fall of France.

BELOW: Torpedoes in storage at the shore base at Cuxhaven. The picture clearly shows the control surfaces and the screws on the torpedoes.

CHAPTER THREE

FROM 'HAPPY TIME' TO GLOOM: JUNE 1940 – MARCH 1941

After the 'Phoney War', disaster upon disaster befell the Allies. For the U-boats, this was their 'Happy Time': but British defences were beginning to gain in strength.

The capture of the French ports, especially those in the Bay of Biscay, was absolutely vital to the progress of the U-boat campaign. The most obvious gain was operational, as the U-boats no longer had to make time-consuming transits from Wilhelmshaven into the Atlantic, cutting the journey to the operational area by about a week. This meant that the boats could stay on station for longer, and it had the effect of increasing the number of submarines in the Atlantic by about 25 per cent; previously, the additional U-boats would have been travelling to or from the area. These factors meant that the relatively small number of available U-boats could be much more effective than before. In addition, as the port facilities at Lorient were made operational, returning submarines could be repaired and made ready for operations much more quickly, as this reduced the queues at German dockyards. It also enabled U-boat headquarters to move closer to the action, which it did as soon as circumstances allowed.

LEFT: The menacing shape of a U-boat as it cuts through the water. Although technology had advanced since 1918, the U-boats still found it easier to fight on the surface, using their ability to submerge to protect them from the enemy.

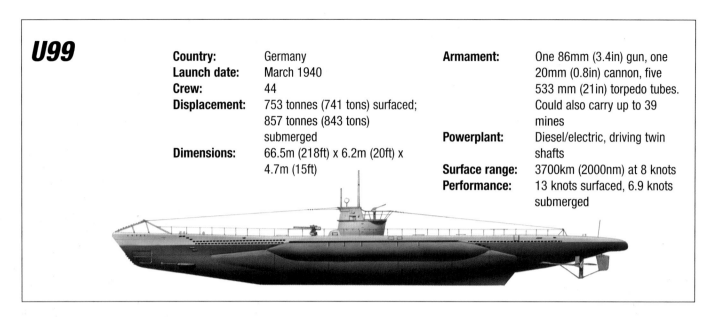

U99

Country:	Germany	**Armament:**	One 86mm (3.4in) gun, one
Launch date:	March 1940		20mm (0.8in) cannon, five
Crew:	44		533 mm (21in) torpedo tubes.
Displacement:	753 tonnes (741 tons) surfaced;		Could also carry up to 39
	857 tonnes (843 tons)		mines
	submerged	**Powerplant:**	Diesel/electric, driving twin
Dimensions:	66.5m (218ft) x 6.2m (20ft) x		shafts
	4.7m (15ft)	**Surface range:**	3700km (2000nm) at 8 knots
		Performance:	13 knots surfaced, 6.9 knots
			submerged

ABOVE: *U99* was commanded by Otto Kretschmer, and enjoyed a distinguished career, making eight patrols. On the night of 16–17 March 1941, *U99* was depth-charged to the surface by the destroyer HMS *Walker*, during an attack on convoy HX112. Forty of the crew, including Kretschmer, were rescued.

These advantages did not mean that the situation was without some difficulties. When the U-boat campaign resumed, the total number of available submarines was six fewer than at the start of the war. Of these boats, a number were in need of refit and repair, and were blocking dockyards that would otherwise be employed in building new craft. Although the facilities in France quickly made a difference, the rate of building the sort of fleet that Karl Dönitz thought necessary was impossible to attain at this stage. Nonetheless, it seemed as though the U-boats would be able to enjoy greater success upon resuming operations against Britain's maritime trade, particularly as the investigation into the torpedo problems had enabled the reliability of the weapon to be improved. On 9 June, 16 U-boats were available in the Atlantic and began operating.

Dönitz was eager to see the development of pack tactics. He placed six boats under the tactical command of Gunther Prien on a patrol line 675km (420 miles) west of Lorient, with the intention of intercepting convoy HX48, which was heading from Halifax, Nova Scotia, to the United Kingdom. Five other boats, controlled by Hans Rösing in *U48*, were sent to hunt for the troop convoy WS3, which contained three liners with 26,000 troops on board. In addition to this potential prize, the battlecruiser HMS *Hood* and an aircraft carrier, along with a number of cruisers, were accompanying WS3.

The planned operations owed much to the development of communications technology. The idea behind the attack groups was simple: one vessel would locate and shadow the convoy and, using radio transmissions, would inform the other boats in the group of the whereabouts of the

RIGHT: German construction crews at work building new facilities for U-boats at one of the French Atlantic ports. The capture of the French ports offered major operational benefits to the U-boat fleet.

convoy. The group commander would coordinate attacks locally from his submarine, so as to evade the defences. In circumstances where the convoy was not heavily escorted, it was hoped that the pack would be able to overwhelm the defences. The U-boat commanders would decide the manner of the attack, although Dönitz had ensured that crews were trained in delivering surface attacks at night.

This caused immense difficulties for the escorts, as the overwhelming faith in the ability to master the submarine was based purely upon the Allied Submarine Detection Investigation Committee's (asdic) ability to detect underwater craft. The surface night attacks robbed the escorts of the means of locating the enemy, and the low profile of the surfaced U-boats made sighting them extremely difficult. U-boat commanders sought to place the silhouette of the merchantmen against the night sky and run in to attack with their targets clearly visible. If the light was too low for this to be effective, a number of commanders, most notably Otto Kretschmer, attacked from the windward side of the convoy, so that the lookouts were battered by the wind and spray, thus reducing their visibility. Planning for the attacks was facilitated by the German radio observation service, or *B-Dienst*, which was to become ever more important in the battle against the convoys.

On this occasion, however, all the planning came to naught. The convoys, HX48 and WS3, went further to the southwest than anticipated and arrived unscathed. After this failure, the packs were broken up and sent out individually against shipping in the English Channel. If Dönitz was disappointed by the latest failure of the attempt at pack tactics, results from the individual boats would soon cheer him. During June 1940, the U-boats sank 58 ships, grossing 288,673 tonnes (284,113 tons). As if to demonstrate the need for the convoy system to be extended, more than 80 per cent of these victims were sailing as independents. This began the 'Happy Time' for the U-boats, when it appeared that nothing that the enemy did would stop them.

THE 'HAPPY TIME'

The development of the Happy Time owed little to tactical developments on the German side, but rather to the broader strategic picture. The fall of France left Britain vulnerable to invasion, and a large number of vessels that would have been employed as escorts were retained in home waters for use against an invasion. Although the Battle of Britain dominates the history of the period from June to October 1940, it is important to note that the Germans would not have invaded from the air, apart from a relatively small number of paratroops. The

ABOVE: The scene inside one of the U-boat pens. The failure of RAF Bomber Command to attack the French ports while the U-boat pens were being built meant that German submarines could survive enemy air attack as long as they were protected by the thick concrete roofs of the pens.

ABOVE: Maintenance personnel manhandle a torpedo towards a waiting U-boat. Although the U-boat crews naturally received the attention of the public, without the supporting crews ashore, their task would have been impossible.

majority of invasion forces would have travelled by sea, with this attack being met by the Royal Navy. This presented the Royal Navy with a dilemma: it could ensure that there were large enough forces to fend off an invasion fleet *or* it could provide convoy escorts. It could not do both. This meant that, in June and July, convoys were enjoying the protection of just one escort vessel.

To avoid the danger posed by air attack, the British Admiralty took to routing convoys through the North West Approaches, but this meant that the smaller *Type IIB* and *IIC* U-boats, which were designed for coastal operations, were able to engage ocean shipping. To make matters worse, the capture of French airfields meant that anti-shipping aircraft were in a far better position to make attacks. Dönitz hoped that aircraft would assist in the development of pack tactics, by providing reconnaissance information. It was fortunate for Britain that this did not go according to plan.

The first major obstacle to success was the lack of an available long-range aircraft. The *Luftwaffe* had dabbled with the idea of long-range strategic aircraft in the aftermath of Hitler's decision to rearm, but the driving

force behind them, General Walther Wever, had been killed in a flying accident before any projects had developed. His successors concentrated instead upon twin-engined, medium-range bombers and dive bombers. As a result, the *Luftwaffe* was forced to cast around for a conversion of an existing type. It decided upon a version of the Focke-Wulf 200. The FW 200, better known to history by the nickname 'Condor', originated as a four-engined airliner. Conversion to military standards was slow, and, when France fell, the available FW 200 unit, *Kampfgeschwader* (KG) 40 had only a few serviceable aircraft. At the end of the month, KG40 moved to the airfield at Bordeaux-Mérignac. A newer model of the Condor, the FW 200 C-1, began to arrive, and it at last appeared that meaningful cooperation between the U-boats and aircraft could take place. Dönitz envisaged that the aircraft would locate and attack enemy shipping, then call up U-boats which could further the attack. Unlike the aircraft, which would be limited in the time that they could stay attacking convoys, the U-boat pack would be able to conduct a series of attacks, possibly over the space of 48 hours.

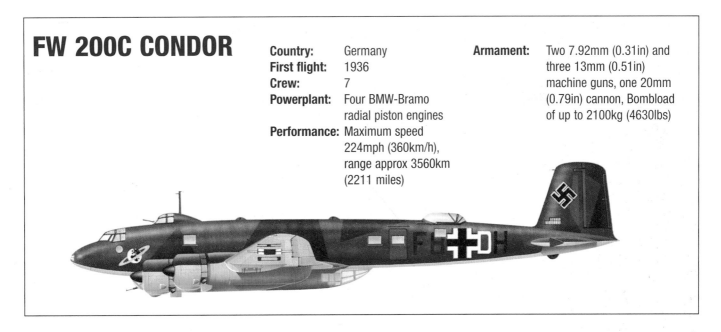

FW 200C CONDOR

Country:	Germany
First flight:	1936
Crew:	7
Powerplant:	Four BMW-Bramo radial piston engines
Performance:	Maximum speed 224mph (360km/h), range approx 3560km (2211 miles)
Armament:	Two 7.92mm (0.31in) and three 13mm (0.51in) machine guns, one 20mm (0.79in) cannon, Bombload of up to 2100kg (4630lbs)

This may have been what Dönitz envisaged; unfortunately for him, Hermann Göring had different ideas. Not only did Göring thwart the rapid construction of the U-boats that Dönitz thought were needed, but he also concentrated upon prosecuting the Battle of Britain to the exclusion of all else. Establishing close cooperation between a single *Luftwaffe* unit and the U-boat arm was hardly his top priority, and Dönitz had to wait. This was frustrating, as the FW 200s managed to sink 22 ships in June. The U-boats sank 58, but what, Dönitz wondered, would the tally have been had better aerial reconnaissance information been available to him?

This was a moot point. Dönitz at least had the satisfaction of seeing the bases at Brest, Lorient and La Pallice come into full use during August, and this meant that his boats could operate with far more effect. The U-boats could now operate as far as latitudes 25° west. The British escorts, thanks to their limited range, could only reach 17° west. Air cover by the longest-ranged Coastal Command type, the Sunderland, extended only as far as 15° west, giving the U-boats a considerable area in which they could attack shipping. Once the convoy escorts had left, the ships in convoy had the choice of continuing without escort or dispersing to sail on to their destinations independently. The opportunity to create absolute havoc as a result of this gap was, as always, limited by the number of available U-boats; even so, the toll they exacted from shipping caused

ABOVE: The FW 200 proved to be a highly effective conversion of a civilian airliner. Heavily armed, its appearance over merchant ships led to a sense of dread amongst those who saw it. The FW 200s record in anti-shipping strikes was impressive, but fortunately for the British, cooperation with the U-boat arm was not as good as it could have been. Once carrier-borne fighter aircraft accompanied convoys, the FW 200 found life far harder.

LEFT: The conning tower of a *Type IIC* U-boat. The hatch is open, and the periscope housing can be seen immediately behind it. The commander would have stood at the front right of the tower, next to the voice tube, while the wheel and compass were for the helmsman.

ABOVE: An unidentified U-boat returns home after a patrol. Note that the background of the photograph has been crudely scratched out by the German censor, to conceal any useful information.

considerable concern to the British and led to a considerable rethinking of how to deal with the submarine threat.

LEND-LEASE

The Royal Navy was perfectly aware that it faced a serious dilemma because of its inability to provide both escorts and anti-invasion forces; even before France fell, it was clear that more ships were needed. Where were they to come from? The First Lord of the Admiralty, Winston Churchill, thought that he had the answer: the United States. Before he was able to pursue this, he was caught up in significant political upheaval. On 10 May, Prime Minister Neville Chamberlain was forced to step down, and Churchill replaced him. Five days later, he wrote to President Franklin D. Roosevelt and made a plea for the loan of 40 or 50 of the US Navy's older destroyers. Churchill pointed out that, while British shipyards were contracted to provide new destroyers and escort vessels, they would be unable to deliver the number required for some time. What was required, Churchill concluded, was a loan to bridge the gap.

A month and one day later, Churchill wrote again, bemoaning the entry of Italy into the war, and repeated his request. When Roosevelt read another letter dated 31 July, it is unlikely that he was surprised to read yet another request for the loan of destroyers, although the figure had increased to 50 to 60 required. Churchill once again pointed out that there would be an increase in the number of destroyers by mid-1941 anyway – but, he gloomily warned, the crisis would have come well before then.

Although historians are generally agreed that reading Roosevelt's thoughts on intervention in the war are difficult, it is possible that Churchill was pushing against a semi-open door, with full opening being prevented by an obstacle behind it: in this case, Congress. In June, a deal to sell torpedo boats to Britain had been cancelled as the result of an outcry in the Senate, and it appeared that there would be no progress until opinion changed. Roosevelt sought to move the obstacle behind the door. It is quite possible that Roosevelt would have been forced to intervene in the war if Britain were about to collapse, as it would hardly have been in the interests of the United States for Europe to be dominated by two ideologically opposed dictatorships, particularly when both appeared eager to spread their influence as far as possible. If we make this assumption, it is not difficult to see that Churchill had a sympathetic ear. Roosevelt was further helped by increasing admiration and sympathy for the United Kingdom as it held out alone against the Germans. On 2 September, Roosevelt announced the signature of the lend-lease agreement. Among other things, Churchill received the 50 destroyers that he so desperately wanted.

The crews of the new craft were not so sure that their Prime Minister's enthusiasm was well placed. The first eight ships were handed over on 6 September, and the first crews prepared to take them to sea. The ships were named after towns, giving them their Royal Navy name – the *Town* class. While they were impressed with the level of home comforts provided on a US destroyer, they were less content when the ships set sail. While the accommodation was good, if cramped, the ships' handling in bad weather – and they were going to have to face a great deal of that – was appalling. When one of them, now HMS *Campbeltown* was packed with explosives and blown up to destroy facilities at St-Nazaire, someone was heard to observe that this was the best thing that could happen to a *Town* class. While the crews may not have liked them, they did perform sterling service. Before they could do this, though, they needed modification so that they could fulfil the anti-submarine role, which caused them to take longer to bring into service than Churchill had anticipated.

PACK OPERATIONS

While Churchill was attempting to persuade President Roosevelt of his case, Dönitz was not idle. The pleasing level of success achieved by only a few boats led him to turn his thoughts to developing pack operations, particularly given that the French ports enabled more of the small force to be at sea at the same time. After the abortive attempts earlier in the war, Dönitz decided to try his luck again.

The process began with the interception of a message from the Admiralty to a convoy. *B-Dienst* had managed to break one of the Admiralty's ciphers and had little difficulty in working out that the message to convoy SC2 (sailing from Sydney, Nova Scotia) was giving details of where the convoy should meet its escort. As a result of the intercept, Dönitz sent four boats to try to intercept the convoy. *U65* did just that at 19° 15' west. The escort vessels drove *U65* away, but were unable to prevent her shadowing the convoy, broadcasting the course and speed to the other three boats in the pack. On 7 September, the erstwhile *U47* attacked and managed to sink three ships. Again, this was through the preferred method of surfaced night attack, making it almost impossible for the escorts to do anything.

At dawn, Coastal Command arrived, in the form of Short Sunderlands. This compelled the U-boats to dive and lose contact. Despite this, the commanders could remain confident that, as long as they were able to regain the convoy, they would be able to attack again: the Sunderlands did not have the endurance to provide the convoy with cover for long. The aircraft did not have any means of locating the U-boats at night.

On the night of 8/9 September, the attack resumed. *U99* and *U28* located the convoy first and attacked. Otto Kretschmer did not enjoy any luck, leaving *U99* empty-handed for once; *U28* managed to sink one ship. Prien arrived on the scene shortly afterwards and sank a third. When the U-boats had broken off, they had sunk five ships out of a convoy of 53. At first sight, this does not seem particularly impressive, but the U-boats had sunk just under 10 per cent of the convoy. There can be no doubt that losing 10 per cent of every convoy would have made the British very worried indeed.

BELOW: The Philadelphia Naval dockyard on 27 October 1940. The impressive array of ships would slowly be depleted as destroyers headed for the United Kingdom under the terms of the lend-lease agreement.

ABOVE: Two of the 'four-stackers' destroyers sent to the UK under lend-lease – USS *Leary* (158) and USS *Shubrick* (268) await the Royal Navy crews who would be arriving to take them over.

SC2 was far from the last victim. HX72 was attacked next, losing six ships, and worse was to come. On 5 October, convoy SC7, comprising 35 ships and just one escort, set out on its journey. The escort vessel, HMS *Scarborough,* was a newcomer to escort tasks, having begun life as a survey vessel. By 9 October, four ships had fallen out of the convoy as a result of the bad weather conditions; three of them fell prey to marauding U-boats. The convoy then lost formation in a gale, and its speed was reduced to 6 knots. Despite this, no attack went in against the convoy during the next week, and, on 16 October, two more escort vessels joined up with the weather-beaten merchantmen and *Scarborough.* This did not mean that the convoy was out of trouble; in fact, its difficulties were only beginning. That night, *U48* located the convoy and started its 'shadower' reports. U-boat HQ sent six more boats to assist. Hans Rösing, commanding *U48,* did not wait for reinforcements and hit two ships before the pack had formed up; this caused the convoy to execute an emergency turn through 45 degrees, while *Scarborough* and HMS *Fowey* went in search of the U-boat. They did not find it, but in the morning, a Coastal Command Sunderland did. Rösing was forced to dive and duly lost contact with the convoy.

The captain of *Scarborough,* Commander N.V. Dickinson, then spent the next 24 hours hunting for *U48.* He did not find it. *Scarborough* did not find the convoy again, either. It would be grossly unfair to be critical of Dickinson, though, as the motivation behind his actions was impeccable – the U-boat represented a threat to the convoy, and it was appropriate for one of the escorts to hunt it down so as to remove the threat. The problem, of course, was that it exposed the convoy to greater risk, as it reduced the number of escorts. Dickinson was not to know that the pack would return to the convoy later – and, even if *Scarborough* had been there, it is hard to see what she could have done. It was not Dickinson's fault that effective training in convoy protection was in its infancy; nor was it his fault that neither the *Scarborough* nor the other two escorts had been given even the basic instruction that was available. The fault lay firmly with the reluctance to embrace convoy as the best approach to the problem of enemy submarines and nowhere else.

Some of the pressure caused by the disappearance of one of the escorts was relieved by the arrival of the sloop HMS *Leith* and the corvette HMS *Heartsease.* They were unable to make much difference.

Before the pack returned, *U38*, which was coincidentally operating in the area, ran into the convoy and made two attacks. These only succeeded in damaging a freighter, but signalled the renewal of the onslaught. *U38*'s signals to Lorient enabled U-boat HQ to direct the pack against the convoy again. The attack resumed late on 18 October. The pack was made up of *U28*, *U46*, *U99*, *U100*, *U101* and *U123*. At 22:06 hours, Kretschmer led the way, sinking one ship as he went head on towards the convoy. About 25 minutes later, he fired another torpedo using the U-boat's torpedo director, which failed to live up to its name. The torpedo missed, and Kretschmer decided that he would fire subsequent torpedoes using his own judgement, but then had to take evasive action before he could fire again. An hour later, he had manoeuvred into a firing position and sank a freighter with one torpedo; five minutes before midnight, another freighter lost its bow, burning with a green flame as Kretschmer scored again. This was Kretschmer's last attack for a while, as he had to evade the escorts; this successfully done, he attacked the convoy from astern and sank another three ships.

By the time the pack had finished, SC7 had lost 17 ships. *U99*, *U101* and *U123* had exhausted their torpedo supply and returned to base to a euphoric welcome; the other members of the pack remained on patrol, just in case they found any more

targets. They did. On 19 October, the boats encountered convoy HX79, made up of 49 ships. The escort was stronger than that afforded to poor SC7, with four corvettes, three trawlers and two destroyers in attendance, along with a minesweeper. While this looks potent, the same problem applied – the crews of these ships were untrained in the art of anti-submarine warfare, and their captains had no plan of coordinated action for the eventuality of running into a pack of U-boats. The attack against the convoy went in at 21:20 hours that night; by the end of the night, 17 ships had succumbed to the depredations of the pack. And this was not the end. Convoy HX79A was unfortunate enough to run into the U-boats and lost seven of its number. This meant that, in the space of three days, 38 merchant ships had been sunk by submarine attack. It was no wonder that Churchill was gravely concerned.

As a result of wartime censorship, the toll inflicted upon the three unfortunate convoys was kept from the public eye, but the next major submarine attack was a serious blow to British pride. The opulent liner *Empress of Britain*, transporting service personnel and their families back to the United Kingdom from overseas postings, was attacked on 26 October by an FW 200. The Condor made three bombing runs, causing a huge fire on board. Incredibly, the *Empress* did not sink, and an attempt was

BELOW: The merchant ship *Lilian* sinks after an attack. *Lilian*'s fate was shared by a large number of merchant ships at this stage of the war, as Britain struggled to update its anti-submarine warfare capability to meet the threat.

HMS *ANCHUSA*

Country:	Britain	**Dimensions:**	62.5m (205ft) x 10.1m (33ft) x 3.5m (11ft)
Launch date:	1940	**Armament:**	One 102mm (4in) gun, up to six 20mm (0.8in) cannon on single mounts. 70 depth charges, plus Hedgehog AS mortar
Crew:	96		
Displacement:	1015 tonnes (999 tons)		

ABOVE: *Anchusa* was one of the *Flower* class corvettes, built by Harland and Wolff in just over five months as part of the wartime programme. *Anchusa*, in common with other later-build ships of the class, incorporated a number of improvements over the earlier *Flower*s to improve the vessel's performance on escort duties.

made to take her under tow. The FW 200s report was passed on to U-boat HQ, while B-Dienst intercepts revealed the desperate efforts being made to save the ship. *U32* was despatched to finish the liner off. The presence of some of Coastal Command's ubiquitous Sunderlands kept her submerged for most of the 27th, but the use of the submarine's hydrophones enabled contact to be maintained – the sound of the escorting destroyers and the towing effort was more than enough. At around midnight, *U32* sighted her quarry; two hours later, the U-boat was in the ideal firing position and hit the *Empress of Britain* with two torpedoes. There was a huge explosion in the mortally wounded liner's boiler room, and she sank within 10 minutes. Unlike the loss of the convoyed vessels, this could not be kept absolutely secret, not least because of the triumphant propaganda from Germany. It marked the end of a terrible period for British merchant shipping. Unfortunately for the British, more of the same was to come.

STRUGGLING TO RESPOND

For the British, the sinkings in October marked the end of an horrendous period. Between June and October, 274 ships had fallen victim to the U-boats. Not unsurprisingly, there was considerable concern as to how to deal with the threat. One of the obvious problems was the lack of escort ships, and although lend-lease offered the likelihood of improvements, the need to convert the *Town* class vessels for their role meant that there would be a delay in their entry into productive service. In addition to a lack of numbers, the problem of locating surfaced U-boats needed to be considered. Asdic was clearly not the answer that had been hoped for.

At a meeting on 21 October 1940, the Defence Committee reached three important decisions. Of most note was the decision to release ships from anti-invasion duties. This would enable convoys to be given increased escorts, although this still meant that the average number of escorts per convoy could

	Hedgehog AS mortar
Powerplant:	Single-shaft, 4-cylinder triple expansion steam unit
Endurance:	6389 km (3500nm)
Performance:	16 knots

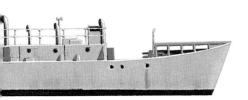

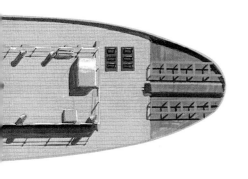

only be raised to two ships. To deal with the problem of finding surfaced U-boats, it was agreed that ships needed to be fitted with a version of the ASV (air-surface vessel) radar that had been developed for Coastal Command. The third decision directly affected Coastal Command, in that it was agreed that urgent steps to improve the command's equipment needed to be taken. Although the release of ships was relatively easy to achieve, the other two matters were rather more complicated.

The reason for this was simple – the ships on anti-invasion duty existed and did not need to be procured. Radar, on the other hand, was brand-new technology, still undergoing development – indeed, it was not, at that point, known as radar, but rather as radio direction finding (RDF). As well as radar sets for ships, there was a need to install similar equipment in Coastal Command aircraft. On top of this, the urgent need for effective aerial night defences meant that radar equipment for night fighters had to be constructed. The

industrial capacity to meet these three needs was simply non-existent. The first ASV radar sets – which were designated by Roman numerals – had been installed in Coastal Command Hudsons in January, but the performance was generally unimpressive. The sets were unreliable as well. Although unwelcome, this was not unexpected – lightweight radar sets had stemmed from work by Dr E G 'Taffy' Bowen in 1937, initially in the form of airborne interception (AI) radar. ASV had followed shortly after. While both types displayed immense promise, they had to be fully tested. Being thrown into operational service barely three years after they had first been thought of was an effective way of perfecting the technology quickly, through a great deal of testing, but was far from ideal. The first ASV I sets had been hand-built, and no two sets were quite the same. The reason for this was simple – as ideas for improvement occurred, they were incorporated into the set being built. This made maintaining the sets a nightmare: importantly, though, it also showed what worked and what did not. By the end of 1940, ASV II was already in the late stages of development and was designed for mass production. Nonetheless, the demands of the Blitz meant that it was difficult to get radar for anti-shipping and anti-submarine work produced ahead of the AI sets needed for the Blenheims and Beaufighters of Fighter Command.

As for the aircraft in Coastal Command, there was competition for labour and resources. Although the Ministry of Aircraft Production was doing sterling work, it could not meet the demands for aircraft for Fighter, Bomber and Coastal commands. The two latter commands required long-range aircraft with similar characteristics. Bomber Command, the only means of striking back at Germany, had priority and jealously guarded its assets. Coastal Command was forced to make do with Bomber Command's cast-offs, starting with the Armstrong Whitworth Whitley. For a cast-off, it was effective and much better than the Anson – nevertheless, it still lacked the asset of really long range to allow greater air cover of convoys. The Whitley was later followed by Vickers Armstrong Wellingtons, as they were replaced by new 'heavy' bombers such as the Stirling, Halifax and Manchester. Although Coastal Command's situation was much improved by the end of 1940, there was still a long way to travel before it could be considered a truly effective force. Given these unfavourable circumstances, it is worthwhile pausing to note how well the Coastal Command crews did with inferior aircraft types or equipment that had yet to be fully proven.

EMPRESS OF BRITAIN

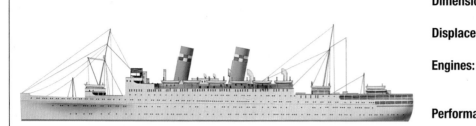

Country:	Britain
Launch date:	June 1930
Passengers:	1195
Dimensions:	231.84 m (750ft) x 29.79 m (98ft)
Displacement:	43,027 gross tonnes (42,348 gross tons)
Engines:	Four Curtis-Brown steam turbines turning four propellers
Performance:	24 knots

ABOVE: The *Empress of Britain* was impressed into war service as a troop transport, in common with a number of other distinguished ocean liners. After being set ablaze by bombing, *U32* arrived to despatch the ship on 12 October 1940. The loss of such a prestigious vessel was a blow to British morale.

BELOW: The Wellington began life as a bomber, but once the four-engined 'heavies' began to join Bomber Command, the type was employed by Coastal Command, both in the form of 'hand-me-downs' and through new production.

ANTI-SUBMARINE TACTICS

The decrease in sinkings by U-boats after October was not, therefore, the result of any sudden change in British tactics. The bad weather and lack of serviceable U-boats after their earlier efforts were primarily to blame. Despite this, there were some successes for the defences. On 30 October, *U32* was sunk by two escort vessels, *Harvester* and *Highlander*. Three days later, *U31* was the victim of HMS *Antelope*, acting in conjunction with an aircraft that was in the vicinity of the convoy. Finally, on 21 November, the corvette *Rhododendron* surprised *U104* and sent her to the bottom.

These three incidents demonstrated the value of convoy escort, yet the idea that the convoy was in some way a regrettable defensive measure had not gone away. Part of the difficulty may have originated from the offensive spirit of Churchill, who spoke vividly of hunting groups acting in much the same way as mounted cavalry did on land – swiftly and decisively. In many ways, the

analogy was apt, as experience had shown that mounted cavalry were unsuited for modern warfare. This was just as true of the hunting group, which enjoyed little success. On occasion, convoy escorts were formed into hunting groups of their own and sent to chase U-boats that they never found, leaving the merchantmen at considerably increased risk. It is possible to understand why the attitude about convoys persisted when placed in the broader strategic context of the war. Apart from the efforts of Bomber Command, it seemed that everything that the Germans did threw Britain onto the defensive at a time and place not of her choosing. Even something as small as pursuing U-boats so as to be pushing some part of the German war effort onto the defensive seemed attractive. This was despite all the evidence from history that the convoy was far more complex than this.

The convoy in fact offered far more benefit to the side that operated it, offering concentration of force. If the enemy chose

VICKERS WELLINGTON

Country:	Britain
First flight:	1936
Crew:	6-7
Powerplant:	Two Bristol Hercules radial piston engines
Performance:	Maximum speed 406 km/h (252 mph), range approx. 2816km (1750 miles)

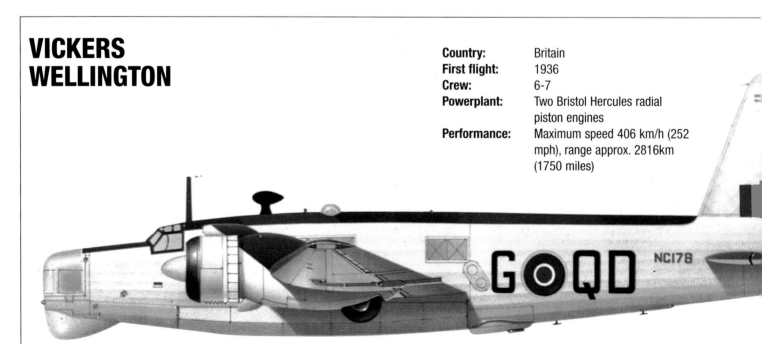

not to engage, it meant that he lost a small battle, in that the vital supplies that were a key target of his strategy were able to reach their destination unscathed. If the enemy did engage, it provided the convoying side with an opportunity to defeat the attack. Furthermore, in certain conditions, the convoy escorts might surprise the enemy and defeat him even before he launched his assault. Despite these nuances, the simple notion that the convoy was a defensive

Armament:	One 7.7mm (0.303in) machine gun on flexible mount in nose (two in power-operated turret in other versions), four 7.7mm (0.303in) machine guns in power-operated tail turret, two 7.7mm (0.3.3in) machine guns in beam mountings, maximum bombload of 2040kg (4500lb)

measure forced upon Britain by Germany and was, therefore, a bad thing proved extremely difficult to shake off.

THE U-BOATS MOVE SOUTH

Although the possibilities for scoring in the North Atlantic dropped away in November, the U-boats that were available were not idle. Five ships were sunk off Portugal, and four off Freetown. There were no properly organized air or surface escorts in this area, and the only available air assets were in the form of the few aircraft in Gibraltar from 200 Group, Coastal Command. These comprised just a single squadron of Saro London flying boats and a few Fleet Air Arm Swordfish biplanes. This was hardly enough to deal with the threat. Although it was obvious that the anti-submarine capability in the region needed to be enhanced, resources did not permit any immediate action.

Sunderlands were finally sent to Freetown in March 1941, and newly procured American Catalina flying boats only reached Gibraltar in May. By this stage, the U-boats had largely returned to northern waters, where they could seek to further the use of pack tactics. Although this appeared to leave the British in as parlous a state as before, circumstances proved to be considerably different.

As 1941 arrived, the U-boat arm could only muster around 21 operational U-boats at any one time, way below the size of fleet that Dönitz thought necessary to wage an effective

ABOVE: A depth charge thrower about to fire against a submarine. The throwers enhanced the fighting power of the escorts, which had previously been limited to dropping the charges over the stern of the ship.

RIGHT: German hydrographers at work. The production of accurate maps and charts was essential to effective operations, but is generally forgotten when considering the U-boat campaign.

U47

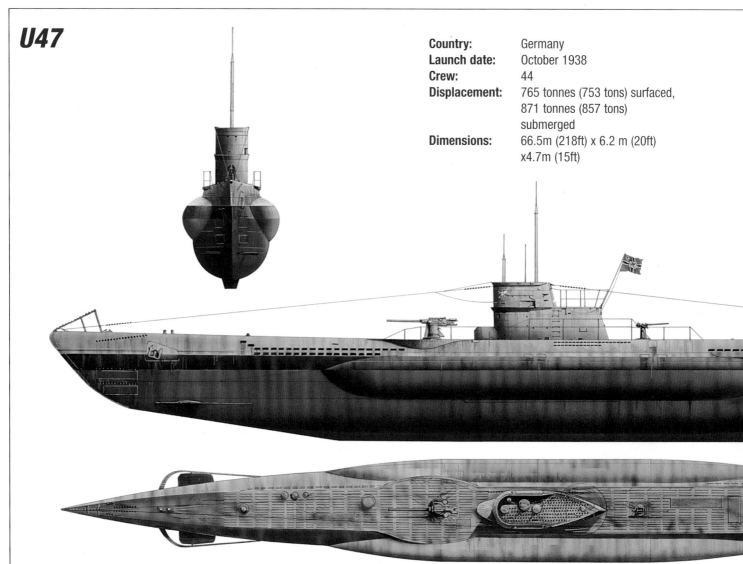

Country:	Germany
Launch date:	October 1938
Crew:	44
Displacement:	765 tonnes (753 tons) surfaced, 871 tonnes (857 tons) submerged
Dimensions:	66.5m (218ft) x 6.2 m (20ft) x4.7m (15ft)

war against the United Kingdom's trade. There were numerous reasons for the lack of boats, most notably shortages of labour and raw materials. These were not made any easier by the interruption caused at docks and factories by air-raid alerts, which caused worker fatigue as well as delay. The shortages of materials for U-boats were exacerbated by the lack of transport available to ferry them to the dockyards. A further difficulty for Dönitz was that Göring was responsible for overcoming these difficulties. Relations between the two men were reasonable to begin with, but this was to change.

In January 1941, Hitler ordered Göring to transfer command of the FW 200s of KG40 to Dönitz. This was a fundamentally sound idea, as it should have enabled effective air–sea cooperation. Göring, however, regarded this as a personal slight inspired by Dönitz. Göring made a jovial attempt to persuade Dönitz to cancel the transfer in command, but was politely rebuffed. This was enough to ensure that the relationship between the two was permanently soured.

Armament:	One 86mm (3.4in) gun, one 20mm (0.8in) anti-aircraft gun, five 533mm (21in) torpedo tubes
Powerplant:	Diesel/electric, driving two shafts
Surface range:	12,038km (6500nm) at 12 knots
Performance:	17.2 knots surfaced, 8 knots submerged

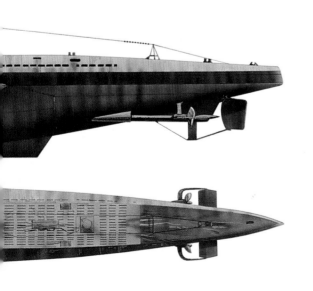

Initially, it appeared that the move was inspired. On 9 February, *U37* spotted convoy HG53 from Gibraltar. After sinking two ships, the submarine called up six FW 200s, which sank five more. While the convoy was recovering from the shock, *U37* pounced again and sent another merchantman to the bottom. Ten days later, an FW 200 alerted a U-boat to the whereabouts of convoy OB288. This enabled a pack to be formed, and five ships were sunk once the escort had turned back at 20° west. The value of cooperation was proved once more on 26 February, when Prien found OB290. He called up Kretschmer and the FW 200s. While the submarines sank three ships, the Condors accounted for a further nine. Sadly for the two parties, these were the only truly successful examples of cooperation during the entire war.

MEETING THE THREAT – BRITISH REORGANIZATION

Despite the serious problems with resources, it was clear that some action could be taken to improve the way in which the fight against the U-boats was conducted. On 7 February, the Admiralty moved its Western Approaches Command from Plymouth to Liverpool. This was more than a movement of personnel, as the Admiral Sir Martin Dunbar-Nasmith, the Commander-in-Chief of Western Approaches, remained in Plymouth as the commander of the new Plymouth Command. Western Approaches Command was taken over by Admiral Sir

ABOVE: Gunther Prien and the crew of *U47*. The daring attack on Scapa Flow made Prien into a national hero, and his loss was a serious blow to the morale of the U-boat arm, particularly coupled with the loss at around the same time of two other aces.

LEFT: *U47* was best known for sinking the *Royal Oak* in Scapa Flow, but enjoyed an extremely successful career under the command of Gunther Prien, accounting for over 30 ships in just over 16 months. *U47* was lost in March 1941, after being rammed by HMS *Wolverine*.

HMS *WALKER*

Country:	Britain
Launch date:	1918
Crew:	127
Displacement:	1100 tonnes
	(1082 tons) standard load

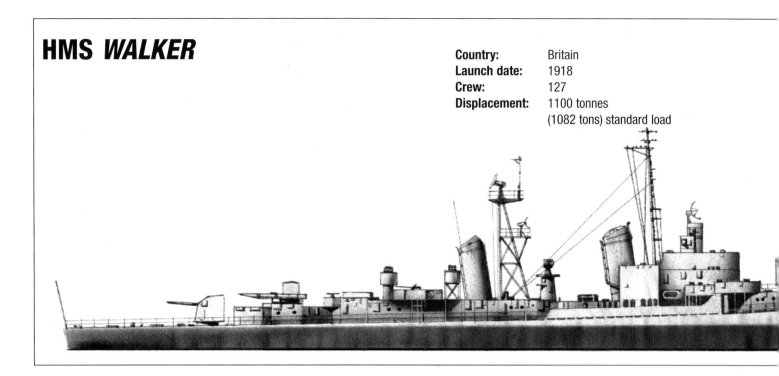

ABOVE: Another of the World War I destroyers still employed by the Royal Navy, *Walker* was converted to long-range escort configuration, and was responsible for sinking Otto Kretschmer's *U99*.

Percy Noble. This owed much to the fact that the German occupation of France meant that the focus of the command had moved away from the dangerous waters of the Channel, but was also to permit the co-location of Western Approaches Command and 15 Group, Coastal Command. This ensured closer cooperation between the Commander-in-Chief Western Approaches and the Air Officer Commanding 15 Group, Air Vice Marshal Sir James Robb.

It also coincided with debate over the future of Coastal Command itself. Some within government circles argued that Coastal Command should be transferred to the Royal Navy, ceasing to be part of the RAF. The Defence Committee considered the proposal too drastic a change in time of war, but reached a compromise: Coastal Command, while remaining part of the RAF, would come under operational control of the Admiralty as soon as possible. In the case of Western Approaches Command, this sealed the close cooperation between the

RIGHT: The size of the welcoming party for this U-boat demonstrates the high regard in which the submarine crews were held.

Dimensions:	95.1m (312ft) x 9m (29ft) x 3.2m (10ft)
Armament:	Four 102mm (4in) guns, one 76mm (3in) anti-aircraft gun, six 533mm (21in) torpedo tubes, depth charges
Powerplant:	Geared steam turbines, driving two shafts
Range:	8350km (4508nm) at 15 knots
Performance:	34 knots

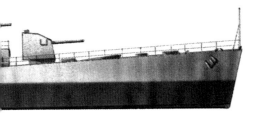

Government Code and Cipher School at Bletchley Park. Using intercepts from U-boats and U-boat HQ, it was possible to work out the location of German submarines. The Naval Intelligence Division's Submarine Tracking Room collated the information and then advised on where the convoys should be routed so as to avoid the submarines.

This new measure had first shown promise in January 1941, when 21 ships had been sunk, almost all of which had been beyond the cover of escorts or which had become detached from their convoys. As the weather improved in February, sinkings increased, with the U-boats scoring 39 kills. Of these, 50 per cent were stragglers. Despite the increase in losses, it appeared that the careful routing of convoys offered some respite from the attack. More by luck than design, the U-boats suffered a series of blows, lack of British resources notwithstanding.

two services, although the painful fact was that neither the Royal Navy nor the RAF – especially the latter – had quite the resources to fulfil their task to its satisfaction.

The absence of resources, however, did not mean that nothing could be done. Instead, the Admiralty turned to the use of intelligence and planning to overcome some of the difficulties it faced. This took the form of relying upon the signals intelligence, much of which was gained through Y-service and the efforts of the

MARCH 1941 – ILL FORTUNE FOR THE U-BOATS

After the successes of air–sea cooperation in February, Dönitz had some cause for optimism. This was to prove to be misplaced. On 6 March, *U47* radioed a report of sighting a convoy – OB293. As a result, a number of other boats were called up, including *U99* commanded by Kretschmer. The pack attacked the convoy at darkness, but found that the escorts were particularly robust in their response. The

LEFT: Some of the crew of HMS *Bittern* manhandle a depth charge onto a thrower, ready for the next engagement with a U-boat.

ABOVE: Otto Kretschmer is reunited with his binoculars. Kretschmer (left) surrendered the binoculars to Captain Donald Macintyre (right) when Macintyre's HMS *Walker* sank *U99*; as seen here, they were returned several years later when the two men met again.

Prien was confident that he had evaded the escorts and surfaced. This was an error: *Wolverine* was waiting and attempted to ram. Prien ordered a crash dive, but it was too late. *Wolverine* released a perfect pattern of depth-charges right on top of *U47*. In among the usual roar of the explosions, a curious red glow was briefly seen from beneath the surface. A few minutes later, some debris, clearly belonging to a submarine, floated to the surface. *Wolverine* was convinced that she had her kill and carried on about her business. Over the next few days, U-boat HQ attempted to contact *U47*, but to no avail. There could be no other conclusion: Gunther Prien, the first U-boat commander to gain hero status in World War II, was dead. For U-boat HQ, matters did not improve.

THE LOST ACES

On 15 March, the new type IXB boat, *U110* under Julius Lemp (who had sunk *Athenia* on the first day of the war), located HX112, about 240km (150 miles) south of Iceland. The convoy consisted of 41 merchantmen and tankers, guarded by five destroyers and two corvettes from Captain Donald Macintyre's 5th Escort Group. The 5th Escort Group was developing a reputation for its tough, methodical approach, although the group's training immediately prior to departure had not been as thorough as it might have been. If engaged, it would need a mixture of firm direction and good seamanship to be successful, along with that vital ingredient, a little luck. As the pack brought together as a result of Lemp's signal was to find, 5th Escort Group was to enjoy all of these things.

Lemp's initial report was slightly misleading, in that he reported only two

unusually designated *UA* was forced to submerge, along with Prien, while Kretschmer was driven off and lost contact. *U70* was vigorously depth-charged by the corvettes *Camellia* and *Arbutus*, and was compelled to surface. The crew just managed to surrender and jump overboard before the submarine sank. As a result of the aggressive actions of the escorts, OB293 escaped with two ships sunk and two damaged, which was a great improvement on the losses sustained in some of the previous pack operations.

Gunther Prien was not prepared to allow OB293 to get away so lightly, and he resumed pursuit the next day. At 00:23 hours, he was detected by the ancient HMS *Wolverine*. Before *Wolverine* could attack, one of the other escorts fired an illuminating shell, prompting *U47* to dive. A five-hour chase followed. At the end of it,

HMS *WOLVERINE*

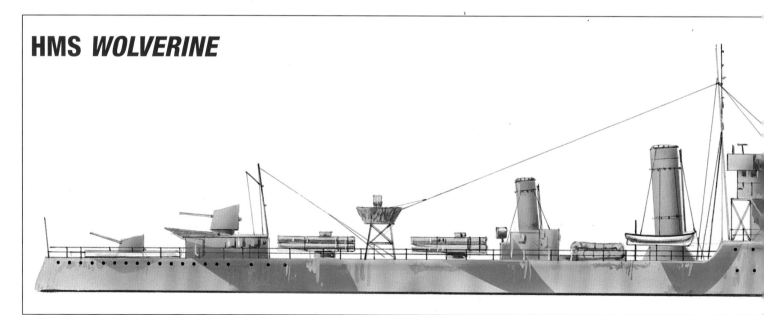

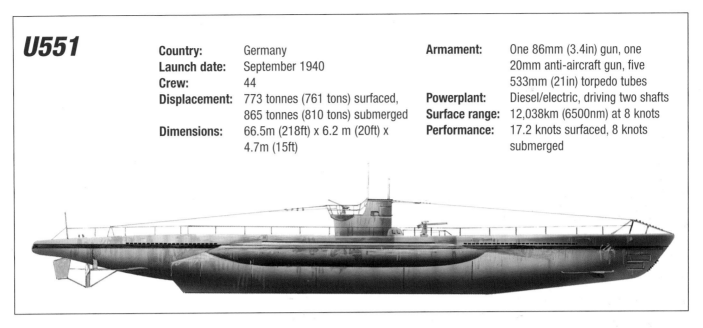

U551

Country:	Germany	**Armament:**	One 86mm (3.4in) gun, one 20mm anti-aircraft gun, five 533mm (21in) torpedo tubes
Launch date:	September 1940		
Crew:	44		
Displacement:	773 tonnes (761 tons) surfaced, 865 tonnes (810 tons) submerged	**Powerplant:**	Diesel/electric, driving two shafts
		Surface range:	12,038km (6500nm) at 8 knots
Dimensions:	66.5m (218ft) x 6.2 m (20ft) x 4.7m (15ft)	**Performance:**	17.2 knots surfaced, 8 knots submerged

destroyers present, thus giving a slightly false picture of the vulnerability of the convoy. At 22:00 hours, he attacked and hit the tanker *Erodona*, which suffered a huge explosion that, to the amazement of those watching, did not sink her – she was later towed to Iceland. The flames from the explosion illuminated *U110,* and the destroyer *Scimitar* attacked, followed by *Walker* and *Vanoc*. Lemp saw them in good time and went deep; although depth-charges were dropped at the point where he dived, they had no effect. After an hour, Lemp resurfaced and chased after the convoy, sending another report (in which he failed to correct the number of escorts given in the first report) before launching a second assault on the convoy just after 04:00 hours. This attack only resulted in a hit on one target, a tanker. Lemp thought that he had scored a victory, but could not be sure. With daylight, Lemp trailed the

convoy and his reports led to orders from Dönitz for all available boats to join him.

U37, U74, U99 and *U100* all responded and headed towards the scene, following homing signals from *U110*. The arrival of a Sunderland forced Lemp to dive, and he lost contact. *U37*, however, was in the area, and soon relocated the convoy, taking over the task of shadowing. Her reports brought up *U99* and *U100*; early that evening, Lemp regained the convoy, and his signals brought up *U74*. Lemp lost contact again, and, when *U74* came alongside, a shouted conversation between the two U-boat skippers led to the decision to head northeast. This was a reasonable assumption of what the convoy *might* have done, but was in fact incorrect. The other three U-boats had made contact, but did not send out any signals to help *U74* and *U110* to join them.

The three U-boats closed in on the convoy and discovered that they were facing more formidable opposition than they had been led to believe. *U100* was sighted by *Scimitar,* forcing Schepke to dive. When he came up an hour later, he discovered that one of the destroyers had waited for him, and he was forced to submerge again as it depth-charged his vessel.

Kretschmer attacked at 22:00 hours, charging into the convoy on the surface, firing his eight remaining torpedoes. One missed, but the others sank five ships and damaged another. The intense, acrid smoke from the tankers hit by his torpedoes enabled Kretschmer to hide from the escorts while working out his line of escape. The flames and smoke may have been helping Kretschmer, but were a distinct problem for his companions. It was now that things started to go seriously awry for the U-boats.

ABOVE: *U551* was an unlucky U-boat. She set off on her first operational patrol on 18 March 1941, and found a merchantman five days later. Before *U551* had the chance to torpedo the ship, the escort trawler *Visenda* attacked her. Although *U551* was submerged, at least one depth charge destroyed the boat, and she was lost with all hands after less than a week at sea.

LEFT: *Wolverine* enjoyed a long career with the Royal Navy, being commissioned just after World War I. In common with a number of similar vessels, she served on through the inter-war years and found gainful employment as an escort vessel. *Wolverine* was sold for scrap in 1946.

Country:	Britain
Launch date:	July 1919
Crew:	134
Armament:	Two 120mm (4.7in) guns, three torpedo tubes, depth charges and Hedgehog AS Mortar
Range:	5778km (3120nm) at 15 knots
Performance:	34 knots

The area of the convoy was brightly lit from the flames, and the escorts steamed purposefully around trying to locate the attackers. Just before 01:00 hours, Macintyre in HMS *Walker* spotted a submarine ahead of him and ordered full speed ahead so as to ram it. It was *U37,* and her commander, Nickolaus Clausen, crash-dived just in time. *Walker* unloaded 10 depth-charges almost on top of the submarine as it ploughed over the top of her. There was a loud explosion, and Macintrye thought that he had sunk his first submarine. In fact, he had not, but *U37* had been seriously damaged. Clausen broke off his attack on the convoy and began the journey home for repairs. This was not the end of Macintyre's work for the night. *Walker* then detected *U100* with her asdic, and Macintyre called in HMS *Vanoc* to attack. *Vanoc* dropped a number of depth-charges; as soon as these had gone off, *Walker* added eight more to the fray. *Vanoc* dropped six more, set for various depths, regained asdic contact after the noise of the explosions had subsided and fired another six.

The unfortunate *U100* was in trouble. The depth-charges had done more than 'rattle the wardroom crockery', smashing vital pieces of machinery and causing flooding. The boat went out of control, and Schepke ordered all ballast tanks to be blown. This was not just a defensive measure to save his boat, as Schepke was convinced that he could torpedo his assailant and effect an escape. He was wrong.

Vanoc had recently been equipped with radar, a ship-mounted version of ASV. *U100* was surfaced in pitch darkness, but may as well have been bathed in sunlight. The radar

operator eagerly reported the contact, and, within a minute, *Vanoc* was on top of *U100,* charging in to ram. *Vanoc* hit the conning tower, and, in the collision, the unfortunate Schepke stood no chance, bearing the full brunt of the attack. *U100* went down rapidly and only seven crew members were saved. *Vanoc* stood by to pick up survivors while Macintyre's HMS *Walker* manoeuvred to protect her.

At this point, the officer on watch on board *U99* happened to turn around. To his horror, he discovered the lookout had not seen the destroyers. Convinced that *U99* had been seen, he ordered a crash dive. Down below, Kretschmer was plotting a course for home; before he could react, it was too late: *U99* was below the waves and a prime target for asdic. In these circumstances, Kretschmer would have sought to escape on the surface, using the speed of the U-boat to evade. *Vanoc* might have detected *U99* with her radar, but the limited field of view for the set would probably have prevented this. No one on the destroyers had seen the submarine, but the dive gave her away. *Walker's* asdic operator reported the contact, and the destroyer ran in to depth-charge her. *Walker* released a pattern of six depth-charges which exploded below *U99*, wrecking machinery and sending her down. Kretschmer ordered all ballast tanks to be blown, and the *U99* shot to the surface.

On board *Walker,* Macintyre saw the *Vanoc* signalling urgently: 'U-boat surfaced astern of me.' The gun crews on the two destroyers opened fire, although their accuracy was not especially noteworthy –

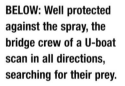

BELOW: Well protected against the spray, the bridge crew of a U-boat scan in all directions, searching for their prey.

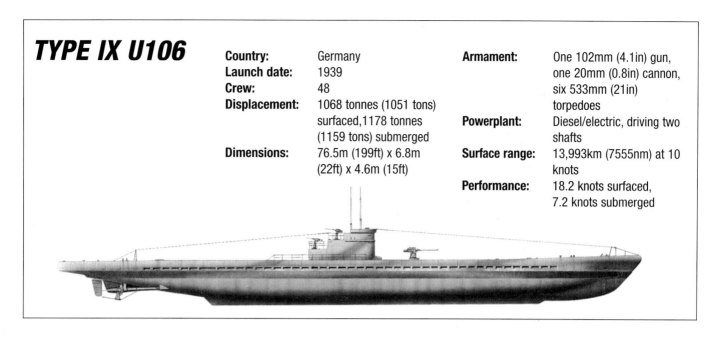

TYPE IX U106

Country:	Germany	**Armament:**	One 102mm (4.1in) gun, one 20mm (0.8in) cannon, six 533mm (21in) torpedoes
Launch date:	1939		
Crew:	48		
Displacement:	1068 tonnes (1051 tons) surfaced,1178 tonnes (1159 tons) submerged	**Powerplant:**	Diesel/electric, driving two shafts
Dimensions:	76.5m (199ft) x 6.8m (22ft) x 4.6m (15ft)	**Surface range:**	13,993km (7555nm) at 10 knots
		Performance:	18.2 knots surfaced, 7.2 knots submerged

they do not appear to have scored a single hit. Kretschmer hoped to escape, but his engines refused to work. He sent off a quick message to Dönitz, announcing that he had been depth-charged and that he would surrender. He then signalled his attackers: 'we are sunking [sic]', at which point the gun crews were ordered to cease fire. A boat was lowered from the *Walker* with the intention of capturing the submarine if possible. As the crew abandoned ship, *U99* slipped beneath the waves. The crew were picked up and taken back to *Walker.* As they disembarked, Kretschmer was last to leave the rescue boat. He was welcomed by Macintrye, who cordially relieved Kretschmer of his binoculars as a souvenir, and then taken below. The action was over.

THE FIRST DEFEAT

Dönitz learned of the disastrous results of what had begun as a promising attack from the battered *U37,* which signalled in reports. Before the escort group had returned home, Winston Churchill told the House of Commons that the Royal Navy had sunk the two leading U-boat aces Kretschmer and Schepke. This meant that the Germans could not hide the losses, and the news came as a great blow to the U-boat arm. The loss of *U47* was not claimed by Churchill, and news of this was suppressed until May, so as to give the impression that the three leading lights of the U-boat arm had succumbed over a greater period of time than they in fact had.

To make matters worse, on 23 March, *U551* attempted to torpedo a merchantman on the surface at dawn. *U551* was spotted, and the freighter radioed an alarm. The escort trawler *Visenda* gamely charged the surfaced U-boat at full speed. *U551* submerged just in time, but was picked up on asdic. The contact was maintained for more than 90 minutes, during which *Visenda* fired 18 depth-charges. At least one of these proved fatal, as the trawler recovered some internal parts from the submarine and, far less pleasantly, some of the internal parts of one of the unfortunate members of the crew of *U551.* This loss was the fifth in just over three weeks. U-boat HQ glumly considered the implications of the loss of three of the most experienced U-boat commanders and feared that the British had come up with some fiendish countermeasure.

The U-boats had suffered an 'exchange rate' of five British ships for every U-boat sunk in March, which was an unsustainable level. Dönitz decided that he would withdraw all his U-boats from the North West Approaches and send them further west, to places where escort cover could not be found. While this was a sensible precaution, it also marked the first tactical defeat of the U-boats, given that they had been forced away from the area in which their commander thought that they could have the greatest level of success.

The major problem still facing the U-boat arm was the lack of craft for the task – Dönitz only had 27 operational boats available at the end of March, or under 10 per cent of the number that he had deemed desirable at the outbreak of war. As if this was not enough, the United States had begun to take a more active part in the war, and the RAF's anti-submarine efforts were improving as new equipment arrived. The remainder of 1941 was to become much harder, both for the U-boats and for Germany itself.

ABOVE: A *Type IXB* U-boat, *U106* was designed for ocean-going operations. The boat possessed high speed, making it very effective for surfaced night attacks. *U106* enjoyed a successful career until it was attacked by Coastal Command Sunderlands on 2 August 1943. The attacks crippled the U-boat, which was lost along with 25 of the crew.

CHAPTER FOUR

A CRISIS OF CONFIDENCE: APRIL – DECEMBER 1941

After the losses of March 1941, the U-boat arm endured an arduous few months as the British appeared to have done just enough to manage the threat posed by the submarine.

As April 1941 began, the British Coastal Command was becoming a far stronger force than before, thus presenting a greater threat to the U-boat arm. It had acquired the first of its Consolidated Catalina flying boats from the United States in March, and they had been instrumental in the hunt for the *Bismarck*. Although the range of the Catalina was impressive, being greater than that of the Sunderland, it was not as well armed as the larger British aircraft. The range was also not quite sufficient to provide as much air cover to the convoys as was needed. As a result, the command was hunting for a very long-range (VLR) aircraft. In March, it found it, with the entry into service of the first Consolidated Liberators.

This did not mark the end of the VLR aircraft problem, as the Liberator was in demand. As the B-24, it was used by the United States Army Air Force as a bomber, and RAF Bomber Command cast covetous eyes upon them. Bomber Command saw the four-engined Liberator as an ideal aircraft for some of its units, and the conflict between the two

LEFT: *U570* shows off its gun: much as in World War I, the gun was an important weapon against those smaller vessels which were not considered to merit the expenditure of a torpedo.

CONSOLIDATED CATALINA

Country:	USA
First flight:	1935
Crew:	8–9
Powerplant:	Two Pratt and Whitney Twin Wasp engines
Performance:	Maximum speed 305km/h (190mph); range 6437km (4000 miles); endurance 17.6 hours
Armament:	Four 7.7mm (0.303in) machine guns, 907kg (2000lb) of bombs or depth charges

ABOVE: The introduction of the Consolidated Catalina greatly enhanced the effectiveness of Coastal Command. Although it did not quite have the endurance to fill the mid-Atlantic air gap, the Catalina proved a tremendously effective anti-submarine weapon.

RAF Commands continued. Bomber Command contended that the diversion of aircraft to Coastal Command was a mistake, as the strategic bombardment of Germany would be the way to win the war. Bomber Command, particularly after Air Chief Marshal Sir Arthur Harris took over in 1942, never quite saw the need for aircraft that would make admirable bombers being sent to Coastal Command. Although it may be easy to understand with hindsight, it was difficult for the members of Bomber Command – which was the only means Britain had to project offensive power against Germany between 1940 and 1944 – to comprehend at the time that their efforts would be for naught if supplies did not get through to the United Kingdom.

This is not to say that the role of Coastal Command was unappreciated. The decision to place Coastal Command under the operational control of the Admiralty had been taken in March, and came into effect in early April. This ensured a greater level of coordination could be achieved. As the command gained new aircraft types, its effectiveness increased. The range factor remained important, as there were still areas that could not be covered. Undaunted, Coastal Command focused its efforts on the Bay of Biscay, which was to become an ever more important hunting ground as the year progressed.

A CHANGE OF APPROACH

On 1 April 1941, Karl Dönitz ordered the nine U-boats at sea to operate further to the west, establishing a patrol line at 30° west, well out of the range of the escorts. As if to confirm the bad luck that the U-boats were encountering, *U76* discovered OB305 in the North West Approaches, some 640km (400 miles) to the east of the new patrol line. Dönitz was faced with a dilemma. Given the strength of the British anti-submarine effort,

he was reluctant to bring his forces further eastwards, but he was equally reluctant to see the convoy escape. He instructed *U76* to track the convoy as it proceeded west, in the hope that the U-boats on their patrol line would be able to intervene when the convoy arrived, guided to their targets by the signals from the shadowing *U76*. This was not without risk, as it was more than likely that the British would intercept the signals from *U76* and re-route the convoy once the location from which the signals originated had been established. As it was, the plan hit difficulties, as *U76* sighted a number of trawlers south of Iceland and was obliged to submerge, losing contact with OB305. *U76* surfaced after nine hours and began the task of relocating the convoy again.

At the same time, *U74* encountered SC26, a convoy of 22 ships escorted by the cruiser *Worcestershire*. Dönitz ordered *U76* to call up other boats, but instructed that no attack should be put in until the other submarines had arrived. Eight U-boats were in a position to form up, making this the largest pack to date. The attack began on 2 April, and five ships were sunk. The convoy commodore ordered the 16 surviving ships to scatter, as the crews made numerous sightings of U-boats, many of which were probably imagined. *Worcestershire* was damaged in the attack, and the Admiralty despatched more escorts to the convoy. *Worcestershire* was escorted to Liverpool by a destroyer, while five other ships formed up the convoy once more to take them to their destination.

By chance, *U76* came across the re-forming convoy and torpedoed a freighter at about 11:30 hours on 3 April – having missed her with her first two torpedoes some five hours earlier. The other U-boats then joined the pursuit of the convoy. *U94* and *U98* sank three ships between them, before HMS *Wolverine* forced them to submerge, ending the attacks for the day. On the afternoon of 4 April, *U76* once again ran into the convoy while running submerged, and she torpedoed the freighter *Athenic*, which was sailing alone. *Athenic* crew abandoned her, but not before they had sent off a warning message. *U76* had not sunk *Athenic* with the torpedo that had caused the abandonment, and her commander, Friedrich von Hippel, came in again and fired two torpedoes that despatched the crippled merchantman. While he was doing this, four of the escorts were rushing to the scene.

When they reached the area on the morning of 5 April, *U76* was on the surface, recharging her batteries. The watch officer saw the approaching ships and crash-dived. *Wolverine* obtained an Allied Submarine Detection Investigation Committee 'asdic' contact, but the apparatus had an intermittent fault that made it impossible to drop more than two depth-charges. The corvette *Arbutus* tried to attack, but lost contact with *U76* among the underwater commotion caused by *Wolverine's* depth-charges. HMS *Scarborough*, the unfortunate companion to the convoy SC7, had better luck, dropping a pattern of eight depth-charges. All the charges, including the initial two from the *Wolverine,* were accurate. The first from *Wolverine* smashed all the instruments, while the next put out all the lights and caused structural damage. Those from *Scarborough* did enough damage to flood the submarine aft. Hippel concluded that his submarine was finished and surfaced so as to scuttle the boat.

Hippel's problems were not over, as *Arbutus* was run in to try to capture the submarine, in the hope of grabbing the Enigma coding machine and any secret papers that might be found. *Arbutus* pulled alongside, and a four-man boarding party led by the first lieutenant, Geoffrey Angus, leapt aboard the forward deck of the submarine. They raced to the bridge, while other members of *Arbutus*'s crew tied cables and a hawser to the submarine to prevent it sinking. When Angus reached the conning tower, though, he discovered that the boat was filling with sea water. This had reacted with the batteries, and a lethal cloud of chlorine gas was emitting from the hatch. Angus slammed it shut in an attempt to stop the air from escaping, hoping that this would prevent the submarine from slipping under. It was not enough, as *U76* continued to fill with water and was going down rapidly. *Arbutus* was in danger of being

capsized, so the wires were let go, and the submarine was allowed to sink. Forty-two survivors were recovered.

The results of the attack on SC26 meant that the decision to withdraw to more westerly longitudes looked less like a tactical reverse than it had done. Eleven ships had been sunk on their way to the United Kingdom, taking their cargoes with them, in exchange for one U-boat. In fact, as Clay Blair observes, this was more a result of good fortune than skill on the part of the inexperienced Hippel. Although a success, the U-boats were still operating away from what could have been the most profitable area of operations.

The fate of SC26 ensured that the development of Allied anti-submarine facilities on Iceland was conducted with even greater urgency. Three escort groups were sent to use the newly established facilities, while Coastal Command sent a number of Sunderlands and Hudsons to use the airfield on the island. Both types were equipped with the ASV II and offered further protection to the convoys. In addition to the long days preventing the U-boats operating safely on the surface, ASV meant that being surfaced at night was not a safe proposition either. This did not mean

BELOW: The Captain and officers of a British destroyer watch the convoy under their protection as it heads for home.

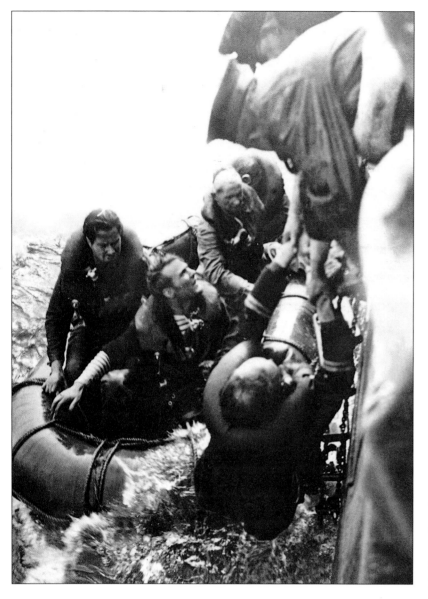

ABOVE: The crew of a British ship help rescue the survivors of a U-boat that has just been sunk by the escort group.

RIGHT: *U76*, a *Type VIIB* boat had a relatively short career, being sunk on 5 April 1941, while attacking convoy SC26. All but one of the crew were rescued.

that the British had established a watertight escort system in the North Atlantic, as there were difficulties in making the system work to full efficiency. Precise routing and timings were required, and these were always at the mercy of bad weather, which could delay the escorts or, worse still, make it impossible for the escorts to find the convoy. Although it would be fair to say that the British were enjoying a small advantage over the U-boats, the submarine threat was still far from over.

CRACKING ENIGMA

A further element in the relatively successful campaign against the U-boats had already been provided by the code-breakers at Bletchley Park, who had undertaken sterling work in analysing the signals sent to U-boats from their headquarters. While this provided valuable insights, it did not provide the ability to read the messages almost simultaneously. It had been this aspect which led to the Admiralty encouraging the capture of U-boats in the hope that they might be able to provide the crucial breakthrough that would allow rapid decryption of signals. This was to come with the attack on OB318.

Convoy OB318 was detected by Herbert Kuppisch's *U94* on 7 May 1941. It was heavily guarded to begin with, as there were 10 escorts assigned. When Kuppisch sighted the convoy, he did so just at the point where 3rd Escort Group had joined the convoy to relieve the first batch of escorts as the mid-point of the journey approached. Five

U76

Country:	Germany
Launch date:	October 1940
Crew:	44
Displacement:	753 tonnes (741 tons) surfaced, 857 tonnes (843 tons) submerged
Dimensions:	66.5m (218ft) x 6.2m (20ft) x 4.7m (15ft)

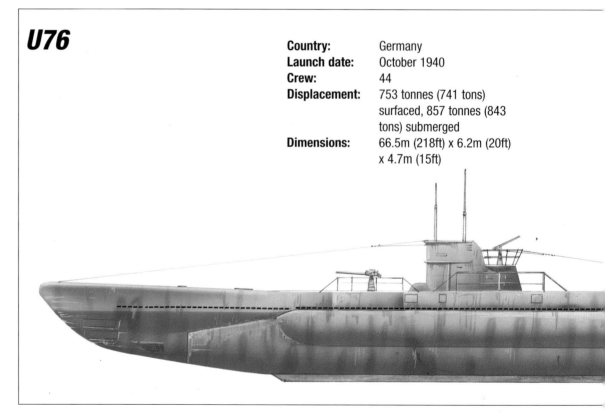

corvettes and the sloop HMS *Rochester* were to remain with the convoy to ensure that the handover was completed with sufficient escorts present. This meant that there were 15 escorts in the area of the convoy when Kuppisch made his report.

The night of 7 May was moonlit, and Kuppisch elected to launch his attack while submerged. He allowed the first escorts to pass and worked his way into the centre of the convoy. He then fired four torpedoes at the passing ships, sinking two. This was to be Kuppisch's only attack, as the destroyers *Bulldog* and *Amazon*, in the company of *Rochester,* made a vigorous counterattack with depth-charges. Over the course of four hours, 89 depth-charges were sent in *U94*'s direction, causing considerable damage to the submarine. Kuppisch was not forced to surface and was able to repair the damage once the escorts had left. He was unable to continue to the attack, however, and instead continued his patrol.

Six other U-boats had been alerted to the presence of OB318, and two of them found the convoy on the night of 8 May. *U110* commanded by Julius Lemp was joined by the new *Type VIIC* boat, *U201*. The two submarines tracked the convoy and surfaced the following morning ahead of the convoy. The commander of *U201*, Adalbert Schnee, held a discussion with Lemp as to the best method of attack. The two agreed that a surface attack at night would be dangerous and decided to attack submerged during the day. Lemp would

LEFT: An Erigma machine. This unremarkable-looking machine was one of the keys to winning the anti-submarine war. When in possession of some of the German code books, the Admiralty was able to use decryptions of messages sent to U-boats to route convoys out of harm's way.

attack first, followed half an hour later by Schnee. At first, the plan worked: Lemp attacked the convoy at about midday, sinking two freighters on the right flank. Unfortunately for him, the corvette HMS *Aubrietia* spotted *U110*'s periscope and attacked with 16 depth-charges. These fell close to the submarine and caused havoc. The submarine's instruments were destroyed; the rudder, diving planes and electric motors ceased to work and chlorine gas began to pour from the forward battery. The submarine began taking on water and started to sink stern first. Lemp realized that he had no hope of saving *U110* and ordered the engineer to prepare to blow the ballast tanks. Before he could give the order, *U110* surged to the surface of its own accord.

Lemp hurried to the conning tower and was confronted with the spectacle of the *Aubrietia*, accompanied by *Bulldog* and another destroyer, HMS *Broadway*, firing at the submarine with every gun they had. *Bulldog* and *Broadway* were coming in at full speed, intent on ramming the submarine. Lemp yelled for the crew to abandon ship immediately, which meant that there was no time to set the U-boat's detonation charges to scuttle her. The quickest alternative means of scuttling the boat was to open the ballast tank vents, but, although the order was given for this to be done, the tank vents remained shut, most likely through a mechanical failure.

The order to abandon immediately meant that the radio operator on the *U110* – who had every reason to assume that the boat would sink – did not destroy the Enigma machine or his code books. The crew began to jump from the submarine amid a hail of gunfire from the escorts.

Armament:	Five 533mm (21in) torpedo tubes, one 86mm (3.4in) gun, one 20mm (0.8in) cannon, up to 39 mines
Powerplant:	Two diesel engines and two electric motors, driving two shafts
Surface range:	12,038km (6500nm) at 12 knots
Performance:	17.2 knots surfaced, 8 knots submerged

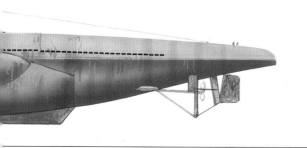

USS *SIMS*

Country:	USA
Launch date:	1939
Crew:	192
Displacement:	1765 tonnes (1737 tons)
Dimensions:	106.15m (348ft) x 10.95m (36ft) x 3.9m (13ft)
Armament:	Five 127mm (5in) Dual Purpose guns, eight 533mm torpedo tubes, two stern depth charge racks
Powerplant:	Geared steam turbines
Surface range:	12,000km (6,479nm) at 12 knots
Performance:	35 knots

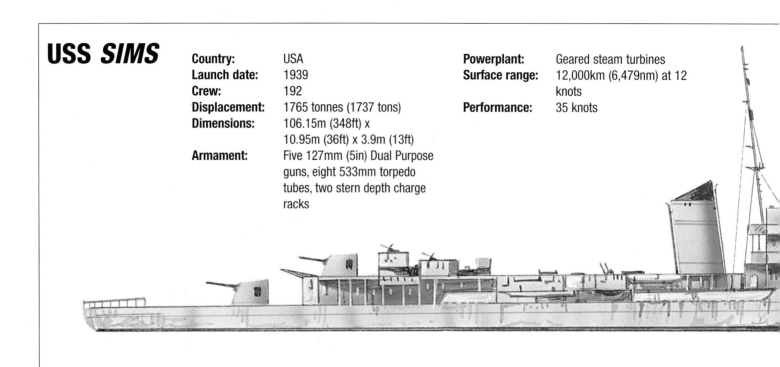

ABOVE: The *Sims* was one of the US Navy's long-range destroyers, and was one of the ships employed as the United States became more closely involved in the Battle of the Atlantic during 1941. The *Sims* herself was sunk at the Battle of the Coral sea in 1942, having been assigned to duty in the Pacific after the United States entered the war.

The commander of the escorts, A. J. Baker-Cresswell, aboard *Bulldog*, noticed that the *U110* was down by the stern, but not sinking. He decided that there might be a chance of capturing the submarine. Baker-Cresswell ordered full-speed astern so as to avoid hitting the submarine and called for a boarding party to prepare. *Bulldog* slowed just in time, coming to a stop not far from the stricken *U110*. *Broadway* also managed to stop after it was realized that the ramming had been cancelled; however, to encourage the Germans to evacuate the boat quickly – and to discourage any efforts to scuttle her that might be taking place – the *Broadway* continued right up to the submarine's bow. Two depth-charges were dropped on a shallow setting just to add further spice to the encouragement, and this appears to have worked. *Broadway*'s approach was not without hazard, and the destroyer fouled one of the diving planes, sustaining damage in the process.

At this point, *U110* was plainly *not* sinking, as Lemp had assumed. He is reputed to have decided to swim back to the submarine in an attempt to scuttle it. What happened next is unclear. According to some sources, the boarding party spotted Lemp and shot him, to prevent him achieving his aim. Others claim that Lemp realized that he had failed and allowed himself to slip beneath the waves. Whatever happened, Lemp was not among the survivors, who were left in the water as the victims of the submarine attacks were rescued first.

Sub-Lieutenant David Balme, who commanded the British boarding party,

jumped aboard *U110*'s foredeck and made his way to the conning tower. To his surprise, he discovered that the hatches were shut – hardly to be expected on a submarine that was in the process of sinking. Balme decided that discretion was the better part of valour and drew his pistol in case there were any of the crew waiting for him when he entered the U-boat. Cautiously, he lowered himself into *U110* and discovered that it was indeed empty. Apart from that, the submarine seemed undamaged – the lights were on, and there was no sign of flooding or of noxious gases.

Balme signalled *Bulldog* that he thought that *U110* was seaworthy and that it could be towed. Baker-Cresswell ordered *Broadway* to send an engineer and manoeuvred *Bulldog* close alongside the abandoned submarine so as to take on board a cable that the boarding party had found in a locker. Below decks, Balme and the rest of the boarding party conducted a search of the U-boat's contents. Although Balme thought that the submarine would stay afloat, he could not be sure. He ordered that all books be collected, apart from those that were obviously read as light relief by the crew. In the radio office, the search party discovered all the code books, signal logs and the coding machine, plugged in just as it would have been if someone were about to sit down and use it. Alan Long, the signaller among the group, was puzzled, as he mistook the machine for a typewriter. When he pressed a few keys and discovered that the machine most definitely was *not* a typewriter, he added it to the boarding party's collection.

While this was going on, *U201* was being depth charged and had some difficulty in escaping. The presence of *U201* caused momentary concern to the boarding party on *U100* when *Bulldog* reported an asdic contact; Baker-Cresswell ordered that the tow cable be released and attacked the contact for a good 90 minutes (accompanied by *Aubrietia* and *Broadway*), before returning to the U-boat. *U110* was taken under tow, with the boarding party now departed, and *Bulldog* headed for Iceland. All seemed to be going well until 11:00 hours the following morning, when *U110* suddenly stood on its stern and went down vertically. Baker-Cresswell was most disappointed at the loss of the prize, but the items removed by the boarding party were of far more significance than the submarine itself.

When *Bulldog* reached Iceland, Baker-Cresswell was anxious to ensure that the captured members of *U110*'s crew were unaware that their boat had been boarded. He transferred all the prisoners from *Amazon* and headed for Scapa Flow. During the journey, he interviewed the surviving officers and discovered that they appeared to believe that the submarine had sunk – they seemed blissfully unaware that the boarding party had managed to enter *U110*. The same was true for the ratings on the submarine. It was clear that some of the Germans knew that a boarding party had been sent across, so a story was put about that, to the regret of the escorts, the *U110* had sunk before the boarding party had managed to effect an entry. The crews of *Bulldog*, *Aubrietia* and *Broadway* were sworn to secrecy, as were the merchant seamen who had been rescued by *Aubrietia*. Not one said anything until after the events were recounted in an officially sanctioned book in 1959.

When *Bulldog* returned home, the search party's booty was piled into two packing crates and sent for examination. It was at this point that the value of the prize was understood. As well as a fully functioning Enigma machine, the keys for the German Home Waters code for April and June (although not those for May) and those for the double-encrypted 'Officers Only' code were present. There were also various charts, signal records, manuals and a whole array of other items including the citation for the Iron Cross, Second Class, that had been awarded to *U110*'s engineer. The reaction from the Admiralty was one of joy. Baker-Cresswell was awarded a Distinguished Service Order and Balme the Distinguished Service Cross, while there were awards for six others (including the captains of *Broadway* and *Aubrietia*), and Mentions in Despatches for 14 more. Given their achievement, reward was merited.

BELOW: An Atlantic convoy, including one of the famous 'Liberty Ships': the BC 2 type cargo ship in the foreground. The speed at which US dockyards could build such vessels made it increasingly difficult for the U-boats to achieve their aim of sinking more merchant shipping than Allied yards could produce.

HMS *Bulldog*

Country:	Britain
Launch date:	December 1930
Crew:	138
Displacement:	1360 tonnes (1338 tons)
Dimensions:	98m (323ft) x 9.8m (32.25ft) x 3.6m (12ft)
Armament:	Three 120mm (4.7in) guns, two 2-pounder anti aircraft guns, five 7.7mm (0.303in) machine guns, eight 533mm (21in) torpedo tubes. Also depth charges
Powerplant:	Two geared steam turbines driving two shafts
Performance:	35 knots

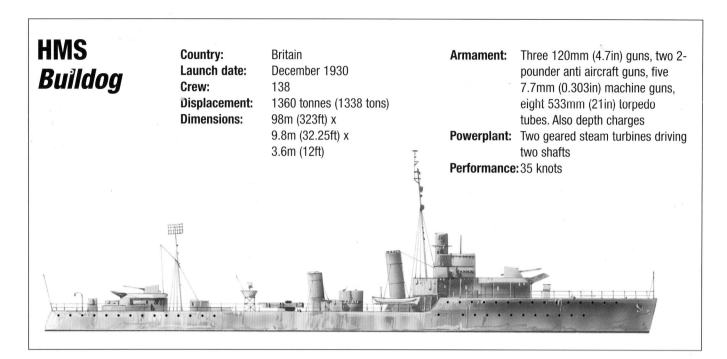

ABOVE: HMS *Bulldog* was built as a fleet destroyer in the inter-war period, but converted for escort work when the war began. Although she appeared a largely unremarkable vessel, *Bulldog* made one of the most important contributions to the war when she captured *U110* and recovered an Enigma machine and its code books.

RIGHT: A U-boat approaches a merchantman. The way in which the crew are dressed would suggest that this encounter took place in warmer latitudes. Independent merchant ships were especially vulnerable to submarine attack.

HIDE AND SEEK

The Iron Cross citation also played a part. It was given to the engineer, who was puzzled. He knew that it had been left on board the supposedly sunken submarine. Did this, he wondered, mean that the British had boarded *U110*? While showing the engineer the citation might appear to have been a potentially colossal blunder, it is more likely that it was a cunning ruse. British (and, before that, English) intelligence services had been releasing documents to

people that, at first sight, should not have been receiving them for centuries before *U110* had sunk. The most obvious victim of this ruse was Mary Queen of Scots. Documents fed to her convinced her that she might soon become Queen of England, rather than remain in the 'protective custody' of her cousin Elizabeth I. As a result, she incriminated herself in her replies and went to a far less pleasant ceremony at the scaffold, not to the coronation she may have been half-

ABOVE: Submarines outside their pens at Trondheim, Norway. The robust construction of the protective pens for the U-boats meant that they were safe from British bombing until almost the end of the war, and ensured that servicing crews were subjected to minimum disruption as they prepared the U-boats for another patrol.

expecting. Given this tradition, the release of the citation appears to have been less of a mistake.

Loewe, the *U110*'s first watch officer, was as suspicious as the engineer and attempted to send a coded message to Dönitz, informing him that the British might have captured *U110*. The message was, naturally, read before despatch. The code used had been broken in World War I, and the British had been able to read all the messages sent in this for years. They were undoubtedly expecting that some attempt to inform Dönitz would be made and were not disappointed when they read Loewe's letter. The letter, of course, did not reach Dönitz. Loewe was later introduced to another *U110* survivor, who told him that the submarine did sink. This prompted another coded letter that told Dönitz that *U110* had gone down – as Loewe noted that a boarding party may have got aboard, the letter did not reach Dönitz's in-tray. Finally, in 1944, another survivor 'happened' to meet another *U110* crewman, who told him that, although a party had reached the submarine, it had only rigged a tow line and had not gone inside. The submarine had

gone down under tow, and there was absolutely no possibility that the submarine had been entered. Loewe – thinking that Dönitz would be reading the third letter in a series – reported that *U110* had sunk, uninvestigated by the enemy. This letter did get through.

This was not enough for British intelligence, which ensured that Loewe was among an exchange of prisoners. The dutiful officer went to see Dönitz and told him directly that the submarine had not been boarded. Dönitz remained blissfully unaware that Enigma had been compromised until well after the end of the war. The fact that it *had* was to pay enormous dividends for the British once Bletchley Park was able to decode all the messages sent and received by U-boat HQ. This marked a serious setback for the German war effort, not just the submarine campaign. Within two months, the situation had become far worse.

BRITISH TECHNICAL IMPROVEMENTS

It was not just the fact that the British had managed to crack Enigma that was not fully appreciated by Dönitz or any of his staff. The lack of success against convoys in the summer

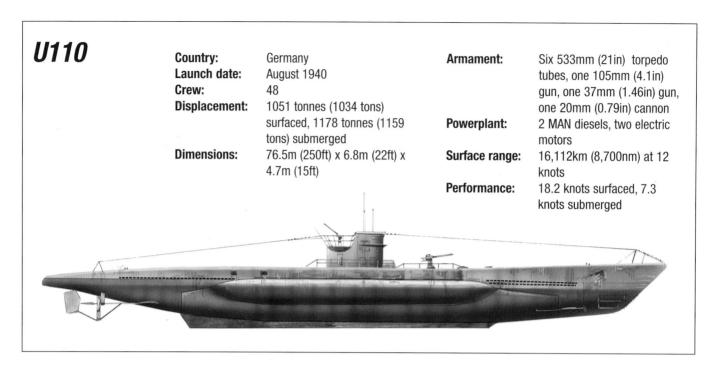

U110

Country:	Germany
Launch date:	August 1940
Crew:	48
Displacement:	1051 tonnes (1034 tons) surfaced, 1178 tonnes (1159 tons) submerged
Dimensions:	76.5m (250ft) x 6.8m (22ft) x 4.7m (15ft)
Armament:	Six 533mm (21in) torpedo tubes, one 105mm (4.1in) gun, one 37mm (1.46in) gun, one 20mm (0.79in) cannon
Powerplant:	2 MAN diesels, two electric motors
Surface range:	16,112km (8,700nm) at 12 knots
Performance:	18.2 knots surfaced, 7.3 knots submerged

ABOVE: *U110* was one of the most important U-boats of the war. The failure of her crew to scuttle her meant that the Royal Navy was able to recover an Enigma machine and associated code books. *U110* sank while under tow on 11 May 1941.

was not only caused by the British having the ability to read the enemy's messages, but also stemmed from improvements in the technology used against enemy submarines.

One of the first methods to receive urgent consideration by the Admiralty was direction finding (D/F) equipment. This had been used effectively in World War I, but the loss of D/F stations in France was a blow. By 1941, a chain of land-based D/F stations had been established, ranging from Land's End, England, through Canada and to the West Indies. This meant that triangulation of U-boat radio transmissions could be conducted with some degree of accuracy. Although Dönitz appreciated that such equipment existed, he seems not to have fully appreciated its significance. U-boat HQ seemed to believe that the evidence from early in the war demonstrated that D/F was only effective over short ranges. It was thought that, beyond about 480km (300 miles), D/F was prone to errors of up to 130km (80 miles), and, at 965km (600 miles), errors of 515km (320 miles) in the triangulated position were thought probable. This completely underestimated the advances in technology that had been incorporated into the equipment. As a result, the U-boats' reliance upon radio communications for sighting reports meant that the British were able to obtain a reasonable idea of where U-boats were to be found. Consequently, the Tracking Room could devise some re-routing even without the assistance of decoded signals.

Radar was also progressing nicely. ASV III, using the 10cm (3.94in) waveband, offered many advantages, and this was to be incorporated in airborne sets in the near

future. Similar radar had been fitted to ships, and the latest model, Type 271M, was fitted to 25 ships in July. Although there were the usual teething troubles to be expected with such new technology, the radars marked a major advance in the campaign against the U-boats, as they would deny them the opportunity of operating on the surface at night. HMS *Vanoc* had already used its Type 271 to good effect against *U100*, in March, and it was clear that this advance offered great promise.

In addition to this, the development of seaborne high-frequency direction finding (HF/DF, or 'Huff-Duff') offered several benefits. This equipment could trace even the shortest signals sent from U-boats, and the first truly effective model, code-named FH 2, went to sea in July 1941. This meant that the U-boats would have to be extremely cautious in emitting signals, as it would give escorts the opportunity to locate and attack the submarine, without any need to receive information – which would be outdated by the time it arrived – from the land-based stations.

The major problem with these advances lay in the fact that the equipment needed tuning and modification to be utterly reliable; it also required the operators to gain experience to have full effect. This took time, and, unlike peacetime where the modifications could be conducted in laboratory conditions, tested in carefully arranged circumstances, modified and tested again until perfect, the equipment received its test in combat conditions. The operators could – and did – receive basic training, but this was hardly of the sort that would have been organized outside a war.

AMERICAN 'INTERVENTION'

President Franklin Delano Roosevelt's decision to send old destroyers to Britain had infuriated Hitler, who viewed this as being tantamount to a hostile act. It had already been clear that the US Government's sympathies lay more towards the United Kingdom than Germany. At the outbreak of war, Roosevelt had authorized the formation of a 'Neutrality Patrol' to report upon and track any belligerent forces approaching the United States or West Indies. At an Inter-American conference on 23 September 1939, the patrol was discussed, culminating in the Declaration of Panama on 2 October. This established a 'Security Zone' which would protect US neutrality. Significantly, this was used as a reason for developing the anti-submarine forces of the US Navy.

While all of this appears to be a sign of absolute impartiality, the creation of the neutrality zone ensured that merchant vessels heading to and from Britain would be safe from attack in the area covered by the United States. There was no reason for the British to risk provoking the Americans by breaching the security zone and every reason for the Germans to avoid doing so. Overall, this meant that the British did not need to worry about covering shipping that had entered the Security Zone.

In the aftermath of lend-lease, Hitler's suspicions that Roosevelt was in favour of Britain were increased. In April 1941, approval was granted for British warships to be refitted in US yards. The implications of this were enormous – although the United States was neutral, it was permitting one of the belligerents to use dockyard facilities, thus reducing the pressures on those in the United Kingdom. On 10 April, the USS *Niblick* was rescuing survivors from a torpedoed Dutch ship when a contact appeared on her sonar (the American name for asdic, later universally adopted). The *Niblick* began a depth-charge attack and reported that the submarine withdrew from the area as a result. As there is no evidence that any German submarine reported being depth-charged on that day, it is probable that the contact was spurious. What was of importance was the fact that the US Navy had willingly attempted to attack a U-boat. On the following day, Roosevelt announced that the US Security Zone would move east, from about 60° west to 26° west.

This announcement was warmly welcomed in Britain and with good cause. As Dönitz bitterly noted, it meant that the Security Zone stretched 4260km (2300 nautical miles) from the US coast and included the Azores. This was an extremely large security zone, as it ended only 1190km (740 miles) off the Iberian Peninsula. This extension made it much more difficult for the U-boat arm, as it would be in danger of being observed by the Americans, who made it clear that they would report the location of all German ships and U-boats, thus giving the British critical information.

The action of U-boat commanders also complicated the situation with the Americans. *U69* had been given approval to mine the African ports of Takoradi and Lagos. As the submarine headed towards Africa, on the evening of 21 May, a ship was spotted by the watch. Although she was lit, there were suspicions on the U-boat that the vessel was an anti-submarine vessel, pretending to be a neutral merchantman. *U69* approached and asked for identification. The ship signalled back *'Robin Moor'*, which merely heightened confusion – there was no ship of that name listed in *Lloyd's Register*. When daylight arrived, the name *Exmoor* could be seen on the ship's stern. The

BELOW: *U570*, the first U-boat capture of the war, when she surrender to a Hudson of 269 Squadron, RAF on 28 August 1941.

U570

Country:	Germany	**Armament:**	Five 533mm (21in) torpedo tubes, one 86mm (3.4in) gun, one 20mm (0.8in) cannon, up to 39 mines
Launch date:	March 1941		
Crew:	44		
Displacement:	761 tonnes (749 tons) surfaced, 865 tonnes (851 tons) submerged	**Powerplant:**	Two diesel motors, two electric motors
Dimensions:	67.1m (220ft) x 6.2m (20ft) x 4.8m (15ft)	**Surface range:**	12,038km (6500nm) at 12 knots
		Performance:	17.2 knots surfaced, 7.6 knots submerged

ABOVE: *U570* was another of the multitude of *Type VII* submarines, and was remarkable for surrendering to an attacking aircraft.

captain of the mysterious ship went across to *U69* by whaler, to explain (supported by some documentation) that the ship had only recently been purchased by a US concern and the name had changed. This was not enough. *U69*'s skipper, Jost Metzler, claimed that he could see guns and radio equipment on the ship's manifest. This meant that the *Robin Moor* was carrying contraband and was a legitimate target. Although there were clear orders, originating from Hitler himself, that US ships were not to be attacked, Metzler sank the *Robin Moor*, after allowing the crew to take to the lifeboats. The unfortunate crew, although given extra provisions by Metzler, drifted for two weeks in open boats before they reached land.

The sinking was unfortunately timed. The British were making great play of the news that an Egyptian liner had been sunk by the German surface raider *Atlantis* while on her way to Egypt from New York. The liner, *Zamzam*, was presumed lost with all on board, including 196 Americans. The Americans were all volunteer ambulance drivers, and newspapers led with news that the Germans had brutally sunk a 'mercy ship'. In fact, the propaganda attempt was extremely crude. The passengers and crew of the *Zamzam*, along with all their baggage, were actually transferred to the freighter *Dresden* and taken to France. This gave Berlin the opportunity to show that the British were playing games with information, but, just as they were about to demonstrate that they were showing due consideration to innocent passengers, the news of the *Robin Moor*'s sinking broke. This meant that the correct version of the *Zamzam* incident did not reach the public eye, and the Americans were left with the impression that the

Germans had brutally sunk a ship, killing 196 Americans (there were only 138 US citizens aboard). To make matters worse, they had then sunk the *Robin Moor*.

Dönitz was furious, and his signals to Metzler made the unfortunate U-boat skipper fear a court-martial upon his return. By the time he returned in July, he had been forgiven. As well as a number of conventional sinkings, he had accounted for the armed freighter *Robert L. Holt* with his deck gun, in an incredibly risky artillery duel. When Metzler reached port, Dönitz rewarded him with the Knight's Cross, rather than a trial.

Not unconnected with the sinking of the *Zamzam* and the *Robin Moor* was the announcement by Roosevelt of an Unlimited National Emergency. He told Americans that it would be suicidal for the

United States to wait for the war to come to them before taking action. The end result was to provide the British with what was effectively an undeclared ally, who provided some assistance in maintaining the safety of convoys.

THE ATTACK ON U-BOATS

The intelligence windfall from *U110* enabled Bletchley Park to read naval Enigma for June promptly and in its entirety. An amazingly comprehensive picture of the U-boat arm was built up, including the number of boats at sea. The signals to and from these boats were read easily, giving the Admiralty the ability to go out and hunt down the submarine force. This was a tempting idea and certainly in keeping with the offensive spirit, but was rejected. It seemed obvious that a simultaneous assault on U-boats spread across the ocean, while ending the threat from submarines for a considerable period, would give the Germans compelling evidence that Enigma had been broken. They would surely change their codes, or possibly even the code machine employed, which would force Bletchley Park to begin again the laborious business of working out how to break the codes, with a consequent loss of insight into German plans while this was done. Instead, the supply ships that were to be used to refuel and rearm the U-boats – thereby extending their endurance – were to be attacked. This would not arouse such suspicion, as these ships were always under threat from aggressive patrolling. When assessing the loss of these ships, the Germans were more than likely to believe that some factor other than the breaking of Enigma was responsible for the British success.

On 3 June, the supply vessel *Belchen* was attacked and scuttled; in the next two days, four others were attacked. Three were scuttled and one, the *Gedania*, captured. The *Gedania* provided a wealth of intelligence information among papers found on board. The loss of the four ships was a major blow to Dönitz, as it meant that operations in West African waters were seriously hampered. This was not all: by the end of the month, the Royal Navy had five more successes, including the capture of a weather-reporting trawler, which provided yet more Enigma-related information that would allow Bletchley Park to read the signals traffic for July. These losses had aroused some suspicions, and a more complex code for reporting the positions of the U-boats was introduced. Bletchley Park took some time to break the code, reducing the effectiveness of the information obtained during the latter half of the month; the U-boat skippers were also baffled for a while, as to begin with they found the new system deeply confusing.

The British ended June, then, with a major intelligence advantage that would assist in the short-term prosecution of the campaign against the U-boats, if not for longer. They also ended the month having gained a new ally: the Soviet Union.

BARBAROSSA

Hitler's fixation with destroying communism meant that it was as inevitable as any event can be that he would attack the Soviet Union at some point. Operation Barbarossa began on 22 June 1941, and, for the first few weeks, it appeared that the Germans might come close to victory. Ultimately, of course, this was not the case,

BELOW: After her capture and repair, *U570* was pressed into British service as HMS *Graph*. She was used on one operational patrol, and then relegated to training duties. She was wrecked in 1944, but salvaged for scrapping in 1961.

RIGHT: Sir Philip Joubert de la Ferté, AOC-in-C of RAF Coastal Command from 1941 to 1943. Joubert flew the first ever recon- naissance mission by the Royal Flying Corps in 1914, and forged Coastal Command into a fully effective force.

and the decision to invade Russia cost Germany an almost incalculable amount. In the short term, it had major effects on the way in which the U-boat campaign was conducted.

The first aspect of this came with Hitler's instruction that no incidents with US vessels were to take place, in case this provoked the United States into war. On 20 June, this policy was severely tested, when Rolf Mützelburg, the commander of *U203*, sighted a battleship escorted by a destroyer. The battleship was the USS *Texas*, part of a task force that the United States had formed to assist the British in anticipation of a sortie against merchant traffic by the *Lützow*. *Texas* had unwittingly entered a zone where Hitler had granted permission for neutral vessels to be attacked, and Mützelburg began a pursuit of the battleship. After 16 hours, it was clear that he would not catch it, so he abandoned the pursuit.

The news of the *Texas* sortie provoked much comment in Berlin. Dönitz and Raeder felt that this represented nothing less than a challenge to Germany by the United States. The correct response would be to attack any US ships that entered more than 32km (20 miles) into the zone of operations (*U203* had abandoned the chase when *Texas* was nearly 240km (150 miles) inside the zone). Hitler initially agreed, but changed his mind, ordering that no US ships would be permitted without his authorization; also, U-boats were to attack only recognizable British battleships, carriers and cruisers. This may have been a sensible precaution to avoid offending the United States, but Dönitz complained that it

meant that the U-boats were prevented from attacking the convoy escorts that presented the greatest threat to them. This said, the U-boats did not usually seek to attack the escorts, and Dönitz's complaint related more to the principle of not being allowed to attack them.

This was not the only effect of Barbarossa, as Hitler demanded the presence of a number of U-boats in the Baltic, where they were of little use. The U-boats did, though, have some success against the Arctic convoys that were run by the British – although there have to be doubts as to whether this was an effective use of the boats, as they were diverted from their main operational area as a result. It also suggested to the British that they need not worry about any invasion attempt against them in 1941 (although they suspected that the Soviet Union might be defeated by the end of the year), which meant that the ships still assigned to anti-invasion duty could be released to join the Battle of the Atlantic.

THE OCCUPATION OF ICELAND

On 6 June, President Roosevelt ordered that US forces be sent to occupy Iceland. They did so under Operation Indigo, arriving at Reykjavik on 7 July; within hours, bases were being constructed on the island. On 6 August, the US Navy's Patrol Wing 7, equipped with Catalinas and Martin Mariner flying boats, arrived, joining Coastal Command's three squadrons made up of Hudsons, Catalinas and the now almost forgotten Northrop seaplanes of the Norwegian-manned 330 Squadron. Two weeks after the first landing, six battleships and nine destroyers arrived; in August, another 21 surface units were sent to Iceland. By the end of the month, Iceland had been turned into a virtually impregnable base.

Dönitz was incensed, proposing that the occupation be countered by a U-boat offensive. Hitler, determined to keep the United States out of the war, refused. This meant that the entire U-boat campaign in the vicinity of Iceland was adversely affected, given the massive amount of coverage from the forces now based there. Even though the United States was not a combatant, it was already making a major contribution to the anti-submarine campaign through the presence of its forces. Thanks to Hitler's reaction, nothing was done.

THE LOSS OF *U570*

The U-boats found little success during July, as the British ability to read Enigma enabled the re-routing of convoys to avoid the known dispositions of U-boats. This meant that the summer's results were far below Dönitz's expectations. There seemed to be some hope of intercepting a convoy passing to the south of Iceland, when the B-Dienst service detected signals suggesting that a large body of ships was in the area. In fact, it was three convoys, being given considerable air escort. Despite Hitler's orders limiting U-boat operations, and notwithstanding the threat posed by the substantial forces based on Iceland, Dönitz decided to launch an attack on the 'convoy'.

The results were not good. *U452* was sunk by a combination of a Catalina from 209 Squadron and the trawler *Vascama*, and then disaster befell *U570*. *U570* sailed from Trondheim at 08:00 hours on 24 August 1941, in a rather dilapidated state and with a very inexperienced crew. When she reached the open sea, a large number of the men became seasick, grossly lowering the efficiency of the crew. *U570* was directed to search for the 'convoy' and duly did so. The U-boat's hydrophones were not working, so the skipper, Hans Rahmlow, had to conduct visual searches. At about 10:50 hours on 27 August, he conducted a periscope search for enemy surface forces, found nothing and ordered that the submarine surface. Fatally, Rahmlow had forgotten to make a check for aircraft, and, as soon as he opened the hatch, he heard the sound of engines. He ordered a crash dive, and *U570* began to go under.

The aircraft was a Hudson from 269 Squadron, RAF. The pilot, James Thompson, had been directed towards the U-boat by signals on the aircraft's ASV set, and he was heading towards the submarine even as Rahmlow ordered the emergency dive. Thompson managed to release his depth-charges right on top of *U570*, even before she had the chance to submerge. The depth-charges were set for 15.24m (50ft) and straddled *U570*. The explosions from the depth-charges knocked out the lights and instruments, sending panic among the inexperienced and demoralized crew. Someone reported a leak of chlorine in the aft section of the submarine, and men rushed forwards. Rahmlow attempted to dive again, but discovered that the bow planes would not work. The explosion had damaged the electrical system, which required resetting – as there was no one aft, this could not be done. Rahmlow made the mistake of assuming that he had no option but to abandon ship, and he gave the order. The Enigma machine and secret papers were dumped over the side, but the crew was reluctant to jump into cold, unforgiving seas with no prospect of rescue.

In the Hudson, Thompson saw the Germans tumbling out onto the deck and assumed that they were hurrying to man the deck gun and machine guns against him. He duly made several strafing runs, just as he was about to make his fourth pass, he realized that one of the crew was waving a white shirt at the aeroplane, while others were holding white painted boards. It took a moment for him to comprehend that the U-boat was *surrendering* to him. What was he to do? He circled the submarine and sent a message asking for help. Another Hudson shortly

BELOW: Despite its obsolescence, the Supermarine Stranraer gave sterling service until 1941, when the last one was replaced by the far more effective Catalina.

STRANRAER				
Country:	Britain	**Performance:**	Maximum speed 265km/h (165mph), range 1609km (1000 miles), endurance 9.6 hours. Service ceiling 5640m (18,500ft)	
First flight:	1934			
Crew:	6			
Powerplant:	Two Bristol Pegasus X piston engines	**Armament:**	One 7.7mm (0.303in) Lewis gun in the bow, amidships and tail positions. 1000 pounds of bombs or depth charges	

appeared on the scene and was joined by the Catalina which had sunk *U452*. They orbited the submarine, awaiting assistance. The Admiralty were fully aware of the possible importance of the capture of a submarine, and Admiral Noble sent two destroyers and four trawlers to conclude the capture.

The first vessel to arrive was the trawler *Northern Chief*, which was instructed to prevent the U-boat from scuttling. It arrived at 22:00 hours, guided in by flares being dropped by the still circling Catalina and newly arrived Hudsons. Thompson had returned to base when his fuel ran out; his day was slightly spoiled when the aircraft was caught by an unexpected and ferocious gust of wind as he came in to land and crashed. The most serious injury to the crew was wounded pride, although no one could really blame Thompson for the mishap.

Northern Chief took control, and the crew of *U570* were told that they would not be rescued if they made any attempt to scuttle their craft. The by-now thoroughly miserable Germans had little intention of doing this, such was their state, but the British had no way of knowing this. During the night, the rest of the task force despatched by Noble arrived on the scene, allowing the crew of the Catalina to return home after what must have been an incredibly tedious 13 hours circling *U570*.

Commander S.R.J. Woods, captain of one of the destroyers (HMS *Burwell*), assumed command of the situation and took the view that, if he allowed the Germans to leave *U570*, they would almost certainly scuttle it. As a result, he kept the crew on board, much to the dismay of Rahmlow and his men.

Woods attempted to get a line across to the submarine, but the heavy seas made it difficult, particularly given the lack of cooperation from the Germans. At this point, the proceedings almost became farcical as one of 330 Squadron's Northrop patrol planes appeared on the scene and attacked *U570*, despite the presence of six friendly warships. To make matters worse, it then turned on the *Northern Chief*, which returned fire. Woods quickly contacted the plane by radio and asked them to desist. The enthusiastic Norwegians asked if they might try to bomb *U570* again, but were politely – and firmly – turned down.

The attack by the Norwegians had a positive effect, as it greatly disturbed the Germans, who became much more cooperative, agreeing to assist in attaching a tow line. When the line was sent across, however, it parted. Woods suspected that the line had been sabotaged and ordered a machine-gunner to fire a burst over the heads of *U570's* crew. Regrettably, the heavy seas meant that the gunner was less than accurate, and he hit *U570's* conning tower instead, wounding five of the crew. This at least convinced the Germans that the British were serious, and they cooperated from this point on. The crew blew the ballast and fuel tanks to create maximum buoyancy. Rahmlow asked for the wounded to be taken off, and Woods agreed.

There was some difficulty in getting in close to *U570*, and Woods ordered the trawler *Kingston Agathe* to send a boarding party to oversee the transfer. *Kingston Agathe* proved just a little too enthusiastic, as it took off some of the officers, including Rahmlow, before

BELOW: Designed to the same specification as the Stranraer, the London undertook many routine maritime reconnaissance missions during the first two years of the war. The last was withdrawn from service in Gibraltar in June 1941.

SARO LONDON

Country:	Britain	5.2 hours. Service ceiling 6065m (19,900ft)
First flight:	1934	
Crew:	6	
Powerplant:	Two Bristol Pegasus X piston engines	**Armament:** One 7.7mm (0.303in) Lewis gun in the bow, amidships and tail positions. 2000 pounds of bombs or depth charges
Performance:	Maximum speed 250km/h (155 mph), range 1770km (1100 miles), endurance	

removing the wounded. This ruined Woods's scheme of keeping the crew hostage to ensure that they kept the boat afloat, as the three men removed were those who were responsible for ensuring that it remained seaworthy. The Canadian navy destroyer *Niagara* then sent across a raft, and the Germans were told to evacuate *U570*. The Germans were confused, having been told to stay aboard, but were informed that they should disregard that instruction. They did and went aboard *Niagara*. By that time, the boarding party had secured tow lines from the submarine to the *Kingston Agathe*, which took *U570* under tow. The line parted during the night, and Northern Chief took over the task. After a worrying day, *U570* was grounded in the harbour at Thorlakshafn.

Unlike the capture of *U110* – which was listed as having been sunk even in the British official history of the war at sea published nine years after the end of the conflict – the British saw no reason to keep the surrender secret. They doubted very much that the capture could be kept quiet and were rather pleased to be able to use the news to place the German submarine force in a poor light. The Enigma machine was not captured, of course, and this information was allowed to find its way back to Dönitz. *U570* was studied carefully by the British and the Americans. Churchill toyed with the idea of allowing the Americans to repair the submarine, but this was opposed by the Admiralty. In the end, *U570* became HMS *Graph*, serving under the White Ensign.

COASTAL COMMAND

The capture of a U-boat by an aircraft marked something of a change in the fortunes of Coastal Command. Aircraft had enjoyed little success in the attack against U-boats by June 1941. The major difficulty, as alluded to above, was that Coastal Command was initially not given the same level of attention as Bomber Command, and this meant that there were only about 200 aircraft available to it. Even though the first Liberators had begun to arrive to permit the formation of 120 Squadron, there was still a lack of suitable aircraft. Coastal Command had certainly ensured that the U-boat attacks in the North West Approaches were more difficult, but it is hard not to observe that they could have made an even greater contribution with more suitable aircraft. The transfer of a number of Vickers Wellingtons to the command was welcome, but this type was still range limited, even if it could carry a larger load of depth-charges than the Hudson or Whitley.

Air Chief Marshal Bowhill was replaced as Air Officer Commanding-in-Chief in June by Air Marshal Sir Philip Joubert de la Ferté, who had conducted the first ever reconnaissance mission by what was then the Royal Flying Corps in 1914. Joubert wished to see an increase in offensive patrolling and asked that his command be strengthened. He particularly wished to carry the war to the Bay of Biscay, where aircraft could make a major contribution against the U-boats transiting to and from their operational areas. Joubert was not foolish enough to believe that his request would be acceded to immediately, and he set about seeking other ways of improving Coastal Command's success rate.

He turned to a number of scientists, most notably Professor P.M.S. Blackett, later a Nobel Prize winner. This began the vital use of operational research (OR). Blackett and a team of assistants analysed thousands of pages of data relating to Coastal Command's operations to date and produced a number of recommendations.

First, it was noted that the standard of navigation in Coastal Command was poor. Aircrews seldom knew exactly where they were, which meant that they did not always patrol the areas that they should have done.

ABOVE: Professor P.M.S. Blackett played a key part in developing operational research in Coastal Command. His careful study of combat reports followed by recommendations for improvements led to a considerable increase in the effectiveness of Coastal Command's aircraft against U-boats.

They were also prone to failure to find convoys that they should have been escorting as a result of this. This failing owed far more to the lack of funds for training before the war rather than any inability of the aircrew, who had simply not been trained sufficiently. The lack of training was also noted in the second point, which concluded that ASV operators were being asked to do too much considering how little instruction they had received. Furthermore, the aircraft were flying too high to benefit from the radar's capabilities. This meant that crews were not finding submarines and did not fully trust ASV.

There were also difficulties with attacking U-boats. The submarines usually saw the aircraft first, and the depth-charges in use were inadequate. Also, the charges were set to explode at too great a depth. Blackett's solutions were simple. Radar operators and navigators were to receive proper training, while the undersides of the aircraft should be painted white, so as to make them less visible against the sky. The altitude at which operations were conducted should be reduced, and the depth-charges should be given more powerful explosive (TORPEX), set to explode just beneath the surface of the water. Finally, they should be dropped with greater spacing between the release of the depth-charges, providing a longer 'stick' of weapons.

The suggestion that many small depth-charges were better than a few large ones was not fully accepted by Coastal Command, and parallel development of better small depth-charges and a larger 900kg (2000lb) type was undertaken. Despite this disagreement, Blackett's work – which continued – provided the RAF with its first real insight as to how to attack U-boats effectively. The successful capture

of U570 by a Hudson flying lower and using depth-charges set to explode at 15m (50ft) rather than at 30m (100ft) or more demonstrated just how effective such work could be.

CONVOYS IN THE ARCTIC

The Soviet Union's entry into the war was viewed with a mixture of optimism and pessimism in London. Churchill insisted that supplies should be sent to the hard-pressed Russians, beginning with the despatch of Hawker Hurricane fighters. The Hurricane was becoming outclassed against the latest German aircraft, but was better than many of the aircraft available to the Soviet Air Force at the time. Although the Soviet aircraft industry would produce some superb aircraft of its own, the supply of aircraft from Britain – and through lend-lease, which was extended to the Soviet Union by Roosevelt – was of great importance.

The sailings began when the old aircraft carrier *Argus* and merchant ships were used to carry 48 Hawker Hurricanes to Archangel. The convoy was assembled at Reykjavik on 21 August, with six escorts including the carrier *Victorious*. *Argus* flew off her cargo, which landed in Murmansk, while the merchantmen with the aircraft in packing crates (and the equipment needed for those aircraft that had flown in) arrived safely at Archangel. This was not the first PQ (United Kingdom to Russia) convoy, though. The first official convoy on the Russian route was QP1, which was the designation for the convoy as it returned. The first outward bound convoy, PQ1, set sail on 28 September, beginning an epic series of journeys. The convoys had to cover some 2250–3200km (1400–2000 miles) in ferocious conditions. There was no available

BELOW: One of Britain's most famous aircraft carriers, the *Ark Royal* had a lucky escape from submarine attack in the first few days of the war. After providing valuable service in home waters and the Mediterranean, 'the Ark' was torpedoed by *U81* in November 1941.

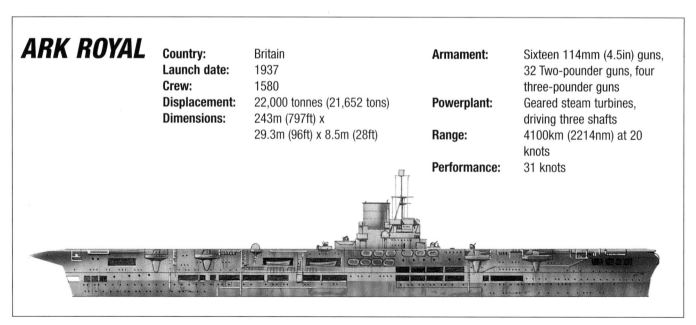

ARK ROYAL			
Country:	Britain	**Armament:**	Sixteen 114mm (4.5in) guns,
Launch date:	1937		32 Two-pounder guns, four
Crew:	1580		three-pounder guns
Displacement:	22,000 tonnes (21,652 tons)	**Powerplant:**	Geared steam turbines,
Dimensions:	243m (797ft) x		driving three shafts
	29.3m (96ft) x 8.5m (28ft)	**Range:**	4100km (2214nm) at 20
			knots
		Performance:	31 knots

LEFT: Sailors take some time to relax, looking out over the convoy that they are escorting. The crews of the escorts endured cold, poor weather conditions and not infrequent danger as they went about their work. Although not 'glamorous', their work was vital to the war effort.

refuelling stop, and the convoys would have to be accompanied by oilers.

It was intended to run the convoys on a 40-day cycle (that is to say, the gap between successive sailings), but, in October, the Admiralty decided to operate a 10-day cycle instead. This posed serious difficulties for the Home Fleet, as it meant that resources were strained to the limit: it took three weeks for the escorts to complete the journey to and from Murmansk, with obvious problems as to how the convoys could be escorted. At first, the scope and extent of the convoys was not fully appreciated by the Germans, and the U-boats were not thrown into battle. As soon as the importance of the cargoes was realized, though, the *Kriegsmarine* threw in heavy forces in an attempt to prevent the convoys from passing through. The rest of 1941 was a quiet year for attacks by U-boats on the convoys, but this would not last for long.

DIVERSION IN THE MEDITERRANEAN

At the end of August, the U-boat arm suffered another blow. Hitler ordered that naval forces should be sent to the Mediterranean. On first examination, Hitler's reasoning appeared sound: there was a serious problem facing the *Afrika* Corps, which was having supply difficulties. German and Italian supply ships were being harried by the Royal Navy and air attack. The problem was that, while the U-boats (and for that matter surface units) might have some impact against the Royal Navy's submarines and surface vessels, there was nothing that could be done against the

anti-shipping aircraft. The main target for the U-boats would be British warships, which were far more dangerous targets than merchant shipping. The lack of operational U-boats meant that diverting any to the Mediterranean would cause a drop in the effort against trade. Dönitz protested to no avail: his forces were to go to the Mediterranean whether he liked it or not.

This marked a major shift in strategy and to no apparent purpose. As Dönitz noted, although victory in the Mediterranean theatre would have been important, it was not in the same league as defeating Britain. Dönitz knew which battle zone was more profitable for the U-boats, but was overruled. This is not to say that the U-boats were not effective. On 13 November, *U81* sank the aircraft carrier *Ark Royal*, which slightly made up for the defective torpedoes that hit the ship in 1939; 10 days later, *U331* accounted for the battleship HMS *Barham*. These successes prompted Hitler to instruct Dönitz that the Mediterranean was now to be considered the main area of operations for submarines, and the entire operational force was to be sent to the Mediterranean forthwith. As John Terraine has remarked, this meant that the greatest blow against the U-boats' attack on British shipping was delivered by their own high command. Success in the Mediterranean against a few surface units, no matter how large they were, was not going to win the war. Within weeks, the scope of the war was vastly extended when the United States was brought into a conflict that it had desperately hoped to avoid.

CHAPTER FIVE

U-BOATS AGAINST AMERICA: JANUARY – JULY 1942

America's entry into the war provided the U-boats with an unexpected opportunity. After nearly a year of disappointment, the U-boat arm took another heavy toll of Allied shipping.

Officially, US military involvement in World War II began only after 7 December 1941, with the infamous attack on Pearl Harbor by the Japanese. However, the United States had committed forces to the Battle of the Atlantic well before that date. Had Karl Dönitz been able to gain acceptance for his plan to attack US forces based in Iceland, the history of US involvement in the war might have been very different.

The attack on Pearl Harbor did not guarantee that the United States would become involved in the war in Europe. The outrage at the Japanese attack meant that there was strong enough public support to take on and defeat Japan. Becoming embroiled in the war against Germany would inevitably mean that resources would be diverted from the Pacific, and it is by no means certain that President Roosevelt would have declared war on Germany in December 1941, even though it is clear that he had no sympathy for Hitler whatsoever. If Roosevelt felt any doubts about war with Germany, though, these were neatly

LEFT: America's war really began before the attack on Pearl Harbor. Here, the destroyer USS _Kearny_ makes her way to Rekjavik after being torpedoed on 17 October 1941.

USS *REUBEN JAMES*

Country:	United States	**Powerplant:**	Geared turbines, driving two shafts
Launch date:	October 1919		
Crew:	150	**Range:**	4023km (2500nm) at 20 knots
Displacement:	1100 tonnes (1082 tons) standard		
Armament:	Four 101mm (4in) and one 3in guns, 12 torpedo tubes	**Performance:**	35 knots

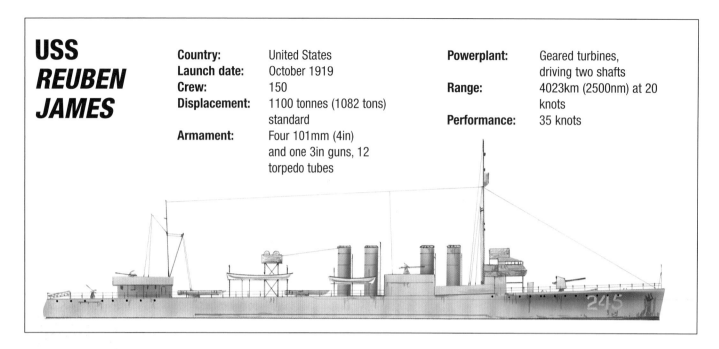

ABOVE: *Reuben James* was one of a large group of destroyers laid down for the US Navy at the end of World War I. Fifty of this group were later transferred to the Royal Navy for use as escort vessels needed to fight the U-boat menace.

RIGHT: An American destroyer encounters heavy weather in the Atlantic, 16 November 1941.

assuaged by Hitler, who declared war on the United States on 11 December 1941. Whether this was in solidarity with Japan or merely a formalization of the undeclared naval conflict between the two countries is hard to tell. The first shots had already been fired. On 10 October, *U552*, commanded by Erich Topp, had found convoy HX156, escorted by five US destroyers. Topp lined up on the USS *Reuben James* and fired two torpedoes. These struck the unsuspecting escort on the port side, and the subsequent explosions ripped the ship apart. Only 45 of the crew of 160 were saved.

The *Reuben James*, therefore, had the unfortunate distinction of being the first US warship to be sunk by enemy forces in World War II. The loss caused considerable dismay within US political and military circles, prompting the Chief of Naval Operations (CNO), Admiral Harold R. Stark, to comment that, although Americans might not be aware of it, 'we are at war'. Despite this dramatic private declaration, little was done to ensure that US shipping was better protected once the formal declaration of hostilities began.

Dönitz recognized that the large amount of shipping made available by the United States' involvement presented a serious challenge. As well as increasing the capacity available to bring supplies across the Atlantic to sustain Britain, the US shipyards would be able to make a significant contribution. Unlike those in Britain, which had come under sustained

LEFT: A T*ype VIIC* in port. The *Type VII* and *Type IX* were numerically the most important U-boat classes. Despite this, it took far longer than Dönitz had hoped for his force to reach a size where it could pose a major threat to Allied shipping.

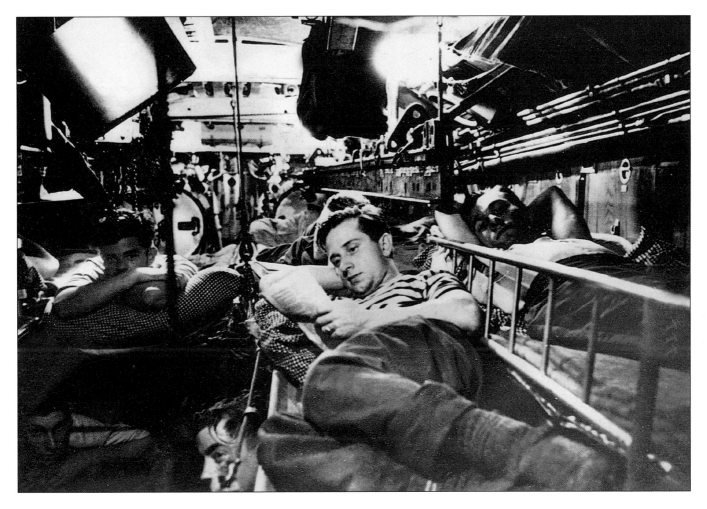

ABOVE: A crew try to relax in the cramped conditions of a U-boat. Men could often be found sleeping where they worked, sometimes using the torpedoes as a make-shift pillow.

attack from the *Luftwaffe,* there was little that could be done to attack the US yards. No ultra long-range aircraft existed to attack the United States from Germany; nor were the Japanese in any position to make a contribution by striking against the dockyards. This meant that the tonnage war would have to be expanded, in the hope of sinking more tonnage than even the US yards could contribute.

Dönitz calculated that around 812,400 tonnes (800,000 tons) of shipping per month would have to be destroyed if the campaign were to succeed. An assessment of the sinkings in the last six months of 1941 did not given much cause for optimism, as, on average, the U-boats had sunk only 15 per cent of that figure per month. Fortunately for Dönitz, the position was more hopeful than it appeared, as U-boats were at last beginning to commission in greater numbers. Ninety-one submarines were in service in January 1942, and this was projected to increase to 138 by July. It is important to stress that this did not mean that this number of submarines was available for operations. Many of them would be refitting after operations, fitting

U123

Country:	Germany
Launch date:	March 1940
Crew:	48
Displacement:	1051 tonnes (1034 tons) surfaced, 1178 tonnes (1159 tons) submerged
Dimensions:	76.5m (250ft) x 6.8m (22ft) x 4.7m (15ft)
Armament:	Six 533mm (21in) torpedo tubes, one 105mm (4.1in) gun, one 37mm (1.45in) gun, one 20mm cannon
Powerplant:	2 MAN diesels, two electric motors
Surface range:	14,000km (8700nm) at 12 knots
Performance:	18.2 knots surfaced, 7.3 knots submerged

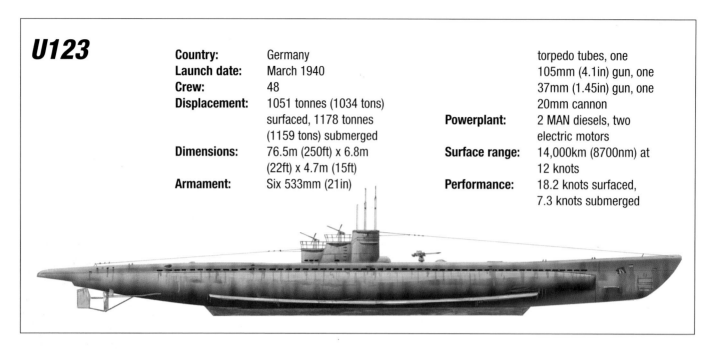

ABOVE: *U123* enjoyed an active career. As well as acquiring an impressive list of victims, she was engaged in a gunnery duel with a US Navy ship in 1942 and managed to escape, and the following year sustained damage from an RAF Mosquito fighter-bomber when caught on the surface. In 1944, *U123* had seen much action and was withdrawn from use as she was unseaworthy. The submarine was eventually blown up at Lorient, but the French Navy salvaged and rebuilt her. Renamed the *Blaison*, *U123* finally retired in 1959.

RIGHT: Eagle boats was a generic term for a large class of anti-submarine vessels built in World War I. They were built by the Ford Eagle Boat Plant, hence their name.

out or used for training duties. In addition, losses and damage in action meant that the number of boats could not be guaranteed. As if to illustrate the problem, of the 266 boats that were commissioned in 1942, half of them did not enter service until the following year. On 1 January, of the 91 submarines in service, only 64 were ocean-going boats. Of these, only six were available for immediate use against the United States.

Dönitz intended to launch an attack against US waters as soon as possible. He did not wish to give the Americans time to build strong defences against the submarine, and

an early attack could have a considerable effect upon morale. Consequently, Operation *Paukenschlag* (Drumbeat) was instigated. The six U-boat commanders available for the operation were briefed on 17 December 1941. Dönitz did not feel that pack operations were required, as there was no evidence that the Americans were operating convoys. Instead, the boats were to conduct individual patrols, giving priority to the largest targets. Any escorted convoys that were found were to be avoided.

The first U-boat to sail was *U125*, which left port the following day. Over the next nine days, the other boats followed. In

EAGLE CLASS

Country:	United States
Launch date:	1917
Crew:	61
Displacement:	508 tonnes (500 tons) standard
Powerplant:	Geared turbines, driving single screw
Armament:	Two 101mm (4in) guns, 12 depth charges
Range:	2091km (1129nm)
Performance:	18 knots

addition to the *Type IX* boats, 10 *Type VIIs* were sent to operate in Canadian waters to see what damage they might inflict. The departure of all of these U-boats was not easy to interpret, and the Tracking Room at the Admiralty experienced some difficulty in defining the boats' intentions. A number of signals were sent to Washington, warning of the likelihood of U-boat operations, but none of them could be particularly informative, as the information available about them was inconclusive. Tracking was not helped by appalling weather in the Atlantic. Several boats were forced to run submerged for long periods to avoid the conditions, surfacing only to recharge their batteries and ventilate the submarine. The need to run submerged meant that navigation was difficult, as it was impossible to take celestial fixes.

By 2 January, the Admiralty had enough information to suggest that there were five or six U-boats heading towards the United States. This was despite efforts by Dönitz to deceive the Allies as to the true focus of operations. *U653* had been sent out to broadcast large numbers of signals, in the hope that this would be interpreted as a concentration of submarines in the North West Approaches. Past experience in the Tracking Room meant that it was possible to see past this ruse and at least give some warning. Having warning of the approach of the submarines was one thing: being able to do something about it was an entirely different matter.

THE SECOND 'HAPPY TIME'
The first U-boats began arriving in American waters on 12 January, and it was not long before they claimed their first victim. Just before 01:00 hours on the following day, *U123* surfaced and went looking for merchant ships. Just after 03:00 hours, it torpedoed an independent, the British freighter *Cyclops*. In the next 48 hours, *U123* sank two armed trawlers. The U-boat crew noted that the amount of shipping traffic in the area was almost unbelievable: there were usually between 120 and 130 ships per day, which meant that it was absolutely impossible to take all the opportunities for attack that offered themselves.

The US response to the threat was not particularly strong. Historians have been prone to criticize harshly the lack of anti-submarine defences, blaming this on inaction and a lack of understanding from senior US Navy officers. In fact, the situation was more complicated than for which they allow. In the first instance, the Pacific

conflict meant that many ships that might otherwise have been employed in the fight against U-boats were not available. Some of the destroyers that might have been had been sent to the British under the lend-lease agreement, and, although they were fighting the U-boats, they were doing so elsewhere. The Commander-in-Chief of the Atlantic Fleet, Admiral Ernest J. King, took the view that it was pointless to send out convoys that were not properly escorted and that it would be better to do so only when the requisite resources were available. The

British remained unconvinced by this reasoning and pressed for convoys to be introduced whatever the level of escort available.

Another reason for the lack of suitable forces could be found in the force structure of the US Navy. Had surface units posed the threat, the Atlantic Fleet would have been despatched to engage them. As the threat was to home waters, the brunt of the work fell upon the Eastern Sea Frontier, commanded by Admiral Adolphus Andrews. Andrews was not in a happy situation. After considerable effort, he managed to muster a motley force of 20 anti-submarine vessels. The best of these ships were seven Coast Guard cutters, although only one of these was truly suited for modern anti-submarine warfare. In addition to these, there were three *Eagle* class submarine chasers dating from World War I, two gunboats that had

ABOVE: The crew of the *U563* pose for the camera beneath the conning tower in the summer of 1942.

RIGHT: The bridge crew of HMS *Wolsey* at work. Of note is the use of the 'Talk Between Ships' set by the officer on the far right of the picture. This enabled far better coordination of the escort ships than had been possible before.

BELOW: The spectacular results of a torpedo attack, somewhere in the Atlantic in 1941. By this stage, the reliability problems with German torpedoes had been overcome.

entered service in 1905 and four large yachts. It is not entirely unfair to suggest that they were not the most obvious ships to conduct anti-submarine operations. They were all Andrews had.

Andrews was also lacking air cover. The US Navy employed its Catalinas for anti-surface vessel operations, scouting for the major units of an enemy fleet, and this meant that they were not to be found in the Eastern Sea Frontier's order of battle. What was more, there was little prospect of Andrews receiving any, as many of the Catalinas coming off the production line were being sent to the Pacific to make good the losses there, while others were sent to the United Kingdom to assist Coastal Command. In the end, King felt compelled to suspend deliveries to Britain between January and March to ensure that his forces had enough of the type.

Andrews was also confronted by the problem that the aircraft that were designated for anti-submarine work were in fact controlled by the United States Army Air Forces (USAAF), which proved to be as reluctant as Bomber Command to divert aircraft from strategic bombing to the anti-submarine role. The US Navy began a relentless campaign to gain control of the anti-submarine assets, but faced resistance from the USAAF. The problem here mirrored that in Britain: the aircraft that would have been most suited for the anti-submarine role – the B-17 *Flying Fortress*, B-24 *Liberator* and B-25 *Mitchell* – were ideally suited for the bombing role (the first two being suited for strategic bombardment).

As a result of the lack of resources and the failure to convoy, the U-boats found that their task was a little easier than anticipated. Radio calls were intercepted every day, giving the submarines ideal clues as to where they might find ships to attack. *U123* continued to be successful, sighting no fewer than 20 ships on 19 January. When the attack went in, two were sunk and one damaged. Out of torpedoes, *U123* headed home, broadcasting its sinking reports. In this, eight successes were claimed, as the crew did not realize that some of the ships they had attacked had only been damaged. Nonetheless, it was an impressive effort and greatly encouraged Dönitz. On the way home, *U123* added to its tally by sinking two more ships with its deck gun. *U66* enjoyed similar success, sinking three ships on 22–23 January, before heading for home. In the space of 10 days, three U-boats had sunk 10 ships without loss. This was not a reason for the Allies to panic, but it was a justifiable cause for concern.

The attacks in Canadian waters had proved similarly successful, despite the cold water and poor weather. *U130* had been surprised on the surface by an aircraft on 12 January, but had managed to crash-dive without sustaining any damage. On the next day, two freighters succumbed to the submarine's torpedoes. The day afterwards, the submarine was attacked again. The crash dive to avoid the enemy ship was successful, but the freezing conditions created a problem. The diesel exhausts had frozen open, allowing eight tonnes (eight tons) of water to pour into the U-boat as it dived. Undaunted, the crew pumped the water out and surfaced to resume their patrol. A signal

BELOW: *U333* had a particularly active career. She shot down three aircraft and was badly damaged twice by escort vessels, escaping each time. She also sank the German blockade runner *Spreewald* by mistake, although it was concluded that the fault lay with the ship for operating in a prohibited area. *U333*'s luck finally ran out in July 1944, when she was sunk by HMS *Starling* and HMS *Loch Killin* with the Squid AS mortar.

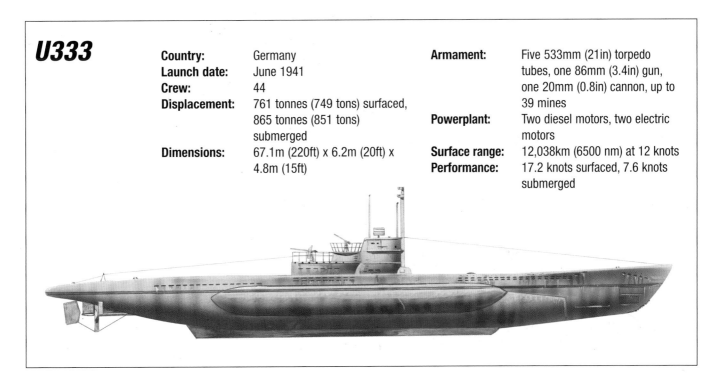

U333				
Country:	Germany	**Armament:**	Five 533mm (21in) torpedo tubes, one 86mm (3.4in) gun, one 20mm (0.8in) cannon, up to 39 mines	
Launch date:	June 1941			
Crew:	44			
Displacement:	761 tonnes (749 tons) surfaced, 865 tonnes (851 tons) submerged	**Powerplant:**	Two diesel motors, two electric motors	
Dimensions:	67.1m (220ft) x 6.2m (20ft) x 4.8m (15ft)	**Surface range:**	12,038km (6500 nm) at 12 knots	
		Performance:	17.2 knots surfaced, 7.6 knots submerged	

USS *DICKERSON*

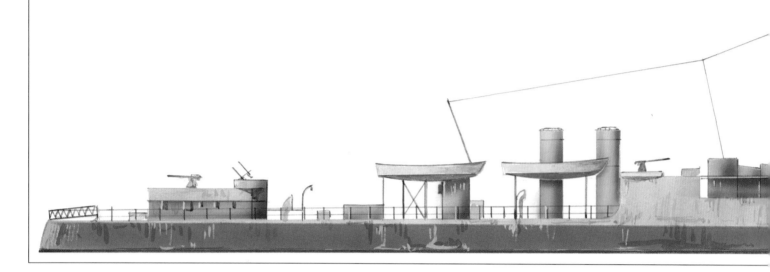

ABOVE: Launched in 1919, *Dickerson* was already in European waters at the outbreak of war. She remained there until being reassigned to the neutrality patrol in 1940. A stint operating from Newfoundland after official American entry into the war was followed by more coastal patrol and escort work, during which the ship was fired upon by the merchantman *Liberator*, which had somehow mistaken the destroyer for a U-boat. In 1943, *Dickerson* was reclassified as a high-speed transport ship, and was reduced to a smouldering wreck by a Japanese Kamikaze on 2 April 1945. Although the fires were put out, *Dickerson* was sunk by the US Navy two days later.

from Dönitz giving discretion as to where the submarine could operate prompted *U130* to head for Cape Hatteras, where more traffic could be guaranteed.

U130 was the last U-boat of the first wave sent to enter US waters. On 22 January, the tanker *Olympic* was sunk, followed three days later by the Norwegian-registered tanker *Varanger*. The *Varanger* exploded so violently that windows were shaken on shore, 55km (35 miles) away. On 27 January, *U130* encountered the US tanker *Francis E. Powell* and despatched her with torpedoes.

There was one serious failure during the first set of operations. *U333* came across a ship running without lights and, making the assumption that the ship was British, torpedoed her. It transpired that the ship was actually the German blockade-runner *Spreewald*. Dönitz was furious at the mistake and directed that the *U333*'s skipper, Peter Cremer, should be court-martialled upon his return. When the *U333* returned, Cremer was brought to trial, but it soon became clear that he had not been as negligent as Dönitz had first believed. The *Spreewald* had been disguised and was sailing in an area in which she was not supposed to be. Cremer's defence counsel suggested that Cremer had acted quite correctly under the circumstances and ought not to be blamed. The court-martial agreed.

This was the only serious blemish, and the first attack on US waters had been a success. Forty-one ships had been sunk without loss to

the U-boats. This prompted concern in London, which was mystified as to why Admiral King would not instigate convoys, even if he were short of the ships with which to do this. The Admiralty offered 10 corvettes and two dozen anti-submarine trawlers to the US Navy. The trawlers were accepted, as it was thought – incorrectly as it turned out – that US shipyards would produce enough ships to overcome the deficit.

Several military missions were sent out to Washington from London, and these returned with gloomy reports. The missions reported that the US forces were at a disadvantage because they had no experience of how difficult it was to locate and sink an enemy submarine. There was little coordination of air and sea assets to deal with the threat; whereas British Coastal Command and the Admiralty were linked, the US Navy and Army Air Forces had not had the chance to put into effect a workable system of cooperation. In addition, there was no central body to formulate anti-submarine doctrine, and research and development in the field had only just begun. Finally, the depth-charges in use in the United States had relatively unsophisticated fuses, as they could only be set to detonate at a maximum of 91m (300ft). While this would not have been a problem in the area around Cape Hatteras, where the waters were shallow, the U-boats were in easy reach of much deeper waters, where the depth-charges would have little effect.

Country:	USA
Launch date:	12 March 1919
Crew:	114
Displacement:	1107 tonnes (1090 tons)
Dimensions:	95.8m (314ft) x 9.3m (30ft) x 3.45m (11ft)
Armament:	Four 126mm (5in) guns, one 76mm (3in) gun, 12 torpedo tubes
Range:	7038km (3800nm) at 15 knots
Performance:	35 knots

Although the situation was not favourable, it was clear that a major effort to improve was under way. The question was whether this could be achieved at a swift enough rate to prevent the sinkings from becoming far worse. Initially, the signs were not good. By the time that the first and second waves

of U-boats had departed, 46 ships had been sunk with only one loss: U82 had been surprised and sunk by the sloop Rochester and the corvette Tamarisk on 6 February. The destruction of one U-boat in exchange for 46 ships was an acceptable loss rate for the Germans.

The U-boats also began to range further afield. From 16 February, they were sent to the Caribbean, to attack any targets that presented themselves, especially those connected with the oil industry. There was some dispute as to how this should be conducted, as Admiral Erich Raeder wanted the U-boats to use their deck guns to shell shore installations. Dönitz felt that this was not the proper way to use his submarines and argued that they would be better employed sinking the tankers and small tenders that served the oil facilities. The two could not agree, and, in the end, Dönitz took the simple expedient of ignoring the instructions.

On 16 February, *U156* attacked three tankers moored in San Nicholas, the harbour of Aruba. One sank, and the other two were seriously damaged. Although this gave away the fact that a U-boat was in the area, it did not deter *U156* from returning to shell the oil refinery and the tank farm next to it once darkness fell. Disaster struck. The gun crew, in their enthusiasm, forgot to remove the plug from the gun barrel. As a result, the gun exploded when the first shot was fired,

LEFT: British and American sailors discuss the finer points of one of the lend-lease destroyers. The lend-lease ships were not altogether popular, but fulfilled a vital role.

killing a crewman and seriously wounding the gunnery officer. The gunnery officer was taken below, and attempts were made to treat him. His leg had been severely damaged, and it was clear that he would need better treatment than could be provided on the submarine. As a result, *U156* headed for the Vichy French island of Martinique and put the unfortunate man ashore. French doctors saved the man's life, although not his leg. The fact that *U156* had been permitted to land its wounded led to a furious reaction from Roosevelt, who felt that this proved that the Vichy French were cooperating in the U-boat campaign. It appeared that the U-boats were operating with impunity against shipping in US waters.

The lack of an effective anti-submarine policy led to a number of unfortunate incidents. On 27 February, *U578* sank the tanker *R.P. Resor,* which prompted the despatch of two destroyers from New York in an attempt to intercept the submarine. The two ships, the *Dickerson* and the *Jacob Jones*, hurried to the area. At 05:00 hours on 28 February, *U578* saw the *Jacob Jones* approaching, and fired two torpedoes. These

both hit their target, and the *Jones* blew up. Worse still, the explosion set off the ship's depth charges, and the concussion from these killed many of the ship's crew as they were in the water. Only 11 men out of a crew of 200 were saved. The *Dickerson* was not to escape unscathed from the U-boat offensive either.

U124, commanded by Johann Mohr, began a run of successes even before she had reached US waters. Just past Bermuda, *U124* encountered the tanker *British Resource*. Mohr attacked it, and it blew up. On the evening of 16 March, a Honduran-registered freighter was sunk; the next day, *U124* approached Cape Hatteras submerged. Mohr found three ships and attacked them. A freighter succumbed first, followed by the tanker *E.M. Clark*. The third ship, the tanker *Acme*, was seriously damaged, although Mohr thought that he had sunk her as well. The *Dickerson* and a Coast Guard cutter were in the area, but concentrated on rescuing the survivors from the attacks, rather than hunting the submarine. A seaplane appeared and released two depth-charges, which fell

BELOW: A depth charge is launched against a U-boat. The depth-charge thrower made a considerable difference to the escorts: whereas previously they had to roll their charges over the stern of the vessel, the thrower enabled wider and more effective patterns to be laid, increasing the chances of damaging or sinking the submarine.

quite near to *U124*, convincing Mohr that it was time to conduct a retreat. He would be back.

Mohr used withdrawal profitably, giving his crew a day's rest before they returned to the shallow water on 18–19 March. *U124* waited on the surface for her next target, which, given the dense nature of the traffic, would surely come. The unfortunate victims soon arrived. They were two US tankers, the *Papoose* and the *W.E. Hutton*. Mohr torpedoed both. The *Hutton* exploded in an enormous ball of flame. This understandably attracted attention, and the *Dickerson* was sent to the scene. On the way, she came across a US freighter, the *Liberator*. The armed guard defending the *Liberator* was completely inexperienced and somehow managed to mistake *Dickerson* for an enemy submarine. They opened fire and, more by luck than judgement, scored two direct hits. These struck the *Dickerson*'s bridge, killing two sailors and mortally wounding the captain. This was not the end of the saga, as the muzzle flashes from the *Liberator*'s guns attracted the attention of *U332*, which torpedoed her.

In the next two days, *U124* damaged two more ships and *U71* sank a freighter. On 23 March, Mohr used his last two torpedoes against the tanker *Naeco*, which sank after a huge explosion. Four US Navy ships hurried to the scene, but, by the time they arrived, Mohr had reached deep water and was heading for home.

U71 remained in the area and sank two more ships. After the second ship had sunk, a Navy aircraft and a destroyer attacked the submarine with bombs and depth charges, but broke off the attack to rescue survivors. On the way home, two more ships fell victim to *U71*, which reached port on 20 April, after 56 days at sea. The success of the U-boat operations in March prompted agonized discussion in London about the effectiveness of US anti-submarine operations. Despite complaints that the Americans needed to introduce convoys, King and others maintained their position that convoys should only be mounted when there were enough escorts to protect them. The British view, perhaps a little unreasonably, was that the Americans were concentrating too much on the Pacific and that this would inevitably lead to disaster, as they would not be able to tackle the serious threat posed by the U-boats until they diverted adequate resources to the Atlantic.

In fact, the situation was beginning to improve. By the end of March, the Eastern Sea Frontier had much larger forces than it had in January. Admiral Royal Ingersoll, who had succeeded King as Commander of the Atlantic Fleet on the latter's promotion to Commander-in-Chief of the US Fleet, did his best to assist the hard-pressed Eastern Sea Frontier, temporarily assigning 14 destroyers. This did not mean that there were 14 destroyers available every day – in fact, there was an average of just two. So,

ABOVE: A merchant ship slowly founders after a U-boat attack. The close proximity of the vessel from which the photograph is taken suggests that any survivors might have been lucky enough to be rescued. In many instances, though, the convoy was forced to sail on to avoid danger, leaving men in the water to face certain death.

although this could be portrayed as an improvement in circumstances, the U-boats still had the chance to make a number of spectacular patrols before they found the defences too difficult to handle. During the first two weeks of March, eight *Type VII* boats sailed for US waters and had huge success. Between 3 and 10 April, Erich Topp in *U552* sank six ships, as did Hans Oesterman in *U754*. The eight boats combined sank 26, demonstrating once again the paucity of effective defences.

There were some successes for the anti-submarine defences, but the most promising opportunity to gather intelligence from a U-boat was lost thanks to overenthusiasm. On the night of 13–14 April, the destroyer USS *Roper* detected *U85*, commanded by Eberhard Greger. Roper had recently been fitted with Type 286 radar (which, despite its higher numerical designation, was an earlier type than the Royal Navy's Type 271). This enabled the *Roper* to obtain a fix on the *U85*, and she charged after the U-boat. Greger was unaware that his pursuer was fitted with radar, and his efforts to outrun the *Roper* were futile. The *Roper* caught the U-boat, and it appears that Greger decided that he would have to scuttle. He turned the U-boat side-on to Roper, which opened fire at point-blank

range. The inexperienced destroyer crew thought that the Germans running across the deck were heading for the deck gun to shoot it out, although it is extremely unlikely that a U-boat would have attempted to engage an enemy destroyer in a gunfight. The unfortunate Germans were machine-gunned as they ran along the deck to abandon their vessel.

U85 began to sink, and the *Roper*'s crew saw many of the Germans in the water. A mixture of excitement and inexperience meant that the opportunity to recover prisoners who could offer valuable intelligence information was not taken. *Roper* went after the submarine with depth-charges, even though the submarine was sinking. The depth charges killed many of the men in the water and inflicted huge damage on the *U85*. This meant that it proved impossible to recover the submarine and its potentially valuable contents, such as its Enigma machine – something that would have been technically possible in the shallow waters.

Although this was a lost opportunity, the defences were beginning to improve. By the middle of April, although the level of experience was lacking, the Cape Hatteras area had become much better defended. After 20 April, none of the *Type VII*s that

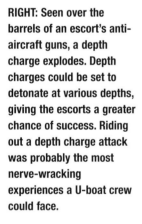

RIGHT: Seen over the barrels of an escort's anti-aircraft guns, a depth charge explodes. Depth charges could be set to detonate at various depths, giving the escorts a greater chance of success. Riding out a depth charge attack was probably the most nerve-wracking experiences a U-boat crew could face.

LEFT: Safely home. The crew of a U-boat gather on deck, tired but within sight of their home port. As the war progressed, fewer and fewer crews returned.

ABOVE: Survivors from a sunken merchant ship approach a U-boat. They would be taken on board and transferred to a German ship if at all possible: if not, they would be taken back to the submarine's home port, facing all the hazards that entailed.

had sailed to the area in March had any success. The 20 *Type VII*s from this group sank a total of 46 ships, but the sinkings had declined in comparison with those that had preceded them. The steady improvement in the defences meant that the U-boats would have to hunt elsewhere.

FURTHER AFIELD

As a result of the improved defences, the U-boats headed for the easier waters of the Caribbean and the Gulf of Mexico. In May, 77 ships were sunk in the two areas, followed by 81 the following month. General George C. Marshall wrote to Admiral King on 19 June to express his fears that the U-boat offensive could threaten the entire war effort of the United States. Although Marshall appreciated that the lack of escorts was a factor, he wondered whether or not some 'improvised means' could be brought to bear. King's reply was to the point: he agreed with Marshall and concluded that using convoys was the only way to deal with the threat from enemy submarines.

King's controversial reputation (Churchill is reputed to have claimed that the war would progress more smoothly if someone took the Admiral outside and shot him)

tends to cause debate about his reluctance to use convoys before this. Historians such as Clay Blair point to the fact that, if you look at King's official correspondence, he appears to have recognized the value of the convoy system even before the war; others such as John Terraine note the curious gap between the claim that escorts were the only answer and the reluctance to employ them from the beginning. It appears that King may have been too closely wedded to the notion that it was only worthwhile using properly designed escorts for convoys. In fact, if enough improvised types were employed, they presented U-boat commanders with the dilemma of whether to attack or not. A naval gun is still a naval gun whether the platform it is mounted on is designed for the task, even if the accuracy and effectiveness of the gun is better on the purpose-built platform. The same is true of the depth-charge. Although there was no guarantee that the escorts would have sunk any U-boats, this was not the point: sinking U-boats was not the aim of convoy – it was to prevent them sinking the merchant shipping. Any possible deterrent to the U-boat was worthwhile. It appears that this was not fully appreciated, and the U-boats were able to enjoy great success owing to the lack of convoying: the deterrent was lacking, and commanders felt much less constrained in their activities as a result.

Marshall's concerns were actually excessive: by the time he wrote, convoys had begun to be employed (from the beginning of May). Convoying was extended to the Caribbean from June, and the freedom of action enjoyed by the submarines since the start of the year declined. The battle was far from over, though, as the U-boats turned their attention to the North Atlantic convoys once more. By the end of June, the U-boats had sunk more than three million tonnes (three million tons) of shipping, in the form of 585 vessels. Although the second 'Happy Time' was drawing to a close, the impact of submarines was still to be felt.

BACK TO WOLFPACK TACTICS

The gradual improvement in the defences on the East Coast of the United States demanded that Dönitz shift the focus of operations to an area where the required rate of monthly sinkings could be achieved. By the summer of 1942, the possibility of achieving greater success had increased, as more U-boats were entering service than before. On the Allied side, the number of escorts remained a cause for serious concern, as the problems of fighting a two-ocean war became readily apparent. The US Navy found that more and more of its ships were required in the Pacific, leading to a steady withdrawal of units in the North Atlantic. This meant that the Royal Navy and the Royal Canadian Navy were forced to bear the main brunt of convoy escort. Some organizational changes helped: the Newfoundland Escort Force, which had previously travelled between its base and Iceland, had an extension of responsibilities. Renamed the Mid-Ocean Escort Force (MOEF), it would henceforth take convoys all the way from Newfoundland to the coasts of Ireland.

In addition, the use of more direct routing – facilitated by the fact that the U-boats were so busy off the US coast – combined with the reorganization to reduce some of the pressures on the escort ships. This could not, however, disguise a fundamental problem: the lack of escorts. Thirty-two destroyers were lost during the first six months of 1942, and, had it not been for the 200 corvettes (reduced to 190 by transfers to the US Navy), it is difficult to see how the anti-submarine war could have been prosecuted effectively. In April, the first super-corvettes, soon re-christened 'frigates', had arrived. These ships were

ABOVE: A member of the crew keeps careful watch for enemy aircraft or shipping. A good lookout could make the difference between escaping unseen or a depth charge attack.

LEFT: A U-boat skipper enjoys a meal. His slightly unkempt appearance suggests that he has been on patrol for some time. As a result, he has decided to eat on deck, rather than have his food spoiled by the unpleasant conditions below.

RIVER CLASS

Country:	Britain
Launch date:	November 1941 (first unit)
Crew:	107 (140 in later units)
Displacement:	1392 tonnes (1370 tons)
Dimensions:	91.9m (301ft) x 11.12m (36ft) x 3.91m (12ft)
Armament:	Two 101mm (4in) guns, two 2-pounder anti-aircraft guns.

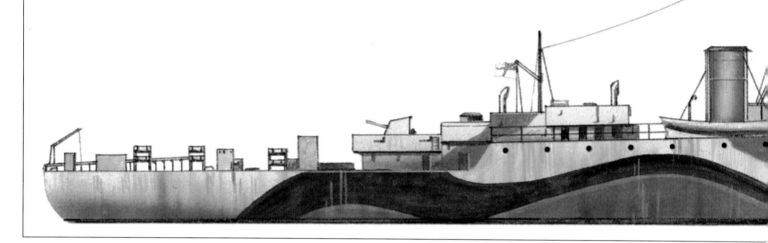

BELOW: A Coastal Command Liberator I. The RAF used a number of different marks of the Liberator, with varying armament fits.

faster than the corvettes and had a larger crew, better armament and better sea-keeping characteristics. The first of the *River* class, HMS *Rother,* was commissioned in April, followed by the Spey shortly afterwards. There was a major problem, though, and this was that the frigates took a long time to build. Even large convoys of up to 50 ships were still being escorted by just five or six warships, a level of protection not really adequate to deal with a large pack of U-boats. Pursuing a U-boat once it was detected was not possible.

Many of the escort group commanders and captains of individual ships were developing in battle-hardened units that operated together to full effect. However, as more warships joined the fray, there was an inevitable lack of experience that had to be overcome. While Admiral Noble's insistence

LIBERATOR

Country:	USA
First flight:	1939
Crew:	8-10
Powerplant:	Four Pratt and Whitney Twin Wasp Radials
Performance:	Maximum speed 434km/h (270mph), range 3685km (2290 miles). Service ceiling 9753km (32,000ft)
Armament:	Four 20mm (0.8in) cannon in under-fuselage pack, up to eight 7.7mm (0.303in) machine guns in nose, beam and tail positions. Maximum bombload 5800kg (12,8000lb)

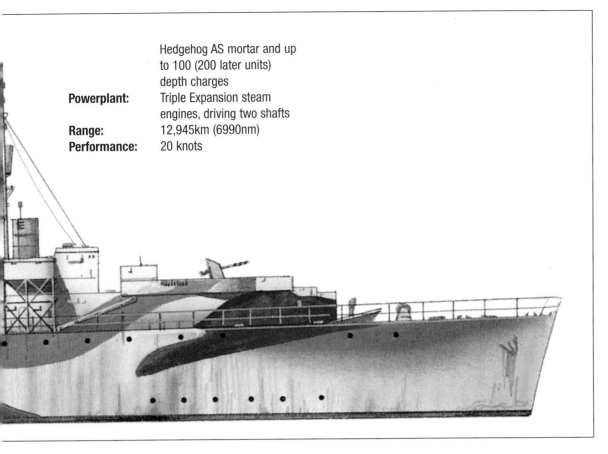

	Hedgehog AS mortar and up to 100 (200 later units) depth charges
Powerplant:	Triple Expansion steam engines, driving two shafts
Range:	12,945km (6990nm)
Performance:	20 knots

LEFT: The *River Class* frigates were a considerable improvement over some of their predecessors. They had good sea-keeping properties, and proved successful against U-boats. Over 130 were built in yards in Britain, Canada and Australia.

on the creation of a school to instruct the finer points of anti-submarine warfare was of inestimable benefit, the adage that there was 'no substitute for experience' held true. The blend of inexperience and lack of warships meant that the battle with the U-boats was far from won.

WAR IN THE ETHER

The Allied situation had not been helped by the loss of the decryption ability at Bletchley Park. Throughout 1941, the relative lack of success enjoyed by the U-boats had caused mounting concern for Dönitz. Although there was a thorough investigation by U-boat HQ, no evidence that the Enigma codes had been broken came to light. None the less, Dönitz saw no reason to remain complacent and authorized additional improvements to signals security. A fourth coding rotor was added to the Enigma machines, while a new code – TRITON – replaced that currently in use. Although the codes for training operations in the Baltic and in German waters were retained, those for the crucial Atlantic operations were completely different. This meant that Bletchley Park could no longer provide the crucial up-to-date information on the location and intentions of the U-boats. In turn, this made the routing of convoys to evade the U-boats a less precise task, thus increasing the risk to the convoys.

LEFT: Admiral Ernest King, Commander-in-Chief of the US naval forces and architect of the naval war against Japan. Throughout 1942 he remained steadfast in his belief that convoys should only be mounted when there were enough escorts to protect them.

At about the same time as Bletchley Park lost the ability to decode the German signals, B-Dienst succeeded in cracking the Admiralty's Naval Cipher Number 3. By February, the Germans were reading some 80 per cent of the signals sent in this cipher, and, when the focus shifted from the Americas back into the Atlantic, it provided the Germans with vital information on the whereabouts of convoys that were using the cipher.

ABOVE: A U-boat crew maintains watch while on patrol in the Mediterranean. The U-boats were far less successful in the Mediterranean theatre, and Dönitz felt that they would have been better used against the Atlantic convoys.

The overall effect was interesting. Had Bletchley Park retained the ability to read Enigma while B-Deinst gained the ability to read the naval cipher, it is far from unlikely that someone in the German service would have noticed that the Admiralty was extremely well informed as to the whereabouts of U-boat concentrations. It is hard to believe that this would not have allowed someone to work out that Enigma had been compromised, with

possibly fatal results for the cryptoanlaytical efforts of the Allies. As Bletchley Park lost the ability to read German signals, there was no clue for B-Dienst that Enigma had been compromised. Conversely, it also meant that the Admiralty was unaware that the cipher had been broken so successfully. These were not the only problems facing the British, as there were continuing problems facing Coastal Command.

HMS
EXMOOR

Country:	Britain	**Powerplant:**	Geared steam turbines, driving two shafts
Launch date:	March 1941		
Crew:	168		
Displacement:	1067 tonnes (1050 tons)	**Performance:**	29.7 knots
Dimensions:	85.3m (280ft) x 9.6m (31ft) x 3.7m (12ft)	**Range:**	2500km (1350nm) at 12 knots
		Armament:	Six 101mm (4in) guns, one quad two-pounder AA gun, two 20mm (0.8in) cannon, 60 depth charges

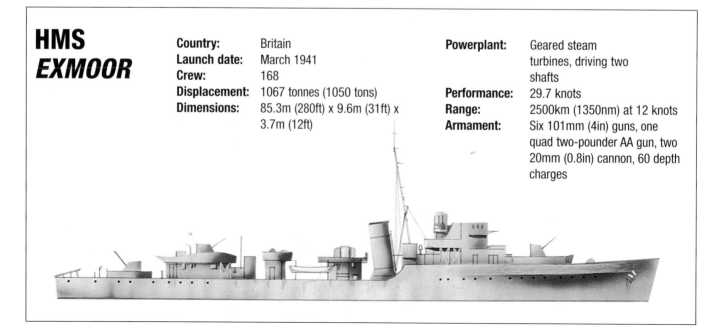

AIRCRAFT AGAINST SUBMARINE

Although Coastal Command had been boosted with the introduction of new aircraft types and better weapons, along with the benefits from Operational Research, it did not begin 1942 in a happy state. Air Chief Marshal Joubert complained that his one squadron of *Liberators* was being allowed to 'die'. Supplies had been diverted to Bomber Command (which did not use them over Europe apart from as electronic warfare aircraft) and overseas. This meant that the one true very long range aircraft available to Coastal Command was not in service in anything like enough numbers. The erstwhile *Sunderland* continued to perform valiantly, although it did not have enough range to cover the air 'gap' in the Atlantic. This gap was caused by the fact that – with the exception of the *Liberator* – there was no aircraft that could go far enough out into the Atlantic to guarantee that, at the point where it had to turn for home, air cover from the opposite shore of the Atlantic would be present.

Although Bomber Command was willing to provide Coastal Command with Whitleys and Wellingtons, this was only because these aircraft were being replaced by larger, longer-range bombers such as the *Stirling*, *Halifax* and *Manchester* (and later the *Lancaster*). Bomber Command, especially

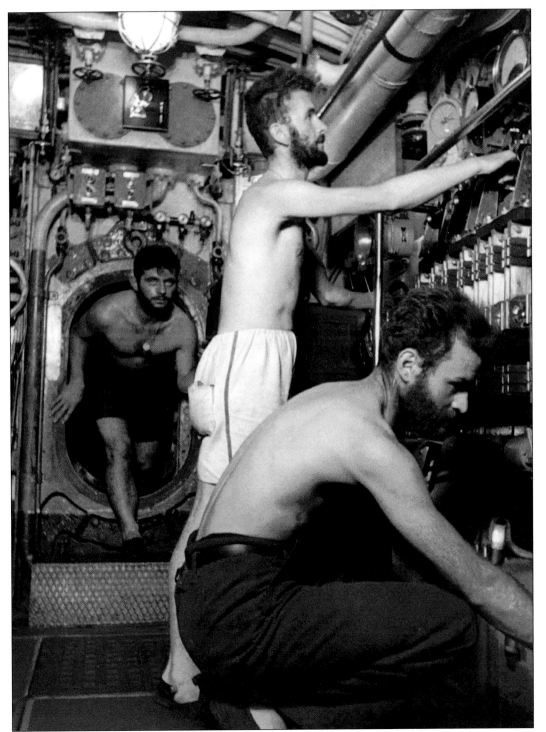

LEFT: Members of a U-boat crew hard at work. The intense heat generated in warm waters is suggested by the way the men are dressed. In the freezing cold of the Atlantic in winter, the picture would have been rather different.

FAR LEFT: HMS *Exmoor* was a Type II *Hunt* class destroyer. The Type IIs had a heavier gun armament than the Type I, but, more importantly, had better seakeeping characteristics thanks to some design changes. Nearly half the *Hunts* were of the Type II variety.

RIGHT: A Sunderland flies over a U-boat as a pattern of depth charges explodes in close proximity. The U-boat has been surprised, and could not help but sustain damage from the explosions.

BELOW: The Short Sunderland (a Mark III is seen here) was perhaps the most famous flying boat to serve with the RAF. It was the mainstay of Coastal Command in the early years of the war, and proved effective in all theatres. The last Sunderland did not leave RAF service until the mid 1950s, when it was only just ceasing to be an effective anti-submarine aircraft.

once Sir Arthur Harris had assumed command, would not accept that long-range aircraft could have as much effect as if they were used for the strategic bombing of Germany. The Royal Navy and Coastal Command took the view that bombing German towns would not offer a solution to the U-boat threat, whereas using air cover over convoys would. They were polite enough to refrain from noting that Bomber Command had refused to attack the submarine pens at the French ports while they were being built. When Bomber Command did return, they discovered that their bombs would not penetrate the thick concrete roofs of the pens. It is hard not to conclude that Bomber Command missed a golden opportunity to have an important strategic effect on the war at a relatively early stage as a result of this failure to act in time.

SUNDERLAND

Country:	Britain	**Armament:**	Eight 7.7mm (0.303in) machine guns, two
First flight:	1937		12.7mm (0.5in) machine guns in beam
Crew:	13-14		positions, four 7.7mm (0.303in) machine guns
Powerplant:	Four Bristol Pegasus radial engines		fixed in bows on later aircraft, 907kg (2000lb) of
Performance:	Maximum speed 434km/h (270 mph), range		bombs or depth charges
	3685km (2290 miles). Service ceiling 9753m		
	(32,000 feet)		

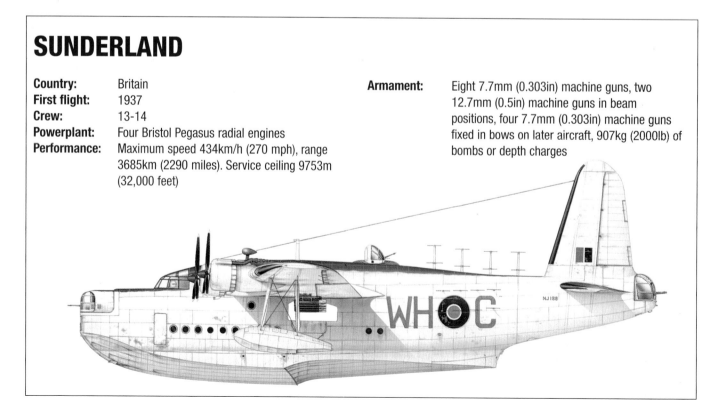

LOSSES INCREASE

On 8 June 1942, OS100 was located by U-boats, and, at 02:00 hours on 9 June, the convoy was startled by the sound of two explosions. The source for these was not hard to guess. Although there appeared to have been no hits, it was concluded that the sound must have originated from torpedoes exploding at the end of their run. When dawn broke, however, it became clear that the torpedoes had found a victim – the Free French corvette *Mimosa* was missing from the convoy. It transpired that the ship had been sunk by Johannes Mohr, enjoying more success in *U124*. The reduced escort then battled its way onwards. Two more ships

were sunk by *U94*, followed by another on the 11th. Shortly afterwards, Captain J.D. Prentice, RCN, arrived on the scene with two ships from his training group. Another ship was lost to *U124* on 12 June, but the convoy was then able to escape without further loss, helped by the bad weather that was afflicting the area at the time. Four days later, an attack on ONS102 was repulsed with one loss and damage inflicted upon *U94* and *U590*. This was a clear sign that the convoy war in the North Atlantic was about to resume. The fighting was to be bitter, and, during the course of the next 12 months, would result in the climactic convoy battles of the war.

ABOVE: This view of the U-boat pens indicates the thickness of the reinforced pen roofs, enabling U-boats to shelter from bombing raids in safety. RAF Bomber Command failed to take the opportunity to destroy the pens while they were being built, and the U-boats enjoyed virtual immunity from air attack for almost all of the war as a result.

CHAPTER SIX

THE BEGINNING OF THE END: AUGUST 1942 – MAY 1943

German successes against shipping in American waters declined as effective convoying was introduced. As the defences improved, the battle of the Atlantic entered its final phase.

The institution of convoys in US coastal waters achieved the desired reduction in Allied losses to submarine attack, and did so again when they were instituted in the Caribbean. Admiral Sir Dudley Pound confidently expected that the majority of shipping in these waters would pass through safely. Despite this, he was concerned. Pound considered that the war against the U-boat was about to reach a turning point. He reasoned that Karl Dönitz would ultimately reach the conclusion that the defences in the Western Atlantic were too strong to continue the offensive there. In these circumstances, continuing operations in US and Caribbean waters would cease to provide a worthwhile return on the effort made.

Pound's assessment was accurate. Dönitz was fully appreciative of the fact that he would be able to conduct a more profitable campaign back in the Western Approaches. For every single U-boat sent to US waters, there could be three in the eastern Atlantic. The strength deployed against convoys in the Western Approaches could be greater,

LEFT: A U-boat enters a patch of debris left from an American steamer, sunk in the Barents Sea. In the middle distance, survivors sit on pieces of wreckage, waiting to be rescued.

U459 TYPE XIV

Country:	Germany
Launch date:	September 1941
Crew:	53
Displacement:	1715 tonnes (1688 tons) surfaced, 1963 tonnes (1932 tons) submerged
Dimensions:	67.1m (220ft) x 9.35m (30ft) x 6.51m (21ft)
Armament:	Two 37 mm (1.4in) guns, one 20mm (0.8in) cannon or one 37mm (1.4in) gun, four twin 20mm (0.8in) cannon and one single 20mm (0.8in) cannon
Powerplant:	Diesel/electric motors
Surface range:	22,872km (12,350nm) at 10 knots
Performance:	14.4 knots surfaced, 6.2 knots submerged

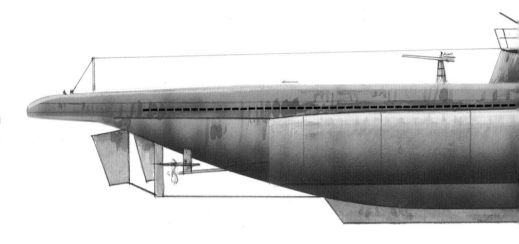

ABOVE: The *U459* was representative of the *Type XIV* 'Milch-cow' tankers employed to extend the range of the attack boats. The tankers became prime targets for anti-submarine efforts, and *U459* was sunk on 24 July 1943 in a dramatic engagement with aircraft of Coastal Command.

enhanced by the use of the *Type XIV* supply U-boats, the so-called 'Milch-cows'. The British position was less favourable, as reinforcements, including two escort groups, had been sent to US waters just as the threat was moving eastwards, towards British waters again.

Signs that these fears were about to be realized came on 24 July 1942, when *U552* intercepted ON113 as the result of a B-Dienst intercept. ON113 consisted of 33 ships, escorted by two *Town* class destroyers (HMS *Burnham* and HMCS *St Croix*), along with four corvettes drawn from both the Canadian and British navies. Thanks to direction finding, the Admiralty Tracking Room was able to alert the escort commander (Acting Captain T. Taylor) that U-boats were in the vicinity. The two destroyers took up screening positions, and there was a subsequent sighting of two surfaced U-boats by the *St Croix*. One of the U-boats was duly pursued, until it dived some 5480m (6000yds) ahead. This was well outside the Allied Submarine Detection Investigation Committee's 'asdic' range, but did not mean that the U-boat had escaped. The captain of *St Croix*, Lieutenant-Commander A.H. Dobson, was experienced in these matters and predicted the U-boat's movements.

Dobson's predictions were accurate, and the *St Croix* found the submarine on asdic. Contact was maintained, and depth-charges were fired against the submarine. Although oil and wreckage were seen on the surface,

an experienced escort captain would know that this did not mean that the chase was over. U-boats had developed the art of firing debris from their torpedo tubes in the hope that this would convince their assailant to leave, thinking that they had succeeded in sinking the submarine. Dobson ran in for another attack and dropped more depth-charges over the point where contact had last been made. The explosions produced a mass of debris, not just oil and other wreckage, but food, clothing and, at the end, the remains of some of the crew as well.

This success did not mean that the threat to the convoy had gone. The remainder of the U-boats stayed in contact and enjoyed success during the night. The escorts were not equipped with high-frequency direction finding (HF/DF) or radar, so there was little that they could do. Three ships were lost before deteriorating weather and visibility forced the U-boats to break off. This type of battle, with the advantage shifting from side to side, was to become typical in the months ahead.

On 27 July, Dönitz made a broadcast to the German people which appeared to confirm the Admiralty's suspicions. Dönitz talked about the nature of submarine warfare, and he appeared to be preparing the German population for increased losses in the campaign. He talked of the 'harsh realities' of submarine warfare and of 'even more difficult' times ahead. British intelligence monitored German radio broadcasts to the public just as assiduously as they did military

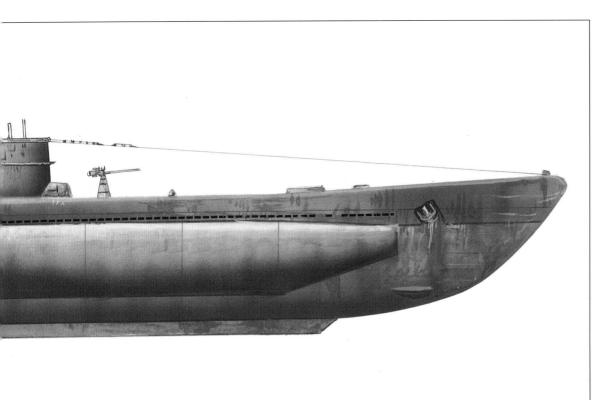

BELOW: Two U-boats rendezvous in the Atlantic, April 1943. Once a convoy was located by a U-boat, it would track it until other boats in the area combined to launch a joint attack. By doing so, they could swamp the defences.

traffic and made a number of conclusions. Dönitz's comments suggested that the U-boats would be operating in areas where the threat to their safety would be greatly increased. This could only mean the main convoy routes. Satisfied with this tip 'from the horse's mouth', the Admiralty waited to see if its predictions would hold true. They did.

In early August, the first signs of the new German approach came when a pack attacked SC94, escorted by the Canadian destroyer *Assinboine* and six corvettes. The Canadian ships in the escort were not equipped with HF/DF or Type 271 radar, making them less versatile than their Royal Navy counterparts. On the night of 5 August, the convoy was hindered by thick fog, which led to it becoming broken up. When this was realized, the convoy began to re-form, but *U593* had sighted them. The U-boat darted in to attack and sank a ship.

Assinboine returned the compliment: it encountered *U210* in the fog and closed in to prevent the U-boat from obtaining a suitably straight course for diving. The two vessels engaged each other with gunfire. The U-boat used its 40mm (1.57in) gun to effect, striking petrol drums by the destroyer's wheelhouse. The blaze did not deter the coxswain, who continued to follow the orders from the captain as they chased after the submarine. *Assinboine*'s gun crew then hit *U210*'s conning tower and killed the commander. The U-boat faltered and *Assinboine* charged in to ram. Two ramming attacks crippled the U-boat, which was sent to the bottom with more gunfire. Unfortunately for the convoy, the

ramming attacks also damaged *Assinboine*'s bows, so that she had to head for home.

There was some respite as convoy managed to keep the U-boats out of range during the next day; however, on 8 August, two of the U-boats in the packs adopted new tactics to delay effect. *U176* and *U379*, running submerged, attacked together during the day. Between them, they accounted for five ships. The crews of three merchantmen, mistakenly believing that they were under attack, abandoned ship. While two of the crews returned to their vessels when it became clear that they had not been torpedoed, the crew of the SS *Radchurch* refused to do so. This meant that a completely undamaged ship was left to drift until *U176* returned to sink her.

As night began to fall, the Royal Navy corvette *Dianthus* saw two surfaced U-boats some nine-and-half kilometres (six miles) away. *Dianthus* immediately opened fire, which forced the submarines to dive. A search with asdic began, but, just after dark, a lookout saw the shape of a U-boat on the surface. Although the U-boat – *U379* – dived instantly, a depth-charge attack was accurate, and the submarine came to the surface. *Dianthus* rammed the U-boat, but this appeared to have no effect. After four such assaults, *U379* went down. Once again, the ramming also seriously damaged the escort, and *Dianthus* was forced to join the merchantmen, as she was no longer able to offer any defence to the convoy. This was not such a blow as it might have been, as two further destroyers had been sent to join the convoy, and they met it in the course of the next 24 hours. On 9 August, a *Liberator*

BELOW: *U210* was another of the multitude of *Type VII* U-boats. She took part in the epic convoy battle of SC94, being lost when the Canadian destroyer *Assinboine* rammed her.

U210 TYPE VII

Country:	Germany
Launch date:	December 1941
Crew:	44
Displacement:	773 tonnes (761 tons) surfaced, 878 tonnes (865 tons) submerged
Dimensions:	67.1m (220ft) x 6.2m (20ft) x 4.8m (15ft)

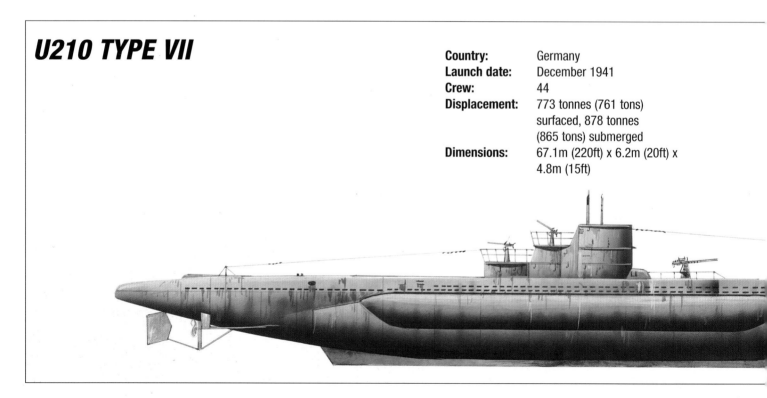

was sighted overhead, providing a welcome reinforcement to the escorts.

The Liberator squadron could not provide aircraft to remain with the convoy all the time, however, and it was absent on the 10th, as poor weather prevented flying. The U-boats launched another combined attack at 10:20 hours and sank another four ships. The weather lifted in the afternoon, and the *Liberators* returned. From this point, there was virtually continuous air escort, and further escort vessels were sent out. The U-boats did not return. Although SC94 had suffered the loss of nearly a third of its ships, this had been slightly offset by the

sinking of two U-boats. The manner of the sinkings, in a fashion that would have been recognized by the ancient Greeks, caused some comment, suggesting that the Canadian ships urgently required newer and more effective equipment. The problem of equipment still taxed the British Admiralty, even three years into the war.

EQUIPMENT DIFFICULTIES

It was appreciated that the escorts were still too weak to be able to deal with the U-boat threat effectively. The lack of numbers meant that it was impossible for escorts to leave the convoy to pursue enemy submarines, as this would leave the convoy vulnerable to further attacks. The escort commander guarding SL118 reported that there had been numerous opportunities to pursue attacking U-boats, but that pursuit had been

ABOVE: HMS *Enchantress* on escort duty in 1942. The station keeping between the ships in convoy can be seen to advantage here. Attacking U-boats would attempt to move between the convoy, using the merchant vessels as cover.

BELOW: Seen through the periscope of an attacking submarine, a merchant ship slips beneath the waves after being torpedoed.

Armament:	Five 533mm (21in) torpedo tubes, one 86mm (3.4in) gun, one 20mm(0.8in) cannon and up to 39 mines
Powerplant:	Diesel/electric motors
Surface range:	12,038km (6500nm) at 12 knots
Performance:	17.2 knots surfaced, 7.6 knots submerged

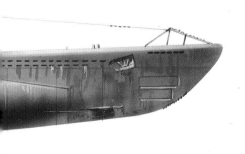

ABOVE: A convoy enjoys protection from a Coastal Command Liberator. The extended range of the Liberator meant that air cover could be provided to convoys all the way across the Atlantic. The overwhelming presence of air cover meant that the Germans began to look at ways of building submarines that could remain submerged for most of their patrol.

MAC SHIP

Country:	Britain
Launch date:	1942
Crew:	105
Displacement:	8128 tonnes (8000 tons)
Dimensions:	147m (482ft)x 18m (59ft) x 8.4m (27ft)
Armament:	One 101mm (4in) gun and a number of small calibre anti-aircraft weapons
Performance:	13 knots
Powerplant:	Diesel engine, driving single shaft
Aircraft:	4 Fairey Swordfish

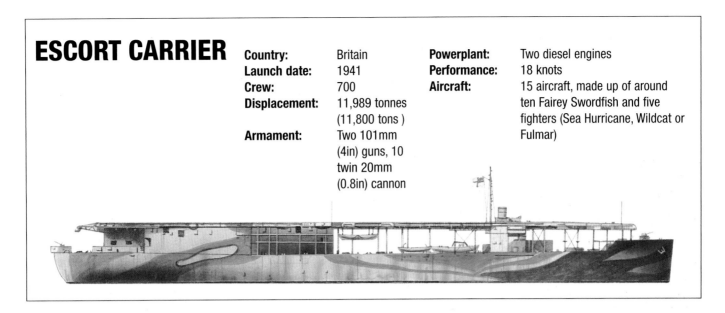

ESCORT CARRIER

Country:	Britain	**Powerplant:**	Two diesel engines
Launch date:	1941	**Performance:**	18 knots
Crew:	700	**Aircraft:**	15 aircraft, made up of around
Displacement:	11,989 tonnes		ten Fairey Swordfish and five
	(11,800 tons)		fighters (Sea Hurricane, Wildcat or
Armament:	Two 101mm		Fulmar)
	(4in) guns, 10		
	twin 20mm		
	(0.8in) cannon		

broken off in every case to ensure that an adequate number of escorts remained with the convoy. In addition, it became clear that the speed of the escorts was inadequate. Generally, they were only four knots faster than ships in convoy, which meant that any diversion to run down and attack a U-boat could leave them so far behind the convoy that they were unable to catch up with it again. The need for faster escorts could be met by the production of more destroyers; however, these took time to build and were already in short supply. As a result, the possibility of obtaining greater numbers of fast escorts appeared to be slim.

This meant that some other approach was required. The method adopted was the creation of the support group. The first of these was the 20th Escort Group,

commanded by Commander F.J. 'Johnnie' Walker, which was brought together in September 1942. This did not mean that the group was immediately deployed, as the need for ships to escort convoys to North Africa meant that there was no alternative but to put every available ship to use, denying the support group a chance to operate together for some time. It would take another six months for the concept to come to fruition.

The lack of destroyers was not the only problem facing the Allies, as escort carriers were also entering service too slowly for the Admiralty's liking. As a consequence, an alternative was sought. The answer came in the form of the merchant aircraft carrier, or '*MAC* ship'. These were conversions of merchantmen that were fitted with a flight deck to enable the carriage of a handful of

ABOVE: The specialized escort carriers came mainly from American shipyards, since those in Britain were at full stretch producing merchant tonnage. As a result of this, only five were built in the United Kingdom. Unlike the *MAC* ships, they were large enough to carry a mix of fighter and anti-submarine aircraft.

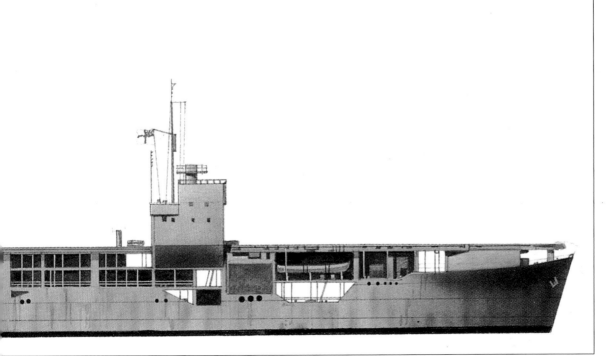

LEFT: The *MAC* ships were designed as stop-gap vessels while escort carriers were still being built. The *MAC* ship retained most of its cargo capacity while being fitted with a flight deck topside. Although the complement of aircraft was small, it was sufficient to provide a convoy with an organic anti-submarine aircraft capability.

SWORDFISH

Country:	Britain
First flight:	1934
Crew:	2 or 3
Powerplant:	One Bristol Pegasus XXX engine
Displacement:	11,989 tonnes (11,800 tons)
Performance:	Maximum speed 222km/h (138 mph), range 878km (546 miles), service ceiling 5867m (19,250ft)
Armament:	Two 7.7mm (0.303in) machine guns, One 457mm (18in) torpedo, four 250-pound bombs/depth charges or eight rocket projectiles

ABOVE: The Fairey Swordfish gave vital service. Designed as a torpedo bomber and reconnaissance aircraft, it was responsible for crippling the Italian fleet at Taranto. As the Swordfish became less able to defend itself against enemy fighters it was employed as an anti-submarine aircraft.

aircraft. Normally, three or four Swordfish were carried. The *MAC* ships were still able to carry their cargoes as well as the aircraft. It was hoped that three of them could be made ready for use at around March 1943; it in fact took until May before even the first of them was ready.

BRAZIL

The U-boats' next major attack proved to be a strategic disaster. A foray by *U507* resulted in the sinking of five ships on 16 and 17 August 1942. All of them were Brazilian, and a furious neutral government joined the Allies five days later. This meant that the Allies had complete control of the narrow part of the Atlantic between Brazil and West Africa. Air and surface cover would now be provided all the way across, making the task of submarines considerably more difficult.

THE LACONIA INCIDENT

On the evening of 12 September 1942, *U156*, commanded by Werner Hartenstein, sighted

U156 TYPE IXC

Country:	Germany
Launch date:	May 1941
Crew:	48
Displacement:	1137 tonnes (1120 tons) surfaced, 1251 tonnes (1232 tons) submerged
Dimensions:	76.8m (251ft) x 6.8m (22ft) x 4.7m (15ft)
Armament:	Six 533mm (21mm) torpedo tubes, one 105mm (4.1in) gun, one 37 mm (1.46in) gun, one 20mm (0.8in) cannon
Powerplant:	Diesel/electric motors
Surface range:	37,729km (20,372nm) at 12 knots
Performance:	18.3 knots surfaced, 7.3 knots submerged

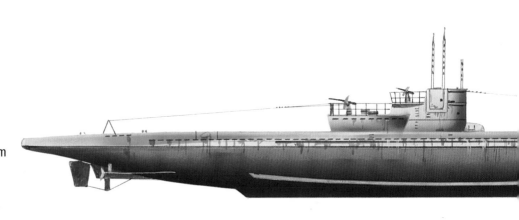

LEFT: A Hawker Hurricane is hoisted onto a catapult on board a 'CAM-ship'. The CAM ships were merchantmen fitted with a catapult track to enable them to launch a fighter against any shadowing aircraft. Once the aircraft had been launched, there was no way of landing back on board. The pilot either had to ditch or parachute to safety. The CAM ship was another stop-gap until escort carriers could be provided.

the liner *Laconia*, an armed merchant cruiser that was now being employed as a troopship. Although this was a legitimate target, Hartenstein was not to know that the majority of those on board were Italian prisoners of war, being taken from North Africa to internment in the Americas. *U156* crippled the *Laconia* with a single torpedo, and the U-boat's crew watched as the ship's passengers and crew took to the lifeboats. Hartenstein moved in closer and, as he did so, realized that the shouts from the stricken passengers were in Italian. There have been questions as to whether Hartenstein was initially driven to save his allies or by simple humanitarian instinct; whatever the motivation, he moved in and began to take aboard survivors. No discrimination between Italian and enemy survivors was made as they were hauled aboard *U156*. Although *U156* was a *Type IXC* and therefore one of the larger U-boats, there was no way that all the passengers could be taken on board.

Even if Hartenstein had initially been merely concerned with saving the Italians, his next action was prompted only by a desire to save as many of the survivors as he could. He sent a request for help to U-Boat HQ and made repeated broadcasts on the international distress frequency. In his message, Hartenstein gave his location and called for any ships that were able to come and assist. He undertook that he would not attack these ships unless he was attacked. Dönitz ordered the three other boats in *U156*'s group to go to Hartenstein's assistance and asked the Vichy French authorities to send help. *U156* slowly proceeded towards the Ivory Coast, loaded with survivors, towing some of the lifeboats and trying to shepherd the others. The other boats in the group failed to find any survivors and were sent back on patrol; *U506* and *U507*, returning from their patrols, were ordered to assist instead. They met up with *U156* on the 14–15 September, and a transfer of survivors was carried out, reducing the burden on *U156*. The three boats continued

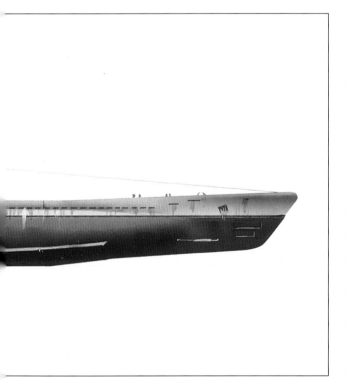

LEFT: *U156* was from the *Type IXC* class of U-boats, and came to prominence in controversial circumstances. After sinking the liner *Laconia*, *U156* rescued survivors, but was attacked by a Liberator of the USAAF while transporting them towards a rendezvous with a German ship. The incident prompted Dönitz to order U-boats commanders not to assist survivors in future.

towards a rendezvous with Vichy French ships that had been arranged by Dönitz.

On the morning of 16 September, disaster struck. A US aircraft appeared and roared over *U156*, which was displaying a Red Cross flag. About an hour later, at 12:30 hours, the aircraft returned and attacked *U156*. Hartenstein ordered the lifeboats to be cast off, and, as this was being done, one of the *Liberator*'s depth-charges fell among the lifeboats, capsizing one as it went off. The pilot of the *Liberator* had spotted the U-boat and the lifeboats while on a routine patrol from Ascension Island and had radioed back for instructions. He was told in no uncertain terms that he should attack and did so. After the first attack failed, the pilot attacked again, inflicting some damage on the submarine. Hartenstein, realizing that to stay on the surface could be fatal, bundled the survivors on board *U156* into the lifeboats and then dived, heading away from the scene. *U506* and *U507* were able to continue towards the rendezvous – although *U506* had to dive to avoid another air attack on the way – and handed some 1200 survivors over to the French ships that had arrived.

Dönitz was furious. His crews had risked their safety to assist survivors, and the Allies had responded by attacking them. On 17 September, he issued an order to all submarines that instructed them to leave survivors from sinkings to their fate, unless it was determined that interrogating them would benefit the German war effort. The

WELLINGTON

kCountry:	Britain
First flight:	1936
Crew:	6
Displacement:	11,613 tonnes (11,430 tons)
Armament:	One 7.7mm (0.303in) machine gun in nose, four 7.7mm (0.303in) machine guns in tail turret. Some aircraft with single 7.7mm (0.303in) machine gun in each beam position. Up to 2041kg (4500lb) of bombs or depth charges
Powerplant:	Two Bristol Hercules XVII piston engines
Performance:	Maximum speed 406km/h (252mph)
Range:	2816km (1750 miles), service ceiling 4877m (16,000ft)

order was to form the basis for a charge against Dönitz at the Nuremberg trials after the war, although he was not convicted of this. The submarine war would now be prosecuted with even greater aggression on both sides.

BATTLE IN THE BAY

British Coastal Command's role in the anti-submarine war was to take on greater

RIGHT: A Swordfish from the carrier HMS *Archer* seen on 9 July 1943. Just visible under the wing are the racks which could be used for flame floats, depth charges and bombs.

importance as 1942 progressed, not least thanks to the efforts of Air Marshal Joubert to ensure that his forces were deployed where they might have best effect. The lack of very long-range (VLR) aircraft was still a major concern, not least since Bomber Command's demands on aircraft production were a serious obstacle to Coastal Command obtaining the aircraft it needed. Sir Arthur Harris, as has been recounted, was even more reluctant to see aircraft diverted from bombing duties to anti-submarine work. He did, however, have to sacrifice six Lancaster bombers for patrol tasks for three weeks – these were drawn from No. 44 Squadron and based at Nutt's Corner in Northern Ireland. Two U-boats were attacked, but not sunk, and the aircraft returned to bombing duties shortly afterwards. This was not through lack of success, but because of Harris's insistence that they were better used under his control.

Joubert decided that the lack of VLR aircraft would not prevent him using his forces, and it became clear that the Bay of Biscay was the best operating area. Although air-surface vessel (ASV) radar was extremely useful, its display was not sufficiently clear to assist air crews running in to attack their targets. The U-boat had to be acquired visually, which was an extremely difficult task at night. Sir Frederick Bowhill had requested that members of his command should send any bright ideas to him, and the solution was offered by Squadron Leader Humphrey deV. Leigh. Leigh suggested that a trainable searchlight be mounted in aircraft.

Coastal Command staff officers were enthusiastic, and Leigh was given the opportunity to develop his scheme further.

A 61cm (24in) searchlight was fitted into a modified Frazer-Nash gun turret. This turret had been designed for fitting into the belly of the *Vickers Wellington* (although very few Wellingtons were so equipped), so it was natural that this was the first airframe to be fitted with the light. After successful testing in March 1941, there was considerable delay following arguments over the type of searchlight that should be used, along with opposition from the Royal Aeronautical Establishment, which favoured a towed flare. Eventually, this was overcome, and the Leigh Light entered service with number 1417 (Searchlight) Flight on 21 February 1942. The flight was equipped with Wellingtons and then raised to squadron status (No. 172 Squadron), although it still only had five Wellingtons.

Joubert initially intended that the Leigh Light be kept in reserve until there were large numbers available, whereupon Coastal Command would achieve maximum surprise by 'swamping' the Bay of Biscay with Leigh Light–equipped aircraft. He was not prepared to wait until he had enough lights, however, sensibly deciding that it was better to put what he had to use. The first Leigh Light operations took place on 3–4 June, and Squadron Leader J.H. Greswell found a submarine. Following up an ASV contact, Greswell found himself virtually on top of the U-boat before he had a chance to

ABOVE: Originally the mainstay of RAF Bomber Command, the Wellington was employed in increasing numbers by Coastal Command as the war progressed. A Mark XIV is seen here, with ASV radar under the nose. The housing for the Leigh Light can be seen under the fuselage beneath the code letter 'G'.

U553 TYPE VII

Country:	Germany
Launch date:	November 1940
Crew:	44
Displacement:	773 tonnes (761 tons) surfaced, 878 tonnes (865 tons) submerged
Dimensions:	67.1m (220ft) x 6.2m (20ft) x 4.8m (15ft)
Armament:	Five 533mm (21in) torpedo tubes, one 86mm (3.4in) gun, one 20mm (0.8in) cannon and up to 39 mines
Powerplant:	Diesel/electric motors
Surface range:	12,038km (6500nm) at 12 knots
Performance:	17.2 knots surfaced, 7.6 knots submerged

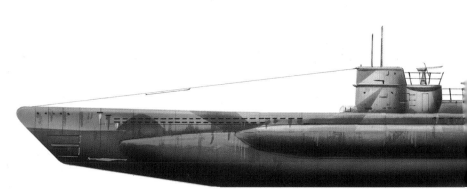

ABOVE: In December 1942 *U553* was fitted with increased anti-aircraft armament. The installation proved unsatisfactory, having an adverse effect on the U-boat's handling. *U553* was lost little more than a month after testing the modified armament.

BELOW: Designed as a long range fighter aircraft, the Beaufighter became the mainstay of Coastal Command's fighter and anti-shipping strike units. The Beaufighter remained in RAF service until 1950.

use his light. His altimeter had been set incorrectly thanks to erroneous pressure forecasts, and he was higher than intended. Greswell rapidly overcame the confusion, and, as he was at least 30m (100ft) higher than planned, he hauled the *Wellington* around to make a proper attack run. The submarine was still on the surface, but suddenly began to fire flares into the air. Greswell was nonplussed and wondered whether the submarine might be firing recognition signals to identify itself as British. He dismissed the idea (being certain that British submarines used different coloured flares) and continued the attack run. At about one-and-a-quarter kilometres (three-quarters of a mile), the Leigh Light was switched on. Greswell could clearly see the submarine and eased down towards an

altitude of 15.25m (50ft). The Wellington roared in, and Greswell released four 110kg (250lb) depth charges. These straddled the submarine – the Italian *Luigi Torelli*. The submarine suffered damage to the steering gear and compass, and had to make for port.

Joubert immediately demanded that Leigh Light production be stepped up, and his confidence in the searchlight was proved correct. During June, No. 172 Squadron illuminated seven U-boats in the Bay of Biscay, while Whitleys using flares failed to make a single sighting. The use of the Leigh Light, even by the small number of Wellingtons, had a profound effect on U-boat skippers. Aware that they could be detected at night and attacked, they began to transit the bay submerged. On 24 June, Dönitz ordered all U-boats to cross the bay

BRISTOL BEAUFIGHTER

Country:	Britain		**Armament:**	Four 20mm (0.8in) cannon in nose and six 7.7mm (0.303in) machine guns in wings. One torpedo under centreline or two 250-pound bombs. Eight rocket projectiles under wings (wing machine guns not carried in this configuration). One 7.7mm (0.303in) machine gun in observer's dorsal position.
First flight:	1939			
Crew:	2			
Powerplant:	Two Bristol Hercules radial piston engines			
Performance:	Maximum speed 488 km/h (303 mph), range 2365km (1470nm), service ceiling 4572m (15,000ft)			

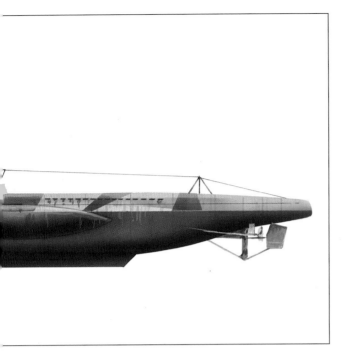

underwater whether during day or night, surfacing only to recharge their batteries. This increased transit times to the convoy routes and helped to reduce the endurance of the submarines. All this was achieved without a single 'kill' by Leigh Light-equipped aircraft, demonstrating once again that important results could be achieved even without actually sinking the U-boats. The first success came on 6 July, when *U502* fell victim to the Wellington flown by Pilot Officer W.B. Howell.

The Leigh Light threat also meant that the number of U-boats to be found during daylight hours increased. The submarines could not remain under water all the time and had to surface even in daylight to recharge their batteries. This meant that the air threat was increased still further, demanding that some action be taken to deal with it. As a result, in September, plans were made to arm the U-boats with two twin 15mm (0.59in) machine guns on the upper platform of the conning tower, with a twin 20mm (0.78in) cannon on the lower platform. It was quickly appreciated that the 15mm (0.59in) weapons would not provide anything like enough firepower against an attacking aircraft, so it was decided that the U-boats would be given an armament of a quadruple 20mm (0.78in) mounting taken from army stocks, along with a 37mm (1.46in) gun. These had to be treated with anti-corrosion coatings before they could be used on the submarines.

From December 1942, they were fitted to a number of U-boats, but there were problems. *U553* was the first boat to be fitted out with this arrangement, and it was reported that the gun platforms produced too much spray when the U-boat was running on the surface. This gave away the boat's position far too easily. In addition, the lower platform affected the U-boat's depth-keeping characteristics, a factor which was felt to outweigh the benefits of having the guns aboard. It was clear that the boats still required some form of anti-aircraft armament, so a programme to modify the conning towers for appropriate weaponry began in January 1943. By April, all operational boats had been fitted with two 20mm (0.78in) cannon – this had the unfortunate effect of tempting some skippers to stay on the surface to fight it out with attacking aircraft when they would have been better served by submerging.

COASTAL COMMAND FIGHTERS

A further problem for the U-boats arose when the Junkers Ju88s employed to attack anti-submarine patrols began to be mauled by marauding Bristol Beaufighters. Initially, the Ju 88s, fighter versions of a bomber aircraft, were extremely useful. They were equipped with an armament of cannon and machine guns and enjoyed a notable performance advantage over Coastal Command's aircraft. Unfortunately for the Luftwaffe (and therefore the U-boats), Coastal Command began to increase the number of guns carried by its aircraft. The Sunderland's armament was increased dramatically, so that it carried at least 14 machine guns, and attacking one became an increasingly difficult prospect, particularly if the pilot was able to dive towards the sea, thus preventing an attack on the only part of the aircraft without guns.

The increased armament meant that the

ABOVE: A U-boat comes alongside lifeboats from the American steamer *Carlton* after she was torpedoed North of Norway on 5 July 1942.

ABOVE: An airman polishes the lens of a Leigh Light, mounted beneath the wing of a Coastal Command Liberator. The Leigh Light could be used in conjunction with ASV radar, greatly increasing the effectiveness of aircraft patrols against submarines at night.

that Noble was not removed from command, but rather sent to Washington as head of the British Naval Mission. Unlike many other senior officers moved at Churchill's behest during the course of the war, this was by no means a case of Noble being promoted to a 'non-job'. He was to become a key figure in Anglo-American naval relations, having done much to tackle the problems posed by the submarine danger. By the time he left Western Approaches Command, Noble had forged a command that was lacking only enough resources to overcome a threat that had appeared almost insuperable when he had taken over when Western Approaches had been moved to Liverpool.

Horton, like Martin Nasmith, had been a submariner, and Churchill appears to have been motivated by the principle of appointing a 'poacher come gamekeeper'. The adage was to prove apt. Horton had a reputation for decisive leadership and probably had more experience of submarine warfare than anyone else on the Allied side. His style proved to be robust (which is usually a euphemism to cover the terms 'direct' and 'abrasive', among others). Whereas Noble had the personal touch – going to sea with escorts and flying with Coastal Command – Horton preferred to make it clear that he did not suffer fools gladly, and it sometimes seemed that he made the assumption that everyone he met was a fool until they had demonstrated otherwise.

Importantly, Horton did not hold this opinion of the Operational Intelligence Centre's (OIC) Submarine Tracking Room for more than a short while. He expressed his irritation with the Tracking Room at one of the first meetings of the Anti-Submarine Warfare Committee he attended in his new post. Horton berated the organization for its apparent failure to interpret recent information correctly, with the result that a convoy's re-routing plan had failed. Rodger Winn, the head of the Submarine Tracking Room, was not one to crumble in the face of such complaints.

Winn had become head of the Submarine Tracking Room in unusual circumstances. Before the war, he had been a barrister, his ambition to serve in the Royal Navy having been thwarted by illness. In 1939, when war seemed likely, he volunteered his services to the Admiralty in the hope that he might be of some use. In August, he was directed to the Submarine Tracking Room. The Submarine Tracking Room was a relatively new creation, as the Royal Navy had allowed its intelligence gathering capabilities to fall

Ju 88s were compelled to attack in pairs or even larger numbers. By the middle of 1942, the *Bristol Beaufighter* was joining Coastal Command in large numbers. The *Beaufighter* had been designed as a twin-engined long-range fighter, but had been pressed into service with Fighter Command to counter the night Blitz launched against Britain between September 1940 and June 1941. It was heavily armed, with four 20mm (0.78in) cannon and 10 7.7mm (.303in) machine guns, and proved more than a match for the Ju 88. As time went on, Beaufighters were fitted with torpedoes or rocket projectiles, and they became formidable anti-shipping (and anti-submarine) weapons. Although pleas for assistance were made to Hermann Göring, he failed to provide an answer. This meant that air opposition to the Biscay patrols was far less than it might have been.

SIR MAX HORTON

On 19 November, Churchill appointed Admiral Sir Max Horton as Commander in Chief of Western Approaches Command, replacing Sir Percy Noble. It must be noted

LEFT: Another Liberator tests its Leigh Light. The Liberator and Wellington made great use of the Leigh Light, driving the U-boat arm to distraction, as surface transit at night became highly dangerous. The solution was to come later, with U-boats that could operate for long periods without having to surface. Fortunately for the Allies, these boats arrived too late in the war to be a serious threat.

away in the inter-war period. In 1937, when Admiral Sir William James had firmly restored the convoy to the Royal Navy's strategy in time of war, he had taken the opportunity to deal with the lack of intelligence-gathering capability. The OIC had been formed, and among its responsibilities was the tracking of enemy submarines.

The Tracking Room had been placed under the leadership of Paymaster-Commander E.W.C. Thring, a veteran of the intelligence-gathering efforts of Room 40 in World War I. By the end of 1940, Thring's health was in a state of near collapse, and it was clear that he needed to be relieved. Thring had become ever more impressed with Winn's ability to master an array of information and arrive at often uncannily accurate conclusions. At first sight, many naval officers felt that Winn's judgements sometimes seemed to be based on little more than intuition. It did not take long for them to be convinced that there was more than that to his judgement, and there was considerable support within the OIC for Thring's recommendation that Winn should succeed him. This was a novel step – placing a civilian in charge of a vital department within the Admiralty. The raised eyebrows that this might have caused were prevented by giving Winn a commission in the Royal Naval Volunteer Reserve, in the rank of commander.

This varied background proved to be of considerable value when confronting Horton for the first time. Winn's legal career had placed him in front of a number of judges who were, if anything, even more cantankerous than Horton. When faced with the accusation that the Tracking Room was failing in its task, Winn politely told Horton that he would, in half an hour, muster all the information that was available at the time the routing suggestion had been made. He would then give it to the Admiral to study, and Horton could tell him whether he would have made a different conclusion. Horton agreed, and appeared in the Tracking Room 30 minutes later. Winn sat him down in front of a huge pile of signal intercepts, weather reports and a host of

BELOW: Royal Navy destroyers practise using their own illuminants, known as 'snowflakes'. These gave escort vessels the means of illuminating U-boats to allow them to be attacked. Care had to be exercised in using them, though, since they could provide the U-boats with brightly lit targets.

ABOVE: A German boat, seen operating in the Atlantic in December 1942. By May 1943, the 102 available U-boats would have sunk somewhere in the region of 3.8 million tonnes (3.7 million tons) of Allied shipping as the Battle of the Atlantic reached a climax.

other messages, and set the admiral to work. A few minutes into proceedings, Winn quietly informed Horton that the Chief of Staff at Western Approaches was eager to receive the situation report. Horton battled on for an hour and a half, before pushing the papers away. He stood up, smiled at Winn and patted him on the shoulder. 'A bit outside my field,' he is reported to have concluded, adding 'It's yours, Rodger.' From this point on, Horton showed an unbreakable trust in Winn's judgement. It also ensured that the Tracking Room would continue to play a vital part in the prosecution of the war.

ATTACK FROM THE AIR

Horton's arrival also meant that there was some progress in the constant struggle to ensure that Coastal Command received the aircraft that it needed. Although there had been some progress, the equipment programme continued at a slow pace. Churchill had created the Anti U-Boat Warfare Committee, which met weekly, starting from 4 November 1942. Once Horton was in place, its meetings became interesting, to say the least. The Admiralty and Coastal Command pressed their plea for VLR aircraft, in the face of opposition from Harris. The Air Officer Commanding-in-Chief of Bomber Command claimed that, by bombing the German submarine pens, his forces were making a far more decisive contribution to the Battle of the Atlantic and had delayed submarine production by six months. Quite how Harris arrived at this

conclusion is open to debate, as the submarine pens were then completed and covered with layers of thick concrete.

Coastal Command, unlike Harris, had the advantage of being able to use Operational Research (OR) to assist in its claims. Professor P.M.S. Blackett had continued with his work and produced a huge amount of valuable information. This included further work on the settings for depth-charges, which were reduced to 7.62m (25ft) from the 15.24m (50ft) that early OR reports had suggested. It is worthwhile recalling that the recommendation to set the charges at 15.24m (50ft) had met with strong opposition: it is a mark of how attitudes changed when the ideas were put into practice that this suggestion passed almost without comment. Blackett's team also came up with a streamlining of the maintenance programme for Coastal Command squadrons, increasing the availability of serviceable aircraft by more than 50 per cent. Significantly, Blackett came up with further discoveries related not to Coastal Command, but to convoys.

Blackett had assessed the statistics for convoys and concluded that the bigger the convoy, the more effective it was. The mathematical relationship between the circumference of a circle and its area, when applied to convoys, demonstrated that doubling the size of a convoy meant that fewer escorts than thought were required to offer adequate protection. Although the number of merchant ships was doubled, the number of escorts only needed to be increased by 33 per cent: a circle of eight ships around 48 merchantmen was as effective as a circle of six around 24 merchant ships. Using mathematical analysis even further, Blackett and his team showed that increasing the size of convoys but reducing the number of convoys that sailed would reduce the number of targets for the U-boats to attack. If a convoy were attacked, it would not suffer any more losses than a smaller one, as the number of victims gained by the U-boats was limited by the number of boats that attacked and their torpedo stowage. They could, therefore, sink only about the same number of ships in a larger convoy as they could in a smaller convoy. However, because the larger convoy would replace two or three smaller ones, the U-boats would have just one chance to sink the ships rather than three. The notion of the large convoy with far fewer escorts than initially thought necessary took time to be accepted; as we shall see, the results were dramatic when finally implemented.

THE MEDITERRANEAN

Dönitz's plan to take the war back to the Atlantic convoys encountered a setback in October 1942. On the 23rd, the British 8th Army, under General Bernard Montgomery, launched a massive attack against the Axis forces at El Alamein in Egypt. General Erwin Rommel, the famed 'Desert Fox', was not

with his men when the attack was launched, as he was ill in hospital. He returned to the battle area on 25 October and came to the conclusion that the position was hopeless. He proposed a withdrawal to the west, but found the Führer in one of his obstinate moods. Hitler's less-than-helpful order was 'stand fast'. This was bad news for Rommel and Hitler made it a double blow when his proposals for the U-boats reached Dönitz. Hitler insisted that the U-boats in the eastern Mediterranean move to the western Mediterranean with immediate effect.

On the face of it, Hitler's plan was not outlandish, as the Mediterranean force had enjoyed poor fortune in September and October, sinking just one merchant ship. Also, German intelligence thought that the aircraft carrier HMS *Furious* and other warships were at Gibraltar, perhaps intending to fly off fighter aircraft to reinforce Malta or to support an invasion of Sardinia. The former assessment was correct, and Furious set sail on 28 October. Seven German and seven Italian U-boats waited for the force, which raced towards Malta at more than 20 knots. Although the force was sighted by three U-boats, only *U565* was able to attack, and all four torpedoes failed to hit. The speed of the convoy made it impossible to pursue, and a change of plan was required. It was decided

BELOW: An early model Bristol Beaufighter seen on patrol. The Beaufighter was just the aircraft needed by Coastal Command, given its versatility. Beaufighters quickly gained superiority over the Junker 88 fighters used by the Luftwaffe to protect U-boats in the Bay of Biscay against Coastal Command anti-submarine aircraft. Beaufighters were not averse to attacking U-boats, and caused havoc amongst surface shipping later in the war.

RIGHT: Professor PMS Blackett, the man who did much to make Operational Research a truly effective tool in the prosecution of the anti-submarine war, seen here in 1964.

RIGHT: Professor PMS Blackett, the man who did much to make Operational Research a truly effective tool in the prosecution of the anti-submarine war, seen here in 1964.

that the U-boats should try to sink the carrier on its return, but this plan was again thwarted by the speed of the convoy as it transited the area. Another four torpedoes were fired, this time by *U431*, with a similar lack of success.

FINDING ENIGMA AGAIN

This plan left just one U-boat in the eastern Mediterranean, *U559*. In the early hours of 29 October, a *Sunderland* detected the submarine. This prompted the destroyer HMS *Hero* to head for the area, but a search with asdic proved unsuccessful. This was not the end of the story, though, as the 12th Destroyer Squadron, upon hearing the report, set out to see if it could lend assistance. About seven hours after the

BELOW: Seen through a porthole, the guns of an escort vessel nose menacingly skywards as a convoy slowly progresses towards port.

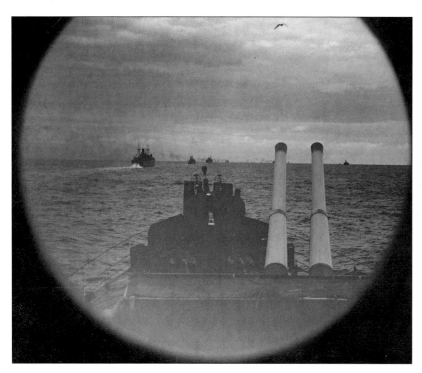

report, the four destroyers arrived in the area and were immediately rewarded. An ancient Vickers Wellesley bomber (a type which had been withdrawn from Bomber Command before the war) had been assigned to anti-submarine duties, and the crew spotted the outline of a submarine. To say the Wellesley 'raced' in to attack would be to credit the aircraft with a greater turn of speed than it possessed, but the pilot dived down towards the completely unsuspecting target and released three depth charges, before firing flares and circling to attract the destroyers' attention.

The destroyers sped to the area covered by the circling aircraft at 31 knots, slowing rapidly to conduct an asdic search. HMS *Dulverton* obtained a contact immediately and began a hunt that lasted for 10 hours. *Dulverton* made six attacks, with 56 depth-charges; HMS *Pakenham* and *Petard* made four attacks each, dropping 62 depth charges between them, while Hero – which had joined the squadron for the search – made three attacks using 17 charges. HMS *Hurworth* dropped 15 charges in its two attacks. Hans-Otto Heidtmann, *U559*'s commander, tried to ride the attacks out on the bottom, but the last five of the 150 depth charges caused serious damage and the boat began to flood. At about 2240 hours, Heidtmann surfaced, hoping to escape in the darkness. He was immediately spotted by *Hurworth*'s radar, and a searchlight was trained on the submarine. *Hurworth* and *Petard* were too close to engage with main armament, so opened fire with every 20mm (0.79in) and 40mm (1.57in) cannon they had. The barrage raked the conning tower of *U559*, probably killing Heidtmann and several others. With no chance of escape, the crew scuttled the vessel and began jumping into the sea. They had failed to destroy any of the Enigma material aboard.

Petard's captain, Lieutenant-Commander Mark Thornton, thought that there might be a chance to capture *U559* and brought *Petard* in close. Some of the crew jumped onto the deck in an attempt to secure a line, while a party was sent away in whalers for a more conventional means of boarding the stricken submarine. Lieutenant Francis Fasson, *Petard*'s boarding party commander, decided not to wait, dived into the water and headed for the submarine, accompanied by Able Seaman Colin Grazier. When they arrived, one of the men already on the submarine, Canteen Assistant Tommy Brown, joined them, and they went into the submarine. They discovered an array of

secret documents, which were passed up the conning tower by Brown to the *Petard*. Brown returned to find Fasson trying to prise a machine – quite what is uncertain – off a bulkhead, but he failed.

Fasson was not especially unhappy about this and proceeded to send a box containing something – probably the Enigma machine – up the conning tower. As this was being done, *U559* suddenly began to sink. Thornton ordered full ahead to attempt to put tension into the towline, to keep the submarine afloat, but saw one of the whalers directly ahead. Realizing that he would sink the whaler and lose the documents, Thornton belayed his order and cut the line. Those on deck yelled for Fasson and Grazier to abandon ship, then leapt for their lives. The box was dropped, and the water pouring into the submarine overwhelmed the unfortunate Fasson and Grazier. The award of posthumous George Crosses marked their courage, while Brown received a George Medal, an award that, coincidentally, ended his naval career. It was discovered that he was only 16 and therefore underage. He was discharged immediately, but, in a tragic irony, this cost him his life, as he was killed in 1944 when

attempting to rescue his sister from a burning building. Although their stories each ended tragically, the three men – along with their colleagues topside of the submarine – had made a major contribution to the war against the U-boat. They had captured key items that would allow Bletchley Park to break back into the Enigma codes.

The process of breaking the code was not made simple, as the Mediterranean boats used a different cipher to those in the Atlantic. The haul from *U559* provided valuable clues to breaking the Atlantic TRITON code, but this would take time to achieve.

TORCH AND THE NOVEMBER DISASTERS

On 8 November 1942, the Allies launched their invasion of North Africa, Operation Torch. This led to the despatch of heavy concentrations of U-boats into the Mediterranean, never their favourite operating area. Given the importance of the task, Dönitz insisted that the U-boats be equipped with the new FAT torpedo, which had a new steering device, allowing the torpedo to make a long looping path through a convoy, thus increasing the

ABOVE: At the stern of his ship, a sailor prepares to release depth charges. Releasing depth charges in this way called for precise timing and limited the field of fire of the ship. The introduction of depth charge throwers meant that the escorts were able to engage contacts to port and starboard without having to manoeuvre into a position to run over the top of the submarine.

chance of a hit. There were only 24 of these torpedoes available, and they did not seem to make much difference to the U-boats. On 10 November, *U81* sank the freighter Garlinge, this success being followed two hours later by *U431's* sinking of the destroyer HMS *Martin*. Other attacks failed thanks to torpedo malfunctions.

The Allied response was robust. On 13 November, the corvettes HMS *Starwort* and *Lotus* sank the *U660*. The next day, RAF Hudsons sank *U605*, while an attack on *U595* seriously damaged the U-boat. The submarine's skipper, Jürgen Quaet-Faslem, appreciated that his craft would be unable to continue and ran her aground, in the belief that the Vichy French forces would help his crew to escape. In fact, they were handed over to the Allies, and a US Army tank unit had the peculiar distinction of being the first ground unit to capture a submarine. On 15 November, a Hudson from No. 500 Squadron sank *U458*, but the blast from the depth-charges brought the aircraft down as well. Two days later, Squadron Leader Ian Patterson, also from No. 500 Squadron, found *U331* and attacked, wrecking the boat. Two other Hudsons joined in the attack, and it became clear to *U331's* commander, Hans-Dietrich von Tiesenhausen, that he could not escape. He ran up the white flag, but while the *Hudson* crewmen were watching, a Fleet Air Arm *Martlet* (the Royal Navy's name for the *Grumman Wildcat*) appeared and, completely misjudging the situation, strafed the U-boat. The dismay of the

Hudson crews was compounded when an *Albacore* torpedo bomber followed the *Martlet* in and sank *U331* with a torpedo, killing many of the crew. Fortunately, a destroyer and a Supermarine *Walrus* rescue aircraft appeared on the scene and recovered 17 of the crew, including Tiesenhausen.

The foray against Torch was singularly unsuccessful, thanks to the heavy level of escorts provided by the Allies; however, even the limited numbers of U-boats that were available in the Atlantic were able to take a ferocious toll on enemy shipping. The concentration of escorts off North Africa meant that shipping in the Atlantic proved to be uniquely vulnerable. During November, while the boats in the Mediterranean enjoyed little success, the submarines that were free for Atlantic operations enjoyed their best successes yet. During the month, 126 ships were lost, and concern in the Admiralty increased yet again. Rather than marking the start of a new and deadly phase in the war, November 1942 was the climactic point. The Admiralty noted that the situation regarding escorts had 'never been tighter'. The losses sustained meant that fuel stocks in Britain had fallen to 304,815 tonnes (300,000 tons), while consumption was running at 132,100 tonnes (130,000 tons) per month. British imports had fallen to a third of the figure in 1939. The Admiralty took the view that the early months of 1943 would be the crisis point of the convoy battles. It was not far wrong.

BELOW: Seen from an escorting aircraft, a convoy progresses across the Atlantic. The photograph gives some idea of the area covered by the convoys. Although convoys offered the U-boats a far larger target than ships sailing independently, the U-boats had to find the convoy first – and this was far more difficult than chancing upon a ship sailing by itself without escort.

LEFT: An 'H'-Class destroyer, HMS *Hero* seen escorting a convoy. *Hero* sank two U-boats in 1942, before being transferred to the Royal Canadian Navy.

ENIGMA

On 13 December, Bletchley Park reported that it had broken the TRITON code used by the U-boats' Enigma machines. This news filled the Admiralty with relief, although this was offset by the news that Rodger Winn's health had collapsed. Winn's blood pressure was dangerously low, and his doctors told him to take prolonged rest or to risk never working again. He was also told that returning to his job in the Admiralty would be out of the question. This was a potentially

serious blow to the Tracking Room, but Winn was made of sterner stuff. He proceeded to make an almost miraculous recovery in the space of a month, then promptly ignored all medical advice and went back to his desk. The breaking of the code did not present immediate benefits, as there was a mountain of previously undeciphered material to go through. This had to be done to work out the different settings of the Enigma machine and took time to achieve. None the less, the ability to

ABOVE: At work in the torpedo room of *U331*: the U-boat's identity can be ascertained from the 'kill' marking on the upper torpedo tube. HMS *Barham* fell victim to *U331* in the Mediterranean on 25 November 1941.

ABOVE: The USS *Benson* ablaze after colliding with the USS *Trippe* during a Trans-Atlantic convoy crossing on 19 October 1942. She survived the accident and went on to escort convoys in the Meditteranean throughout 1943 and 1944.

read German traffic once more was to be of considerable assistance as time went on. In the short term, though, the need to penetrate the code as quickly as possible was demonstrated by the disasters that befell convoys ONS154 and TM1.

ONS154 AND TM1

On 19 December, ONS154, made up of 45 ships escorted by Escort Group C1, set sail. The escort group was inexperienced and had not been given the opportunity to take part in an exercise before leaving. In addition to this, the Tracking Room made one of its rare errors, in an attempt to direct the convoy away from the appalling weather in the North Atlantic. While the idea was sound in principle, the lack of knowledge regarding the whereabouts of enemy submarines proved to be fatal. ONS154 sailed into the midst of two U-boat groups totalling 20 boats.

The first sighting of ONS154 was made by *U154* on 26 December, and Dönitz ordered both groups of U-boats to attack. The first attack came that night, when *U356* made two runs through the convoy and inflicted mortal damage on four ships. The escorts responded by sinking *U356* with depth charges, but this was to be their only success. The following day, *U225* sank the tanker *Scottish Heather* while she was refuelling a corvette. On the 28th, 13 U-boats closed in on the convoy, and, at one point, four were seen approaching in line abreast. At least five of the boats managed to get amongst the convoy, and carnage ensued. Within the space of two hours, nine ships were sunk.

The next day saw no action, and the convoy was joined by two destroyers – although these had to break off the next day because of a shortage of fuel. On 31 December, the destroyer HMS *Fame* arrived and took charge of the convoy. The battle had cost 14 ships for the loss of only one U-boat.

As the climax of the battle of ONS154 was being reached, TM1 set sail from Trinidad, heading for Gibraltar. It consisted of nine oil tankers and was protected by the rather weak escort of one destroyer and three corvettes. Bletchley Park located a group of six submarines patrolling between the Azores and Madeira, clearly lying in wait for just such traffic as TM1. The U-boat group was unaware of the prize target approaching, as B-Dienst was unable to provide any information based on signals interception. Purely by accident, *U514* spotted the convoy on 3 January 1943. Shortly afterwards, the convoy was advised to divert sharply to the south when darkness fell. Bletchley Park was unable to help, as the rotor settings for Enigma had been changed at noon that day, and it was unable to decipher the signals. The escort commander, Commander Richard Boyle, decided not to follow the advice from the Tracking Room. Boyle's decision was based on the weather forecast. A number of the ships would need to refuel at sea, and the weather promised to be better on the original route. This would make refuelling a much easier task, so Boyle stuck to the original route.

Late that evening, *U125* attacked and fatally damaged the tanker British Vigilance, which exploded in a fireball. Contact with the convoy was lost as *U125* escaped, but an inspired piece of planning by Dönitz meant that TM1 was not to evade further detection. Dönitz placed another group of boats across the last known course of TM1 in the event that the convoy continued in the same direction. On 8 January, Dönitz's guesswork was rewarded. U381 made

contact, prompting the despatch of four more boats. That night, *U436* sank two tankers with a single salvo of torpedoes and then retired from the fray after being damaged by the escorts. *U552* then repeated the trick of crippling two ships in one salvo, hitting the tankers *Norvik* and *Minister Wedel*. A little more than an hour after that, the *Empire Lytton* fell victim to *U442*. Over the next three days, the pack managed to sink 77 per cent of the convoy, along with an unfortunate independent that happened to blunder into the way of the pack.

The events which befell ON154 and TM1 gave Britain's Prime Minister, Winston Churchill, and the US President, Franklin Roosevelt, much to discuss when they met at Casablanca on 14 January. Although Operation Torch had been an outstanding success, there was little doubt that the Battle of the Atlantic had been set back by events since November. The conference went smoothly, and it was agreed – rather to Admiral Ernest King's irritation – that the Atlantic should be reinforced. Although this was obviously most in Britain's interest, there was a certain logic to the plan. Roosevelt was well aware that the loss of shipping between the United States and Britain would make the task of

BELOW: A tanker burns furiously after being torpedoed. Despite the intense fire, the crew managed to extinguish the blaze, and effect makeshift repairs to the gaping hole in the ship's side. The tanker was towed back to the United States and repaired.

opening a second front in Europe a much more difficult task. As Stalin was constantly complaining at the lack of Anglo-American military action in mainland Europe, Roosevelt was prepared to see attention turned towards the Atlantic battle. Churchill identified the requirements for winning the battle as being 65 escorts, a dozen escort carriers and as many Liberators as possible. The role of the Liberators was further clarified, with agreement being reached that some should be based on Newfoundland to close the air gap. This did not mark a sudden change in the fortunes of the Allies, as Admiral King appeared not to have quite the same sense of urgency about matters, and the realignment of resources took rather longer to achieve than was desirable. Potential escorts remained in the Pacific, while Liberators remained on bombing duties in North Africa.

REORGANIZATION

The first signs of reorganization came when the Royal Canadian Navy (RCN) received reinforcement from the Royal Navy. Rather unfortunately, the British took the view – which later mellowed when there was time for more reflection – that the Canadians were inefficient at convoy escort. The reasons for this 'lack of efficiency' were not hard to find. The RCN had expanded greatly in the course of the war, with dramatic reductions in the opportunity to train ships' companies before they put to sea. In addition, the Canadian ships were always last in line for new types of equipment: high-frequency direction finding (HF/DF), Type 271 and other essential tools for tackling the U-boats arrived only slowly, with obvious effects when the convoys faced determined attack. The fact that some of the most disastrous losses were sustained when convoys were escorted by RCN

RIGHT: Escorts from the Royal Canadian Navy (RCN) shepherd their charges into port. The RCN suffered from a number of problems at the start of the war, stemming from a mixture of ships with obsolescent anti-submarine equipment and inexperienced crews who were thrown into an intense battle with no prior training. Once this was overcome, the RCN made an inestimably valuable contribution to winning the Battle of the Atlantic.

LEFT: The crew of a stricken U-boat crowd the conning tower, preparing to abandon their vessel. This became an increasingly familiar sight as the escorts and aircraft exacted an ever-heavier toll of the U-boats.

vessels helped to enhance this impression. The RCN escorts were also assigned to the fast convoys, thus reducing the length of time that they were exposed to the submarine threat. None of this, though, should take anything away from the fact that the RCN's escorts made an invaluable contribution to the Battle of the Atlantic. Sir Percy Noble later said 'the Canadian Navy solved the problem of the Atlantic convoys'. As the Royal Navy began to play an even greater part in the battle, the climax was approaching.

The appalling weather of January 1943 meant that the worldwide shipping losses were reduced to 265,200 tonnes (261,000 tons). The loss of TM1 was a particular blow, but only one North Atlantic convoy – HX222 – was attacked and with the loss of only one ship. This respite was short-lived, as, on 29 January, HX224 was discovered. After three days, a pack formed to attack, and three ships were sunk. In return, a Coastal Command Flying Fortress sank U265. This was a relatively minor event, but a survivor from one of the merchantmen revealed that there was another convoy, SC118, following on the same route. As a result, Dönitz was able to form a pack of 20 U-boats against SC118. To make matters worse, Bletchley Park suffered one of its frustrating temporary blackouts as it still came to grips with the four-rotor Enigma machines. In addition, the Norwegian freighter Vannik inadvertently fired a 'snowflake' illuminant, which could be seen

32km (20 miles) away, giving the U-boats the perfect guide to the convoy.

On the morning of 4 February, the wolfpack closed in. The first action came when the destroyer Vimy, under Lieutenant-Commander Richard Stannard VC, sank U187, after using HF/DF to track it down. By the afternoon, this was a temporary setback for the Germans, as five U-boats were in contact with the convoy. Although heavy air cover prevented attacks on the 5th, on 6–7 February, the U-boats struck. U402, under Siegfried von Forstner sank six ships in four hours (earning himself a Knight's Cross in the process. Air cover returned at daylight, and a Fortress from No. 220 Squadron sank U624, while the Free French corvette Lobelia sank U609. However, on the night of the 7th, Forstner returned to sink his seventh victim. When the battle was broken off on 9 February, SC118 had lost 13 ships, while three U-boats had been sunk and another four seriously damaged. This was one of the hardest fights of the battle so far.

For Admiral Horton, the worrying aspect of the battle was that the losses had been inflicted despite the unusually large escort (including five destroyers). The lesson, once again, was that the escort groups needed integrated training. While the losses to SC118 were a concern, Dönitz – who had replaced Admiral Erich Raeder as head of the entire German Navy at the end of January – was equally concerned with the losses and damage inflicted upon his submarines.

ABOVE: Seen through the attack periscope of a U-boat, a merchant ship just at the moment when the submarine attacks her.

BELOW: The SS *Kemmedine* sinks after being torpedoed by a U-boat. Although the allies were gradually gaining the upper hand in the battle against the U-boat, scenes such as this remained alarmingly common throughout 1942 and 1943.

managed to get the submarine to the surface, where it was rammed by the USCG Campbell, which was damaged. *U606* stayed afloat long enough for the survivors to stand on the deck eating sausage and quaffing champagne while awaiting rescue; in addition, the less-than-popular first lieutenant received a well-delivered punch from one of the crew. This gives a false impression of the success of the escorts. Before *U606* sank, three ships had succumbed to its torpedoes. Despite the experience of the escort group, 14 of the convoy (almost 25 per cent) were sunk. Had the escorts been any less skilled, the tally could have been worse. These losses were extremely serious, and March would become even more critical.

THE HEIGHT OF BATTLE

The crisis point of the campaign came with attacks on four successive convoys – SC121, HX228, SC122 and HX229. Once again, Spencer was in the midst of the action, being the mid-ocean escort for SC121. Heineman was less well served with escorts, as, although he had a destroyer, there were only four corvettes available. The convoy covered an area of 11km (7 miles), making it difficult to defend. To make matters more difficult, the weather was so bad that the escorts' radar would not work; three had defective asdic. Two wolfpacks, made up of 24 boats, lay in the path of SC121, while seven more were in the vicinity. The weather meant that there was considerable difficulty in maintaining the wolfpacks' patrol lines, and SC121 initially managed to pass by unscathed. A redeployment of the boats helped, and the convoy was shadowed. On the night of 6–7 March, *U566* and *U230* made contact, sinking one merchantman. Contact was lost in a Force 10 gale the next day, but regained on 8 March. Over the course of the next three days, 12 more ships were sunk.

The presence of the wolfpacks meant that HX228 was ordered to evade to the south, but the instruction was intercepted and a pack sent in. On 10 March, HX228 was spotted by *U336*. HX228, unlike SC121, was exceptionally well escorted. Escort Group B3, under Commander A.A. Tait, contained four destroyers, along with five corvettes. In addition, the American Carrier Support Group TU 24.4.1 (also known as Escort Group 6), was also travelling with the convoy. This contained the escort carrier USS *Bogue* and two destroyers. With the stormy weather, however, *Bogue* would not initially be able to make a contribution to the defence of the convoy.

The other great convoy battle of February was against ON166, guarded by the US escort group A3, commanded by Captain Paul R. Heineman in the US Coastguard cutter Spencer. Heineman also had one other US Coastguard cutter and five corvettes drawn from the RCN and the Royal Navy. The group was made up of experienced captains, which was fortunate considering what would happen. Signals interceptions (this time by the *Luftwaffe's* listening service rather than B-Dienst) gave the location of the convoy, and a pack was duly deployed against it. Dönitz assembled 21 U-boats, and they attacked on 21 February. The initial attack went badly, when Spencer sank *U225*. The next day, *U606* was sunk, mainly as a result of an incorrectly sealed conning tower hatch. The crew

The battle began when *U336* was located by HF/DF and driven off. *U444* was able to remain in contact. On 10 March, *U444*'s signals enabled *U221* to attack, sinking two ships. Within a few hours, *U336*, *U86*, *U406* and *U757* had also joined in, sinking two more ships. One of the victims was the *Brant County*, which was carrying munitions. The explosion that ripped the merchantman apart damaged *U757*. It was at this point that the battle turned against the escorts. Commander Tait, in HMS *Harvester*, sighted *U444* on the surface and attacked. The submarine managed to submerge, but Tait forced her to surface with a vigorous depth-charge attack. As soon as *U444* surfaced, Tait charged in and rammed the submarine. As *Harvester* hit, the submarine scraped along the keel and became wedged under the destroyer's propellers. *U444* broke free and remained afloat, only to be sunk by the Free French corvette *Aconit* which then steamed in and rammed her.

During the morning, *Harvester's* damaged propellers gave up, and she came to a standstill. *U432* spotted the stricken ship and sank her. The gallant Tait and the majority of his crew went down with the ship. The crew of the *Aconit* saw the smoke from the sinking *Harvester*, and the ship hurried to the scene. *Aconit* obtained an asdic contact and depth-charged *U432*. The U-boat was forced to the surface and was engaged by a hail of gunfire from the corvette. This did not finish off the submarine, and *Aconit* charged in and sank her by ramming. The weather relented on 12 March, and *Bogue* was able to launch aircraft, keeping the U-boats submerged. The arrival of aircraft from Coastal Command made the situation far too dangerous for the U-boats to undertake further attacks, and the battle was called off. It ended with four merchantmen and one destroyer lost, with two U-boats sunk and two seriously damaged.

ABOVE: A depth charge explodes after being released against a U-boat contact. Although the explosion looks impressive, if the U-boat was at a greater depth than the charge was set for, it would escape the worst effects of the blast. Captains of many escorts developed something akin to a sixth sense in judging the correct depth settings for their charges.

THE CLIMAX

While SC121 and HX228 were fierce battles, they were relatively minor compared to the vicious events in which SC122 and HX229 became involved. SC122 left New York on 5 March, covered by Escort Group B5, led by Commander R.C. Boyle in the destroyer Havelock. Boyle had a US Navy destroyer, a frigate, five corvettes and a trawler at his disposal. HX229 left on 8 March, accompanied by Escort Group B4.

As usual, signals interception gave Dönitz the opportunity to deploy eight boats against SC122, followed by a newly formed pack of 18 U-boats. Another 11 boats were sent after HX229. After problems caused by the weather, the eight-boat pack (Group Raubgraf) was guided in by U653 on 16 March, not against SC122, which had been driven past the group by a gale, but against HX229. Three ships were sunk that night; the following morning, five more fell victim to the pack. The 18-boat group (Stürmer) arrived on the scene on the 17th, adding to the convoy's difficulties. To complicate the picture of the battle, SC122 had arrived in the area, providing the wolfpacks with a host of targets. This caused considerable confusion at U-Boat HQ, but gave the

submarines unprecedented opportunities. *U338* sank four ships from SC122 using five torpedoes, gaining a fifth victim later in the day. Two more merchantmen from HX229 went down at lunchtime, and it appeared that the convoy was absolutely at the mercy of the pack. The losses already sustained were serious enough, but the convoys were spared absolute disaster – although it did not seem like this at the time – by the presence of Coastal Command.

CHANGES IN COASTAL COMMAND

On 5 February 1943, Air Marshal Sir John Slessor, who would ultimately become the professional head of the Royal Air Force (RAF), replaced Sir Philip Joubert as head of Coastal Command. Just as Horton had done to Western Approaches Command, Slessor brought new vigour to Coastal Command, building upon the unstinting work of his predecessor. The command had enjoyed success against U-boats for much of 1942, even though it had been lacking all the tools for the job.

The threat from Coastal Command attacks in the Bay of Biscay became so serious that Dönitz was compelled to search for some solution. The solution lay in giving the U-

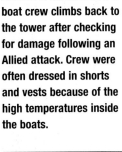

BELOW: A member of a U-boat crew climbs back to the tower after checking for damage following an Allied attack. Crew were often dressed in shorts and vests because of the high temperatures inside the boats.

ABOVE: Elements of an East Coast convoy, seen from the bow of one of the Escorting destroyers, November 1942.

boats early warning of an approaching aircraft, thus allowing them to dive. The answer was found in the French company Metox, which had designed equipment capable of receiving radar signals. This was rushed into production and given to the U-boats, mounted in an extemporized installation. The receiver aerial was mounted on a simple wooden cross, which could be fitted into a socket on the conning tower. As soon as a submarine broke the surface, one of the crew would rush to the conning tower and slot the receiver equipment into the socket. Despite the crude nature of the mounting, Metox was extremely effective, giving just enough warning of ASV-equipped aircraft to allow the submarine to dive.

U-boat skippers were pleased to have the equipment, but were unhappy at its basic nature. When they dived, they had to remember to demount Metox. Also, the wire that trailed from the aerial down to the receiver equipment had a nasty habit of becoming fouled in the tower hatch, slowing the speed of the dive or allowing water in if the hatch was not as tightly shut as it might have been.

For the Allies, the solution to Metox would come with the development of ASV III, which operated on the 10cm (4in) wavelength (also known as centimetric radar) and was undetectable by Metox. The problem, as always, was one of resources. Bomber Command had priority for the centimetric radar in the form of the H2S set (allegedly so called because a senior officer, when asked for his thoughts on the use of radar for ground mapping, said 'it stinks' – scientific humour then meant that the codename was obvious). The centimetric sets were made in the United States, and it was arranged that the Liberators slowly coming off the production lines and reaching British service should be fitted with them. More importantly, Coastal Command began to receive more Liberators. This saved HX229 and SC122 from complete disaster.

SC122 AND HX 229

Coastal Command, so long hampered by the dwindling supply of aircraft to No. 120 Squadron, now found itself with two squadrons. Two of the Liberators, flying from Northern Ireland, arrived over SC122 on 17 March and kept the U-boats underwater for the course of the day.

ABOVE: Two U-boats, surprised on the surface by an allied aircraft. The boat on the right appears to have been subjected to a near miss from depth charges.

Another *Liberator* covered HX229 and had a hectic time, severely shaking the crews of *U221* and *U608*, and attacking another, unidentified boat with its guns once the depth-charges had been expended. The average duration of the *Liberator* flights was 18 hours.

Two more merchantmen were lost from HX229 while its air cover changed over. During the night, SC122 lost two more ships; however, after this, the two convoys lost only three more. The U-boats began reporting that there was a very heavy air escort, and a dozen of them broke off. On the afternoon of the 18th, HMS *Highlander* found HX229. By the morning of 19 March, no U-boat had been accounted for by the escorts or air cover, but by this stage the convoys had entered Western Approaches water, where the shorter ranged aircraft of Coastal Command were able to join in the fray, in the process sinking *U384*.

The results of these convoy battles were received with jubilation at U-Boat HQ. Out of 90 merchant ships, 22 were sunk, for the loss of just one submarine, which had not fallen to the escorts. A total of 148,300 tonnes (146,000 tons) of shipping had been sunk in one battle, and the Admiralty despaired. It appeared that, despite all the

benefits of long-range aircraft, convoys and escort groups, the Germans were about to disrupt communications between the United States and Britain. In the first 20 days, 95 ships were sunk. This took place against the backdrop of a conference where already concerned Allied military leaders debated how to protect the convoys from the apparently rampant U-boats. If they could not find the answer, they feared, they might lose the war.

FINDING THE ANSWERS

The conference began badly, when Admiral King made clear that he was going to withdraw all US Navy forces from the transatlantic convoy routes. The solution worked out was to create a Canadian operational command in the North West Atlantic, which would come into operation in May. King's news was unwelcome, but turned out to be less important than it might have been. The conference was confronted by evidence from Professor Blackett that a force of 200 VLR aircraft might be expected to save at least 400 ships. As we have seen, Coastal Command had two operational squadrons of Liberators, with a third forming. The Canadians had formed squadrons of crews that had no aircraft, while every single US Liberator not in the Pacific Theatre was being used to bomb something – either Germany itself or targets in North Africa. The earlier agreement at Casablanca that 80 VLR aircraft should be assigned to the Atlantic had been subverted, largely by King, who had kept his VLR aircraft in the Pacific. His opposition would have continued to scupper the chances of getting aircraft into the Atlantic Theatre, but he found himself outmanoeuvred. Roosevelt overruled him and ordered that 60 US Navy Liberators would be used to cover the North Atlantic, the Army Air Force would deploy another 75 for anti-submarine duties, while deliveries to the RAF would be expedited, so that 120 Liberators would be available. The first 20 aircraft from this massive increase in resources arrived in the last 10 days of March. The Atlantic air gap had finally been plugged.

Simultaneously, the Admiralty began to appreciate the reason for the apparent failure of convoys. The number of independent sailings had been reduced to such a low level that the U-boats had very little in the way of targets for attack. This meant that they were bound to attack convoys, and, given that there were so few on independent operations, the size of the packs was bound to be larger, creating difficulties for the escorts. The answer was air cover, as this forced the U-boats to submerge, with all the difficulties this entailed for effective operations. It was not just the increase in VLR aircraft that helped, but also the arrival, at last, of the escort carriers. The great German tactical victory against SC122 and HX229 was misleading. The pessimism of the Allies was misplaced, while the jubilation of the Germans at the apparent breakthrough was soon shown to be premature.

April began to give signs that the U-boat threat was being overcome. Between 4 and 7 April, an attack was mounted against HX231, comprising 61 merchant ships. Commander Peter Gretton in the frigate HMS *Tay* led the Escort Group B7, accompanied by a destroyer and four corvettes. Although the convoy was small, and only one ship was fitted with HF/DF, Escort Group B7 beat off a concerted attack. Using an HF/DF bearing, Gretton sank *U635*; a Liberator from No. 86 Squadron accounted for *U632*; and the air and sea escorts damaged another four boats so badly that they had to head for home. For three ships sunk, this was hardly a decent return. May arrived, and the U-boats found that the situation was far, far worse.

On 29 April, ONS5 was sighted, and the convoy ran into the largest pack of the war, made up of no fewer than 40 vessels. A ship was sunk that night, but the battle was truly joined on 4 May. Six ships were sunk, and the night was filled with frantic activity by the rescue trawlers recovering survivors. The next day, a Royal Canadian Air Force *Canso* (the Canadian version of the *Catalina*) sank *U630* ahead of the storm-

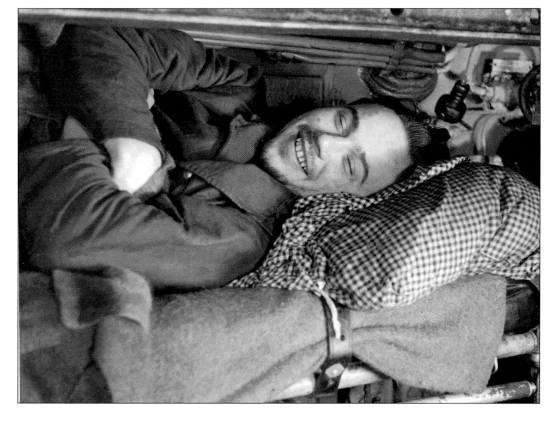

LEFT: Despite the discomfort of his surroundings, this U-boat crewman seems only to need a pillow and the chance to lie down to keep him reasonably happy.

tossed convoy. That evening, the U-boats pounced. Seven more ships were sunk, but the escorts damaged an equal number of submarines. *U192* was sunk by HMS *Pink* on the morning of the 5th, and all attempted attacks were beaten off. After dark, four merchantmen were sunk, but now the escorts gained the upper hand. HMS *Loosestrife* caught *U638* on the surface and charged in towards the submarine. *U638* got beneath the waves, but *Loosestrife* pounded the diving U-boat with depth-charges and destroyed it. HMS *Vidette* located *U125* and used the forward-firing *Hedgehog* anti-submarine bombs to good effect, blowing the U-boat to pieces. *U531* was rammed by HMS *Oribi* and sank. Although fog descended, the sloop HMS *Pelican* used ASV to find *U438* and sank it. At 09:15 hours on 6 May, U-Boat HQ called off the attack. Twelve merchant ships had been sunk, but, crucially, the U-boats had suffered a mortal blow. No escorts were lost or seriously damaged, but eight U-boats had been sunk in the course of the action – two having collided – while another five were so seriously damaged that they limped home in a sorry state.

The supremacy of the escorts was detected by Bletchley Park, which reported ever more urgent exhortations to the U-boat

USS *DUNCAN*

Country:	USA
Crew:	350
Displacement:	3606 tonnes (3549 tons)
Dimensions:	120m (393ft) x 12.5m (41ft) x 5.8m (19ft)
Armament:	Six 126mm (5in) guns, three quad 40mm (1.5in) cannon, six torpedo tubes
Powerplant:	Turbines, driving two shafts
Range:	19,075.6km (10,300nm)
Performance:	35 knots

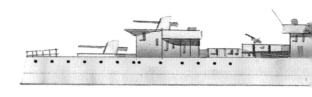

commanders as they carried out their duties. The escorts, by now battle-hardened, became ever more confident, as escort carriers and the VLR aircraft provided them with yet more tools to defeat the submarine threat.

On 16 May, HX237 made port having lost just three merchantmen, with the escorts

HEDGEHOG

Range:	228-250m (250-280 yards)
Mount weight:	13kg (28.780lb)
Sinking speed:	25 f/s / 7.6 m/s
Rate of fire:	1 per 3 minutes
Charge:	30kg (65lb)

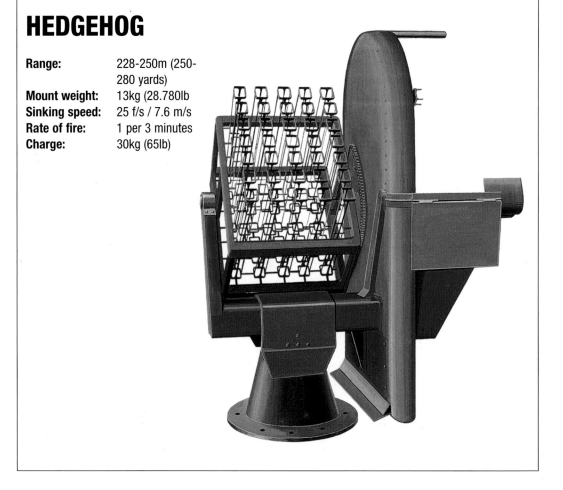

LEFT: The crew of a *Type VII* U-boat take to their dinghies after their submarine has been crippled by an attack.

TINTAGEL CASTLE

Country:	Britain
Crew:	120
Displacement:	1077 tonnes (1060 tons)
Dimensions:	76.8m (251ft) x 11.2m (36ft) x 3.05m (10ft)
Armament:	One 101mm (4in) Dual Purpose gun, two twin, six single 20mm (0.8in) cannon. Squid AS mortar and 15 depth charges
Powerplant:	One triple expansion steam engine
Range:	6910km (3731nm) at 15 knots
Performance:	16.5 knots

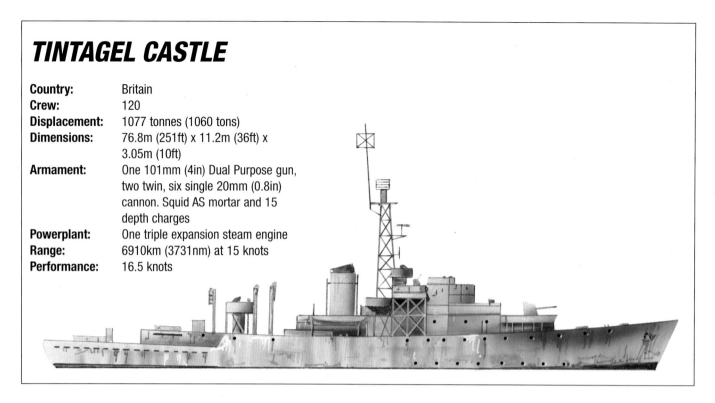

ABOVE: The limitations of the *Flower* class corvettes led to the decision to build an improved corvette, known as the *Castle* class. As well as overcoming many of the failings of the *Flowers*, the *Castles* could carry the Squid anti-submarine mortar. As the *Castles* did not have the speed to match the Royal Navy's frigates, they tended to be employed in homogeneous escort groups.

having accounted for *U89*, *U186* and *U456*, while *U402* and *U223* were seriously damaged. A pack had been decimated for little return. The next convoy of note was SC130, escorted by B7 under the inimitable Peter Gretton. Gretton informed the convoy Commodore, Captain Forsythe, that he did not wish to be held up, as he was getting married when he reached Britain. Forsythe returned that he was due to play a round of golf on the same day. Although Forsythe was keen to help Gretton, there has to be a suspicion that he regarded his game of golf as being the more important of the two functions that day.

SC130 ran into fog and nearly collided with an iceberg, but for the alertness and quick thinking of the crew of the destroyer *Vidette*, which warned the shipping away. The next problem came in the form of a pack of 33 U-boats, which were detected by Bletchley Park and through HF/DF intercepts from the convoy. Nothing was found on 18 May, and, on the next night, HMS *Duncan* ran down an HF/DF bearing just in time to see a U-boat submerging sufficiently far ahead to escape.

At first light, *Liberators* from No. 120 Squadron arrived overhead and reported that there were submarines all around the convoy. In the course of the next 12 hours, the U-boats made repeated attempts to force their way into the convoy, but ran into the escorts. *U381* made one too many attempts and was pounced upon by the *Duncan* and HMS *Snowflake*, which sank the submarine in a veritable storm of hedgehog bombs.

Later that day, the 1st Escort Group joined the convoy, adding a cutter and three frigates to the convoy's strength. This did not deter the U-boats, which attacked again. This was fatal for *U954*, which was dispatched by a Liberator. *U209* was sunk by the escorts, and a Hudson from No. 269 Squadron sank *U273*. On the 20th, *U258* was surprised on the surface by another Liberator and went to the bottom as a result of the attack. On the morning of the 21 May, the pack was called off. Not only had the submarines not sunk a single ship from SC130, but also they had not even fired a single torpedo. In return, five U-boats had been lost, with Dönitz's son Peter among the casualties.

Gretton made the church on time. There is no available evidence relating to Forsythe's round of golf, but it is probable that he enjoyed it. Whether the two men realized the size of the blow they had inflicted upon the U-boats is not certain.

THE BAY OFFENSIVE

While the VLR aircraft were enjoying successes, those conducting operations in the Bay of Biscay were gaining the upper hand as well. The introduction of centrimetric radar meant that it was impossible for the Metox equipment to give early warning, and Dönitz was forced to order U-boat skippers to cross the bay submerged, recharging their batteries during the day. This meant surfacing, and Dönitz's answer to the air threat was to order U-boats to shoot it out with attacking aircraft in daylight. He may have been misled by the success of Peter Cremer, who had managed to shoot down an attacking Wellington when *U333* was surprised on the surface in March. Dönitz had called for a further increase in anti-aircraft armament, and, though this led to deadly duels between aircraft and submarine, it also made life far more dangerous. Seven U-boats fell to Coastal Command in May. The month was becoming worse; by the end of it, Dönitz saw that the writing was on the wall.

VICTORY

Despite the gloomy predictions of early March 1943, the Admiralty had in place almost all the tools it required to defeat the U-boat threat. It was missing two crucial elements – land and organic air power. When used in conjunction with the escorts, aircraft forced submarines to stay submerged, where they were far less effective. Aircraft were not some wonder weapon, but the final tool required to complete the job. Added to determined, experienced escorts, the up-to-date intelligence provided by Bletchley Park, Operational Research and the benefits of developing technology, the balance had been tilted firmly in favour of the Allies. By 22 May 1943, 31 U-boats had been lost, with U-Boat HQ desperately attempting to contact them. On 24 May, Dönitz radioed his surviving commanders, talking of the increasing difficulty of their struggle. He told them that only U-boats could fight the enemy offensively. The German nation, no less, was looking to them as the most decisive weapon the country possessed. The outcome of the war, Dönitz said, rested on the success or failure of the Battle of the Atlantic.

On the same day, Dönitz ordered his boats out of the North Atlantic to the easier waters south of the Azores. Despite his exhortations, he knew something that his determined crews did not. They had lost.

BELOW: A whaler from a Royal Canadian Navy frigate comes alongside having rescued survivors from a U-boat sunk while attacking the convoy which was being escorted.

CHAPTER SEVEN

THE FINAL RECKONING: JUNE 1943 – MAY 1945

The defeats of May 1943 meant that the U-boat was no longer a war-winning weapon for Germany. Despite this, the threat posed by the submarine remained a cause for concern.

The victory against the U-boats in May 1943 came about not because of the sudden introduction of enough Liberators, but as the end result of three years and nine months of incessant and often bloody battle. Although victory had been achieved, it was not a victory that could simply be taken for granted. Another two years of maintaining dominance against the threat posed by German submarines was required. The Allies were in the fortunate position of having rendered the U-boat fleet virtually obsolete by June 1943. Airborne radar meant that staying on the surface was not an option, and the *Type VII* and *Type IX* boats did not have sufficient underwater speed or endurance. They could not catch convoys, nor could they stay in close enough touch with them to be effective. Also, even though the anti-submarine aircraft did not achieve a 'kill' every time that they found a surfaced U-boat, this did not matter: forcing the submarine to dive meant that they had succeeded in dramatically reducing the threat posed by that boat.

LEFT: Dawn breaks over an Atlantic convoy, 1944. Dawn meant a reduction in the threat of a U-boat attack, since the submarines relied upon night-surface attacks to be fully effective. Nonetheless, vigilance was still required.

TYPE XXI

Country:	Germany	**Powerplant:**	Diesel electric motors
Launch date:	April 1944 (first in class)	**Performance:**	15.6 knots surfaced,
Crew:	57		17.6 knots submerged
Dimensions:	76.7m (251ft) x 6.62m (22ft) x 6.2m (20ft)		
Displacement:	1647 tonnes (1621 tons) surfaced, 1848 tonnes (1819 tons) submerged		
Armament:	Six 533mm (21in) torpedo tubes, four 20mm (0.8in) cannon or four 30mm (1.19in) cannon		

ABOVE: The *Type XXI*, which had dramatically more power than its predecessors, was designed as a stop-gap boat while the closed cycle engine developed by Professor Walter (allowing greatly increased underwater operation) was perfected.

BELOW: The *Type XVII* made use of the Walter closed-cycle hydrogen peroxide engine, permitting extended use underwater. Fortunately for the Allies, the engine suffered numerous developmental problems, and the *Type XVII* never reached full service.

The technological war between submarine and aircraft therefore intensified, as the Germans endeavoured to produce submarines that could operate effectively underwater and the Allies attempted to make sure that their technology was adequate to prevent such boats becoming a serious threat. The Germans succeeded in developing the first true submarine – one that could operate effectively while submerged – but it was already too late. Continuing attacks by Allied forces meant that the U-boats were always at a disadvantage, no matter how innovative the technology employed.

Dönitz was convinced that he already knew the solution to these problems. This was a U-boat that could travel at high speed underwater. In 1936, Professor Helmut Walter had put forward the idea of using a hydrogen-peroxide engine, eliminating the

need for the submarine to surface and recharge batteries. Dönitz had been most impressed with the invention, and urged German High Command to investigate further, funding more research. The difficulty, as always, was that of resources. The perceived need to build surface units and the radical nature of Walter's proposals discouraged any further development.

Dönitz did not forget about the engine, and, by 1942, resumed his efforts to have the project accepted. Dönitz explained that a U-boat using the new propulsion system would render useless all anti-submarine measures then in place. This may have been overstating the case in one regard, as the Allies were improving the means of underwater detection (asdic) and their depth-charge technology – both conventional charges and devices such as the Hedgehog would have offered some means of countering the threat. Crucially,

TYPE XVII

Country:	Germany	**Armament:**	Two 533mm (21in) torpedo tubes
Launch date:	September 1943 (first in class)		
Crew:	19	**Powerplant:**	Diesel and Walter closed cycle engine
Dimensions:	41.5m (136ft) x 3.4m (11ft) x 4.25m (14ft)	**Surface range:**	3450km (1862.85nm)
Displacement:	317 tonnes (312 tons) surfaced, 362 tonnes (357 tons) submerged	**Performance:**	9 knots surfaced, 21-25 knots submerged

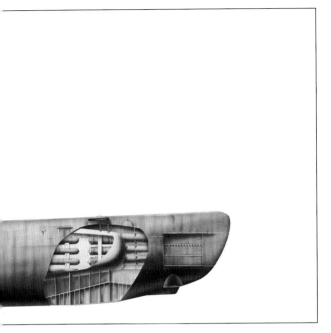

though, maritime patrol aircraft would not have had the means of attacking the new submarines, thus making the life of the escorts far more difficult. Admiral Erich Raeder was convinced, and an order for 180 Walter engine-powered boats was placed in June 1942. The engine did not prove easy to develop, however, and the ongoing problems with it led to the order being cancelled in November 1942. This did not mark the end of the project, as experimental work on it was still funded. What was clear was that the engine would take time to develop as a workable piece of technology, and ordering 180 boats was too advanced a step to take.

The Walter-powered boat was not the only solution to the problem, however, as the first design drawings for the *Type XXI* and *Type XXIII* submarines appeared in June 1943. While these did not offer the same level of underwater endurance that the

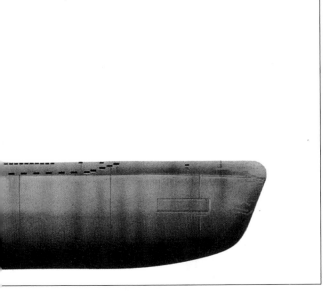

Walter boats promised, the performance was still impressive. Whereas the earlier U-boat types had often been limited to single-figure speeds underwater, the *Type XXI* and *Type XXIII* could offer submerged performance of 18 knots for 90 minutes, or 12-14 knots for anything up to 10 hours. This was a promising development, but there was a major snag. The schedule of production for the new design meant that the first two *Type XXIs* would not be ready until the end of 1944; mass production would commence in 1945, and the type would not be operational until 1946. Dönitz was appalled. It was clear that there was a fundamental problem with procurement, whereby all production other than the German Navy's was under the control of Albert Speer, the head of the Ministry of

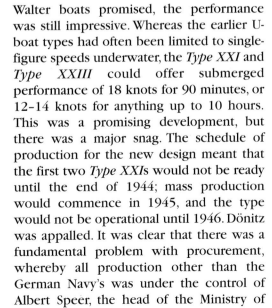

ABOVE: A completed U-boat slides down the slipway. The German U-boat building programme proved inadequate to meet the demands placed upon the submarine arm. Although revolutionary new boats were developed, they came too late to make any impact upon the war.

Speer appointed Otto Merker to oversee the naval programme, and he set to work with a will. Merker's solution to the building problems was simple: delays were caused at the shipyards, so U-boats would not be built there. Merker proposed to build U-boats at inland factories, transport them to the coast in sections and assemble and equip them there. This would obviate the need for space at shipyards and cut the amount of labour required to build the *Type XXI* dramatically. Instead of the agonizingly slow plan initially put forward, the new programme would see the first *Type XXI* enter service in 1944, with sufficient numbers in service by the autumn of that year for a proper campaign to be mounted. Furthermore, rather than continue construction of the old and now outmoded boats, only *Type XXI*s and *Type XXIII*s would be built.

This was a splendid plan in theory, but the practice was rather different. Speer and Merker had not taken into account the disruption that would be caused by bombing. The 10-day long attack against Hamburg, beginning on 25 July 1943, inflicted such devastation that Speer was moved to observe that six more attacks of this sort would destroy German armament production. For the U-boats, the attack on

ABOVE: Admiral Dönitz (left) and Albert Speer, seen in May 1945. Dönitz appreciated that the U-boat building programme would be more likely to achieve success if placed under Speer's control. Despite great efforts, by the time this picture was taken, the U-boats – and Germany – had been totally defeated.

Arms and Munitions. The navy had guarded this division in the past, but Dönitz saw that the system actually worked against his efforts. With Hitler's agreement, Dönitz allowed Speer to take over the running of naval production, with dramatic results.

RIGHT: A line of incomplete U-boats discovered in Bremen harbour by the Allies after they occupied Germany. The scene was repeated on a smaller scale in a number of dockyards.

TYPE XXIII

Country:	Germany	**Dimensions:**	34.1m (112ft) x 3m (10ft) x 3.75m (12ft)
Launch date:	April 1944 (first in class)	**Armament:**	Two 533mm (21in) torpedo tubes
Crew:	14	**Powerplant:**	Diesel electric motors
Displacement:	235 tonnes (232 tons) surfaced, 260 tonnes (256 tons) submerged	**Surface range:**	2500km (1349.9nm) at 12 knots
		Performance:	10 knots surfaced, 12.5 knots submerged

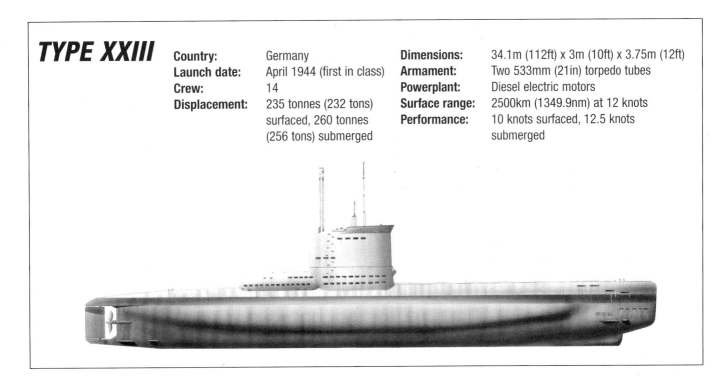

just one city was bad enough: the Blohm und Voss submarine construction facility was severely damaged. Production was delayed by at least four weeks, and it was obvious that further attacks would destroy the submarine-building plan before it had even begun. Merker immediately ordered the construction of a huge submarine factory near Bremen (which included an indoor facility to test submarines underwater), but this took time to construct. In addition, getting the submarines from the factory to the sea demanded the use of the extensive German canal network. By the autumn of 1944, this was under attack. On 23 September 1944, Lancasters from No. 617 Squadron attacked the Dortmund-Ems canal aqueduct and inflicted such damage that traffic was brought to a complete standstill. A huge repair effort saw the canal back in operation in early November: Bomber Command came back and wrecked it again. Such damage meant that Dönitz would never receive the submarines that he needed to reverse the situation in the Atlantic. It was not only through attacking German infrastructure that aircraft played a part in continuing to keep the U-boat threat contained.

AIRCRAFT VERSUS SUBMARINE

By the summer of 1943, Allied aircraft held the advantage over the submarine. Thanks to the slow introduction of the U-boats that would have made their task far more difficult, they were able to make notable advances using new equipment. In the battle for HX237, the destruction of *U266* on 13 May by a Liberator of 86 Squadron had been made possible by a 'Mark 24' Mine.

The Mark 24 was not a mine at all, but a homing torpedo, known as 'Fido', activated by the cavitation of a U-boat's propeller. Although this was a nascent piece of technology, the success on 13 May was followed less than 24 hours later when a Catalina from the VP-84 used the same device to account for *U657*.

The day before Dönitz conceded defeat in the Battle of the Atlantic, a Swordfish flying from the escort carrier HMS *Archer* used rocket projectiles to attack *U752*. Although rockets were an inaccurate weapon, suffering from 'gravity drop', the pilot of the Swordfish scored three hits from eight, rupturing the pressure hull. *U752* surfaced with the intention of driving the Swordfish away with anti-aircraft fire, but found that the biplane was accompanied by a Grumman Wildcat from the carrier, which strafed the boat. The U-boat skipper was killed, and the crew abandoned ship.

The use of rocket projectiles increased throughout the year. Although the weapon is most famous for its use against tanks in the Normandy campaign, the rocket projectile played an important part in the war against submarines. It gave a means of attacking surfaced U-boats outside the range of their increasingly formidable anti-aircraft armament and brought the Bristol Beaufighter further into the battle against the submarine. The Beaufighter had been the mainstay of Coastal Command's fighter operations in the Bay of Biscay, and had been the primary weapon in anti-shipping strikes from late 1941. From 1944, it would be joined by the de Havilland Mosquito, probably the most versatile aircraft of World War II.

ABOVE: The *Type XXIII* was a coastal submarine, and like the *Type XXI* relied upon increased battery power to permit much greater underwater endurance than had been possible before. The *Type XXIII* caused some concern to the Allies in the last days of the war, sinking a number of ships with apparent impunity.

ABOVE: A Sunderland GR V
of 201 Squadron takes off
from Lough Erne, Northern
Ireland, during 1945,
heading on another patrol.

Like the Beaufighter, the Mosquito was primarily used on shipping strikes, but the rocket projectile meant that the aircraft was highly effective against U-boats. The main version used was the FB VI, with 20mm (0.8in) cannon and 7.7mm (0.303in) machine guns, but this was later joined by the Mosquito FB XVIII, fitted with a 57mm (2.24in) Mollins Gun (itself based on the army's 2.72kg (six-pounder) anti-tank gun). The FB XVIII was only produced in small numbers, though, as priority went to the more conventionally armed FB VI, which was in considerable demand throughout the RAF's commands. The FB XVIII also suffered

some structural problems caused by the fierce recoil of the gun. Despite this, it was a formidable weapon. The continuing development of such aircraft gave Coastal Command a great advantage, which would become quickly apparent in the climax of the battles in the Bay of Biscay.

WAR IN THE BAY

Those U-boats that had survived the defeat by the convoy escorts were formed into a new group during June 1943 and given instructions to concentrate their efforts about 970km (600 miles) west of the Azores. This lull in the North Atlantic campaign

RIGHT: A Beaufighter fires
rocket projectiles at a
surface target just out of
shot. A full salvo of eight
rocket projectiles was
claimed to have the same
power as a broadside from
a cruiser.

caused Coastal Command to consider the likely next move by the U-boats. On his own initiative, Sir John Slessor concentrated around 70 aircraft to reinforce the patrols flying against the U-boats' transit routes. Dönitz was well aware of the threat posed by aircraft and ordered that U-boats sail in groups across the Bay of Biscay. The policy of staying submerged during the hours of darkness and surfacing for brief periods during the day remained in place. The intention was for the U-boats to use their anti-aircraft armament against attacking aircraft. Submarines were to be kept in groups so that their combined firepower would present a formidable threat to any aircraft that chose to intervene.

On 1 June, an inbound boat, *U418* was encountered by a Beaufighter, which sank the submarine with its rocket projectiles. The U-boats heading to sea did rather better at first. The Ju 88s became much more active, and, on 2 June, a Sunderland of No. 461 Squadron was attacked by no fewer than eight of these aircraft. The attack lasted for nearly an hour, but demonstrated the Sunderland's now legendary reputation for toughness: the Sunderland's crew shot down three of the attackers and, despite losing an engine and sustaining heavy damage, flew back to Cornwall and landed safely. To counter this renewed threat, Beaufighters, accompanied by a Mosquito squadron from Fighter Command, started to fly patrols in the bay. The Beaufighter had already demonstrated its superiority over the Ju 88, and the Mosquito was even better. The aggressive patrolling by the two squadrons did much to dampen the enthusiasm of the

Luftwaffe, making the task of the anti-submarine patrols easier again.

From 5 June, there were a number of sightings and attacks on U-boats. These resulted in the loss of two aircraft for no submarines sunk, but these figures do not tell the whole story: the U-boat crews suffered heavy casualties in the attacks, prompting Dönitz to instruct that the boats were only to surface when they had to charge their batteries. If located by aircraft, they were still to fight back rather than dive.

On 20 June, the 2nd Escort Group, commanded by Captain F.J. 'Johnnie' Walker from the sloop *Starling,* arrived in the area to cooperate with the Coastal Command patrols. The reason for this increase in force stemmed from a plan to intercept the 'milch-cow' U-boats that were so important to extending the endurance of the U-boat operations. The idea came from the US Navy, which wished to exploit the highly accurate decryptions being made by Bletchley Park. This met with some initial opposition, as the British were desperate not to give any clues that German signals were being read fluently. The plan was saved by implementing a cover scheme that used patrolling aircraft to locate the tankers. The presence of aircraft would suggest that the submarines had been located by regular air patrols that had chanced upon their targets. On 11 June, the tankers *U118* and *U460* had received a signal from *U758,* which needed resupply. The signal was routinely intercepted and gave enough clues to allow an attack to be planned. Task Force 21.12, containing the USS *Bogue,* headed for the area, and her aircraft found *U118* just where the intelligence information had said

BELOW: A *Type XB* minelayer, *U118* was also used as an auxiliary tanker. While operating in this role on 12 June 1943, *U118* was surprised on the surface by aircraft from the USS *Bogue* and blew up after a vigorous depth charge attack.

U118

Country:	Germany	**Armament:**	Two 533mm (21in) torpedo tubes,
Launch date:	September 1941		one-four 20mm (0.8in) cannon one
Crew:	52		37mm gun (1.4in) and one 105mm
Displacement:	1791 tonnes (1763		(4in) gun. 66 mines
	tons) surfaced, 2212	**Powerplant:**	Diesel electric motors
	tonnes (2177 tons)	**Surface range:**	117,987km (63,708nm) at 12 knots
	submerged	**Performance:**	16.5 knots surfaced, 7 knots
Dimensions:	89.8m (295ft) x 9.2m		submerged
	(30ft) x 4.11m (13ft)		

USS *BOGUE*

Country:	United States	**Performance:**	18 knots
Launch date:	1942	**Armament:**	Two 126mm (5in) guns, four
Crew:	890		40mm (1.5in) cannon, 12 20mm
Displacement:	11,176 tonnes (11,000		(0.8in) cannon
	tons)	**Aircraft:**	Up to 28. Usual complement 12
Dimensions:	151.1m (495ft) x 34m		Grumman TBF Avenger and 12
	(111ft) x 7.92m (26ft)		Grumman F4F Wildcat

BELOW: *U464* seen alongside. A *Type XIV* tanker, *U464* was sunk in August 1942 by a Catalina from the US Navy's VP-73 patrol squadron. Two crewmen were lost, but 53 others were rescued.

she would be on the afternoon of the 12th. Nine aircraft assailed the unfortunate *U118*, which blew up after a vigorous strafing and depth-charge attack. Walker struck next.

An aircraft sighting of *U119* led Walker to the Bay of Biscay on 24 June, and he began a search where the last reported sighting had been. Asdic contact was soon obtained, and the unfortunate submarine was plastered with depth-charges. *U119* surfaced, whereupon Walker duly rammed and sank it. The tankers continued to suffer. Once again, an intercept gave away the fact that Dönitz was sending 10 *Type IXs* to operate in the Indian Ocean, which would refuel from *U487*. Four escort carriers were sent to find her, and, on the early evening of 13 July, aircraft from USS

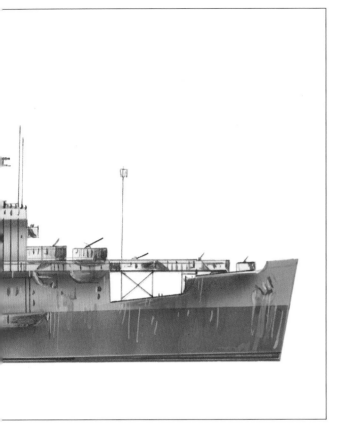

(0.8in) cannon mounting and two twin heavy machine guns. When the Wellington, piloted by Flying Officer W.H.T. Jennings, attacked, it ran into a hail of gunfire, even though the U-boat crew had been totally surprised and had not been able to get to the quad-20mm (0.8in) mount. Jennings was either killed or wounded in this attack, and the Wellington – perhaps aimed by the mortally wounded pilot, perhaps not – slammed into the side of the submarine. Three depth-charges ended up amongst the wreckage on the submarine deck, and the crew threw these over the side. As part of normal procedure, these depth-charges were set to go off at 7.62m (25ft), making it imperative that *U459* vacate the area quickly. As a result of the damage, the submarine could not do this and was caught in the blast from the charges when they went off. *U459* was crippled and could not do anything.

The surviving crewman from the Wellington tried to attract the attention of the Germans, but gave up when he realized that the submarine was out of control. He was glad he did when he heard the sound of engines. Another Wellington, this time from No. 547 Squadron, spotted *U459* and attacked. The return fire from the submarine was far less than before, and seven depth-charges were dropped. The explosion lifted *U459* out of the water, and the crew began to abandon ship as the boat began to go down. It is possible that the commander, Georg von Wilamowitz, had not appreciated that his boat was doomed, as he had set the

LEFT: The escort carrier USS *Bogue* was converted from a mercantile hull, in common with 20 other escort carriers. Eleven of these went to the Royal Navy as the *Attacker* class, with the rest serving with the USN. *Bogue*'s aircraft were responsible for the destruction of 13 U-boats.

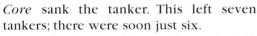

Core sank the tanker. This left seven tankers; there were soon just six.

On 24 July, a Wellington from No. 172 Squadron sighted *U459*. This was not a discovery premeditated by intelligence, but the result of a chance radar contact. *U459* had a heavy anti-aircraft armament. As well as a 37mm (1.46in) gun, there were two single 20mm (0.8in) cannon, a quadruple 20mm

LEFT: Crew members of HMS *Starling* lean over the side to look for debris from a submarine that they have just attacked.

U461
TYPE XIV

Country:	Germany	**Armament:**	Two 37mm (1.4in) guns
Launch date:	November 1941		and one 20mm (0.8in) cannon
Crew:	53		or one 37mm (1.4in) gun, four
Displacement:	1715 tonnes (1688		twin 20mm (0.8in) cannon
	tons) surfaced, 1963		and one single 20mm (0.8in)
	tonnes (1932 tons)		cannon
	submerged	**Powerplant:**	Diesel/electric motors
Dimensions:	67.1m (220ft) x 9.35m	**Surface range:**	22,872km (12,350nm) at 10
	(30ft) x 6.51m (21ft)		knots
		Performance:	14.4 knots surfaced, 6.2
			knots submerged
		Cargo:	Four torpedoes, 423 tons of
			fuel

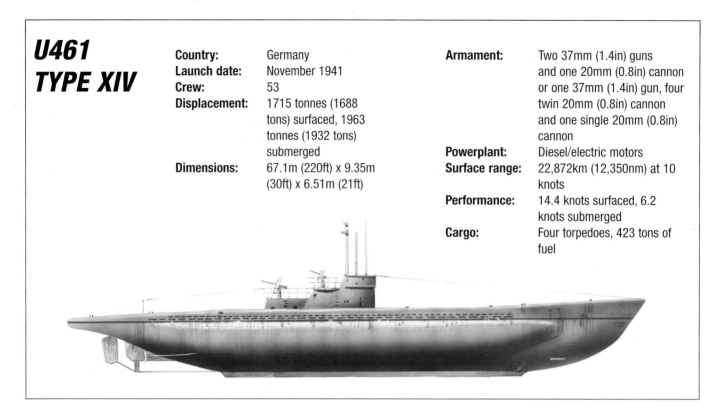

ABOVE: A valuable *Type XIV* 'milch-cow', *U461* was sunk in the Bay of Biscay on 30 July 1943, after being caught on the surface with *U504* and *U462* by a number of Coastal Command aircraft. Dönitz's orders that U-boats should engage aircraft rather than dive sealed *U461*'s fate: assailed by several aircraft at once, she was depth charged to destruction, with only a quarter of the crew escaping.

demolition charges. These went off just as *U459* slipped under the waves for the last time, killing the submarine's skipper.

The threat from the air had prompted Dönitz to experiment with what might be termed a 'flak-boat'. *U441* was given tremendously heavy armament. Two quad-20mm (0.8in) mountings were fitted, along with a 37mm (1.46in) gun. In addition to the armament, the complement of the boat was increased to include not only the gunners needed for the increased armament, but also scientists who would attempt to gain intelligence on the detection methods used by the aircraft. On 12 July, *U441*'s experiment went disastrously wrong. The submarine was spotted, but not by a patrol aircraft. Three Beaufighters from No. 248 Squadron appeared, and *U441* attempted to engage them. The Beaufighters were not lacking in armament themselves, sporting four 20mm (0.79in) cannon each, and they began a coordinated strafing attack. The unfortunate gun crews on *U441* were caught in a hail of cannon fire, and all the officers were killed or wounded. Fortunately, the U-boat had a doctor on board, who took command. He ordered a crash dive and then took the submarine back to Brest. Some Ju 88s came out to assist, and two of them were shot down by the Beaufighters for their trouble. The flak trap U-boat idea was promptly abandoned – but Dönitz persisted with the idea that a group of U-boats could fight it out on the surface. The continuing tanker campaign soon disabused him of this notion.

On 30 July, a group of 11 boats were attempting to transit the Bay of Biscay, including the tankers *U461* and *U462*. At about 09:30 hours, a Sunderland was seen by the U-boat lookouts. The Sunderland stayed well out of range of the anti-aircraft guns, but it was clear from the radio traffic picked up by the U-boats' radio operators that the aircraft was reporting their position. The sensible course of action at this point would have been for the boats to dive, but they followed orders and did not.

In fact, a Liberator from No. 53 Squadron had first sighted the submarines, but the report that had been sent out had proved to be misleading. The Sunderland was the first of a number of aircraft responding to this alert that found the submarines and called up support. It was forced away by a Ju 88, but the German fighter did not have enough fuel to stay in the area. The Sunderland returned, joined by the Liberator from No. 53 Squadron and a new arrival, an American Liberator. The three aircraft circled, trying to contact one another to coordinate tactics, but failed. Into this slightly confused situation arrived a Halifax from No. 502 Squadron, which ignored the niceties of coordination and charged in to attack.

The depth-charges missed, but caused some alarm among the submariners. Another Halifax arrived, closely followed by a Sunderland from No. 461 Squadron, captained by Flight Lieutenant Dudley Marrows. The newly arrived Halifax,

U441 TYPE VIIC

Country:	Germany
Launch date:	December 1941
Crew:	44
Displacement:	773 tonnes (761 tons) surfaced, 878 tonnes (865 tons) submerged
Dimensions:	67.1m (220ft) x 6.2m (20ft) x 4.8m (15ft)
Armament:	Five 533mm (21in) torpedo tubes, one 86mm (3.4in) gun, one 20mm (0.8in) cannon and up to 39 mines
Powerplant:	Diesel/electric motors
Surface range:	12,038km (6500nm) at 12 knots
Performance:	17.2 knots surfaced, 7.6 knots submerged

captained by Flying Officer August van Rossum, attacked *U462* and missed with its first run. Rossum immediately turned about, lost height and ran in for another attack; this time he scored a hit. While this distracted the attention of *U461*'s crew, the two Liberators and Marrows's Sunderland attacked that submarine. The strength of the anti-aircraft fire prompted the Liberators to break off, with the one from No. 53 Squadron taking hits. While *U461* concentrated fire on the Liberators, Marrows decided to attack from low level and thundered in at full throttle, the flying boat's gunners putting down a storm of fire on the deck crew, killing and wounding several of them. Marrows released the depth-charges right on top of the submarine, and this killed *U461*. The U-boat

went straight down, and only a quarter of the crew escaped.

While Marrows turned around to see the results, Rossum made another attack and dropped more bombs near *U462*. His second attack had in fact mortally damaged the submarine, and the other bombs provided the *coup de grâce*. *U504* wisely dived, but, to add to the carnage, Captain Walker's escort group had arrived on the scene and began to shell *U504* as it went beneath the waves. Walker then put his normal plan into operation: one of his ships would track the submarine with asdic, while directing its companions to the best attack position. Once this was done, the second ship would put down a vicious carpet of depth-charges. *U504* was

ABOVE: A *Type VIIC* boat, *U441* was used as a 'flak-boat' intended to shoot it out on the surface with anti-submarine aircraft. The experiment went badly wrong when the U-boat was bombarded by Beaufighters; the ship's doctor was forced to take command to get the submarine into port.

BELOW: Although under attack from Allied aircraft, this U-boat has decided to stay and fight it out; some of the vessel's crew are visible on the deck.

ABOVE: A view of the conning tower of a U-boat, bedecked with anti-aircraft guns. Apart from a brief period when crews were ordered to fight it out with attacking aircraft, if at all possible, the U-boat commander would seek to dive rather than use guns.

boats attempting to take on fuel. It was no wonder that the need for the *Type XXI* and *Type XXIII* became even greater.

NEW U-BOAT TECHNOLOGIES

The *Type XXIs*, despite their underwater endurance, still needed to recharge their batteries. The growth of air cover meant that doing so on the surface was a likely disaster, so alternative means was required. The answer came in the form of another device by Professor Helmut Walter, although it was not of his own design. This was the snorkel. It was invented by a member of the Dutch Navy in 1927 and discovered by the Germans when they overran Holland in 1940. The idea was breathtakingly simple: by using a double pipe system, the submarine could 'breathe' underwater and vent exhaust gases. Attempts to perfect the system were not made until the air threat became almost intolerable. The snorkel was not foolproof, however, as there was always the danger that the cap protecting the pipe could close and cut off the air supply. This meant that careful training had to be given in the use of the device. If handled correctly, the snorkel offered to give the older U-boats a longer effective life by dint of keeping them out of the way of patrolling aircraft.

hunted for two hours and destroyed in just this fashion.

The loss of the tankers was a severe blow to German efforts and marked the nadir of fortunes in the Bay. In June and July, 54 U-boats were lost, all but 10 to aircraft. Of these, six had been tankers. The loss of *U489* on 4 August on its first operational patrol reduced the number of tankers to just three, of which two were in dock. Dönitz was forced to employ some of the *Type IX* boats as tankers instead. This was revealed to the Allies through Enigma, and the attacks continued against these targets. Three temporary tankers were sunk in August, along with two

This was not the only device that was adopted. The U-boat service had no real operational research or scientific support until; the devices that originated from the belated application of science were impressive. The most immediate manifestations came in the form of a new radar detection device, the Hagenuk Wanze and the Zaukönig acoustic torpedo. Wanze was particularly important, as U-Boat HQ began to suspect that the Metox warning receiver gear acted as an emitter which Coastal Command aircraft could detect and therefore attack. This fear was not helped when a captured RAF pilot noted that his interrogators were asking a lot of questions about the RAF's ability to home in on emissions from detector devices. The pilot promptly wove a tale of how air crew never needed to use their ASV, as they could detect Metox emissions. He nearly ruined this brilliant piece of disinformation by claiming that the emissions could be located at a range of 145km (90 miles), but the concern within U-boat command was such that the drift of his story was believed. On 14 August, the use of Metox was discontinued.

The Zaukönig torpedo, known to the Allies as 'GNAT', was designed for the purpose of attacking the escort vessels. This was to be of particular note as Dönitz returned his submarines to their main operational area: the North Atlantic.

ONS18 AND ON202

In the second week of September 1943, ONS18 and ON202, comprising 69 ships between them, became the target for a new pack attack. On 19 September, a Liberator from No. 10 Squadron Royal Canadian Air Force sank *U341*, opening the battle of the two convoys. At 03:00 hours on the 20th, the U-boats attacked and sank two merchantmen. The escorting frigate *Lagan* was hit by a GNAT, causing such damage that the ship had to be taken under tow and returned to her home port. The two convoys had become so close that Admiral Sir Max Horton ordered them to link up, and skilful use of the escorts, combined with the ubiquitous air cover from Liberators, prevented any further loss during daylight. Once darkness fell, the U-boats attacked again, this time with more success. GNATs accounted for the destroyer *St Croix* and the corvette *Polyanthus*.

The next two days brought fog,, when it lifted towards the end of 22 September, the attack resumed. Liberators damaged *U270* and *U377*, which both had to return to base. *U229* was detected from an high-frequency direction finding (HF/DF) bearing and rammed by the destroyer *Keppel*. That night, an acoustic torpedo sank the destroyer *Itchen*

and four merchantmen were sunk. Fog returned the next day and the battle came to an end. The loss of so many escorts caused considerable concern to Horton, but a counter was already being designed. A misunderstanding of a decryption of signal talking about the wandering FAT torpedoes had led to worries that an acoustic torpedo was being developed well before the Germans were actually ready to employ it. The countermeasure came in the form of a towed noise-maker, known as FOXER, while the Canadians worked on a variation known as CAT, which made a noise like a buzz-saw (with a coincidental side effect of unnerving nearby U-boat crews). FOXER was not

perfect, as it demanded that the escorts run at a lower speed, but it was still highly effective.

Dönitz was initially convinced that GNAT offered new hope to his submarines, as the claims of success were impressive. Unfortunately, this impression was mistaken. There was a temptation to believe that the torpedoes always hit their targets, and every detonation heard was logged as being a success. This ignored the fact that FOXER worked particularly well, decoying most, if not all (there is some dispute over the figures), of the torpedoes. This meant that there were claims for the sinking of six destroyers in the first week of October alone – in fact, only one had been hit. The British response was initially one of irritation, and plans to reveal the ineffectiveness of the GNAT were revealed. Before they were enacted, though, a different idea came to the fore. Why let the Germans know that their new 'wonder weapon' was not as wondrous as they thought? Far better to allow them to continue in the misplaced belief that they were having far more effect with a weapon that could be outfoxed than to encourage them to develop something new.

BELOW: A U-boat employs its Schnorchel to recharge its batteries without the need to surface fully. The device enabled U-boats to remain submerged, thus reducing the threat from air attack. Although the Schnorchel protruded from the water, it was not large enough to register a return on the airborne radars of the day.

FAR LEFT: A U-boat succumbs to the efforts of a flight of Grumman Avengers from a US escort carrier. The presence of aircraft with convoys dramatically altered the odds against the submarine.

ABOVE: A close up view of the Schnorchel on *U3008*, a *Type XXI*. The *Type XXI* Schnorchel, unlike those on earlier boats, was telescopic, and raised from a special housing by electric motors.

equally aware that his submarines could have an impact, and he issued orders calling for increased determination on the part of the crews (although not to the extent of ordering de facto suicide missions as some authors have claimed). There were difficulties – first, the Germans did not know when the invasion would come, thus making it almost impossible to have the maximum number of U-boats available; secondly, as ever, there was Coastal Command. Sir John Slessor had moved on to pastures new in a rotation of commanders, and Air Chief Marshal Sir Sholto Douglas had succeeded him. He saw his new command's task as being 'to put the cork in the bottle' holding the U-boats away from the invasion fleet. He had 29 squadrons from No. 19 Group to do this with, including some units from the Fleet Air Arm. In addition, the forces from Nos 15 and 18 groups were ready for any incursions into the English Channel by U-boats based in Norway.

These aircraft kept the pressure on the U-boats, they were aided by the lack of intelligence available to the Germans. When the invasion fleet began its crossing, the U-boats in the Bay of Biscay and Norway were still in harbour and unable to intervene. The Norway boats sailed belatedly, with seven boats without snorkel making for positions between the Scilly Isles and the coast of Devon in England. Nine with snorkel took up positions off the Isle of Wight, while the remainder went on patrol in the Bay of Biscay. Of the seven non-snorkel boats, four were sunk and three severely damaged. Two of these were notable victims of Coastal Command. In the early hours of 8 June, a Liberator of No. 224 Squadron came across *U629* and sank it. Twenty minutes later, while the crew was still enjoying their success, they saw *U373* and sank that, too. This summed up the lot of the non-snorkel boats – no success in return for heavy loss. They were recalled from the area on 12 June.

The boats with snorkel did a little better, but were engaged in an unfavourable exchange rate with the Allies, sinking little and making no real impact upon the invasion. The advance of the ground forces in France was inexorable, and, in early August 1944, the U-boats began to evacuate their bases in the Bay of Biscay. Out of the 36 U-boats there, 12 were sunk in the bay, two more went down in the Channel and six were scuttled. The light surface forces that accompanied them were slaughtered, with 55 falling victim to air and surface forces. U-boat losses now stood at two for every Allied ship sunk, with an overall loss rate of 51.2 per cent. The year of 1944 was characterized by another serious defeat for the U-boat campaign.

Losses of U-boats declined notably in September, but this was because of their running submerged far more. As a result, Allied shipping losses were similarly reduced: in September and October, just nine ships were lost. In October, new packs of U-boats searched in vain for convoys, re-routed thanks to intelligence information from Bletchley Park. Losses among the submarines also increased, with 26 being sunk. On 16 November, Dönitz bowed to the inevitable and withdrew his forces from the convoy routes for the second time. He later recorded that it was obvious that the U-boats could do nothing other than fight a delaying action. In the last two months of 1943, 72 convoys reached their destination without a single loss to submarine attack. The year 1944 would prove to be worse still for the U-boats.

1944

On the Allied side, 1944 was to be of huge significance. It was obvious that the second front might be opened at some point, and the Admiralty Tracking Room was fully aware that any invasion of Europe could be badly hampered by U-boat action. Dönitz was

THE END

The U-boats did not have a completely disastrous year, in that the number of sightings made by enemy aircraft declined. This owed much to the widespread use of snorkel, a development that worried the Allies. The Allies anti-submarine effort had been based upon the fact that the most effective way to counter the U-boats was by using aircraft with Leigh Lights and/or radar in conjunction with escorts with radar, HF/DF and asdic. The use of snorkel meant that the air threat was considerably reduced. The knowledge that the high-speed submarines with much better underwater performance were on their way also caused some alarm. In addition, the U-boats were unable to make radio communication when submerged, which denied an array of information to Bletchley Park and prevented detection by HF/DF. This made the work of the Tracking Room far more taxing, with an inevitable loss of precision.

From September, the U-boats were switched towards British home waters, and they began to make their presence felt from November. The number of casualties from the U-boats began to rise, and the inshore

ABOVE: Slightly different victims: British soldiers are rescued by a destroyer after a U-boat has sunk their transport ship. Attempts by U-boats to sink troop transports were relatively infrequent, with cargo ships taking priority in the tonnage war.

LEFT: A *Type XXI* submarine, still under construction, as discovered by the Allies when they investigated the dockyards at Bremen in May 1945.

U320

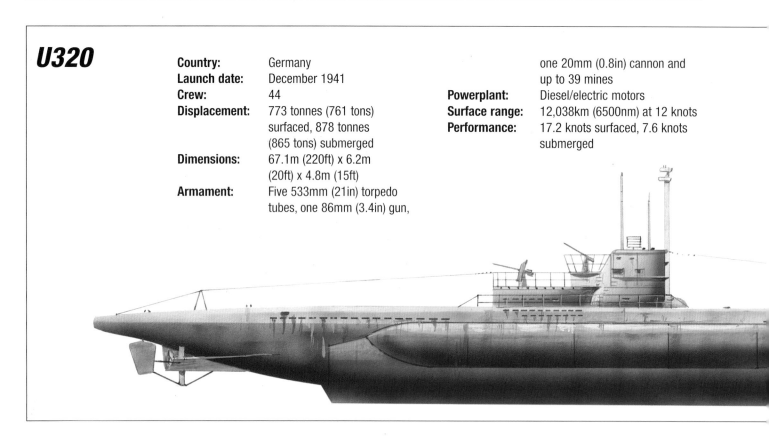

Country:	Germany
Launch date:	December 1941
Crew:	44
Displacement:	773 tonnes (761 tons) surfaced, 878 tonnes (865 tons) submerged
Dimensions:	67.1m (220ft) x 6.2m (20ft) x 4.8m (15ft)
Armament:	Five 533mm (21in) torpedo tubes, one 86mm (3.4in) gun, one 20mm (0.8in) cannon and up to 39 mines
Powerplant:	Diesel/electric motors
Surface range:	12,038km (6500nm) at 12 knots
Performance:	17.2 knots surfaced, 7.6 knots submerged

ABOVE: *U320* was one of an upgraded version of the *Type VIIC*, the *Type VIIC/41*. This had the ability to dive to a greater depth than the *VIIC* thanks to its reinforced hull. *U320* was sunk by a *Catalina* of 210 Squadron, RAF, on 7 May 1945, making her the last boat lost in the war.

RIGHT: Strain showing, a U-boat crewman works in the engine room.

waters meant that it was extremely difficult to use detection devices properly, as these were optimized for ocean-going warfare. Fortunately for the Allies, even this offensive was a case of too little too late. The *Type XXIs* and *XXIIIs* caused concern and some casualties, but it was too late for them to make a difference. Everywhere, the German Army was in full retreat, and the Allies were approaching the Third Reich from two sides. The end was fast approaching. Although the U-boats from Norway operated in some strength even as late as April 1945, there was nothing they could do. In British home waters, 10 merchant ships and two escort vessels were sunk, in exchange for 23 U-boats. Allied bombing reduced the U-boat bases to chaos, forcing the U-boats to head for the Baltic. There, the last five weeks of the war saw the destruction of 83 U-boats by a variety of aircraft. Coastal Command strike wings were joined by rocket-firing Typhoons from 2nd Tactical Air Force, wreaking havoc among the unfortunate submarines. The last U-boat to be lost was *U320*, so badly damaged by a *Catalina* on 7 May 1945 that it sank two days later.

By this point, Dönitz had changed positions once again. This time, it was not a naval job that awaited him, but that of Führer in place of Hitler, who had shot himself on 30 April. Any hope of winning the war was gone. On 4 May, the U-boats were ordered to cease hostilities; also that day, German forces surrendered to Field Marshal Bernard Montgomery in a simple ceremony at Lüneburg Heath. On 8 May 1945, the war in Europe was over.

THE FINAL RECKONING

Despite Dönitz's hopes, the U-boats did not win the war for Germany. There were a multitude of factors behind this basic fact. There were never enough U-boats available to make the sort of concerted effort against the convoys that was required. The work of the large packs towards the height of the

Improved technology, more escorts and the combination of air and sea power meant that the task of the U-boat crews became ever more difficult, culminating in defeat when the defences became just too strong.

Winston Churchill encouraged the use of the phrase 'U-boat' as opposed to 'submarine'. His intent was to make the term a pejorative; he was so successful that the very mention of 'U-boats' can still conjure up a sinister image for people in countries that were part of the Allied alliance. This disguises the fact that the submarine war was fought by an array of brave men on both sides. The U-boat crews knew that they stood little chance of survival if they were surprised and their craft crippled. The merchant seamen and the crews of escorts knew just as well their likely fate if they were sunk by U-boats. For those who escaped their vessel, be it U-boat or ship, the end result could be either a lingering death, drifting in hostile seas, or a quicker demise brought about by ferocious cold. The Battle of the Atlantic was the longest continual battle of World War II. It was ferocious, bloody and vital to the outcome of the war. Many of the participants have no precisely known grave, no headstone to commemorate them in the vast, barren expanse of the seas. Despite this, they cannot be forgotten; their epitaph lies in the fact that their actions shaped the future course of the world. The importance of the wolfpacks, the merchant ships and the escorts and all who were involved in this colossal struggle simply cannot be denied.

campaign demonstrated what could have been achieved had enough been available to swamp the defences of the convoys. The lack of concentration on escort vessels during peacetime could have cost the British dearly, but, by the time sufficient U-boats were available, the situation had changed. The arrival of the United States in the war meant that the shipbuilding might of the US yards would always make the tonnage war a difficult one to win.

BELOW: A *Type XXI*, seen at the end of the war, with the crew lined up on the deck. Unlike thousands of their comrades, these men were lucky: they survived.

INDEX

BIBLIOGRAPHY

J. M. Bourne, *Britain and the First World War*
  (Edward Arnold)
John Terraine, *Business in Great Waters* (Mandarin)
Clay Blair, *Hitler's U-Boat War 1939-1942: The Hunters*
  (Weidenfeld and Nicolson)
Clay Blair, *Hitler's U-Boat War 1942-1945: The Hunted*
  (Weidenfeld and Nicolson)
V. E. Tarrant, *The U-Boat War 1914-1945* (Cassell)

Peter Padfield, *War Beneath the Sea: Submarine Conflict
  1939-1945* (John Murray)
S. W. Roskill, *The War At Sea 1939-1945, Volume I: The
  Defensive* (HMSO)
S. W. Roskill, *The War At Sea 1939-1945, Volume II: The
  Period of Balance* (HMSO)
Jak P. Mallmann Showell, *U-Boat Command and the Battle
  of the Atlantic* (Conway)